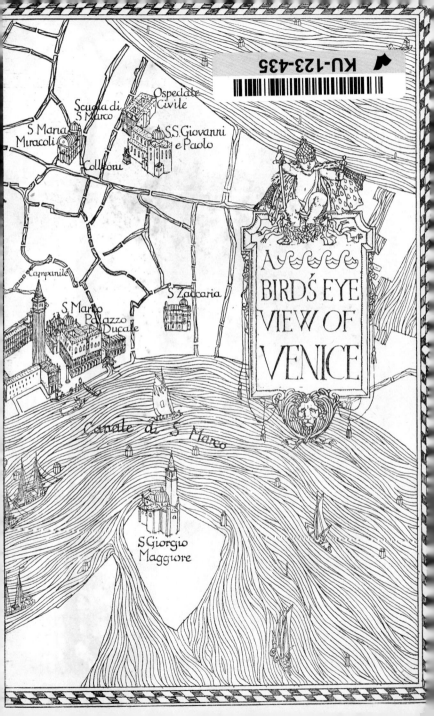

A WANDERER IN VENICE

THE GRAND CANAL FROM THE STEPS OF S. MARIA DELLA SALUTE

A WANDERER IN VENICE

BY

E. V. LUCAS

WITH SIXTEEN ILLUSTRATIONS IN COLOUR BY

HARRY MORLEY

THIRTY-TWO PHOTOGRAPHS FROM PAINTINGS AND A MAP

EIGHTH EDITION

METHUEN & CO. LTD.
36 ESSEX STREET W.C.
LONDON

First Published . . . November 12th 1914
Second Edition . . . March   1915
Third Edition . . . January   1920
Fourth Edition . . . July   1921
Fifth Edition, Revised . April   1923
Sixth Edition . . . . November   1923
Seventh Edition . . . September   1924
Eighth Edition . . .   1925

PREFACE TO FIRST EDITION

FOR a detailed guide to Venice the reader must go elsewhere; all that I have done is invariably to mention those things that have most interested me, and, in the hope of being a useful companion, often a few more. But my chief wish (as always in this series) has been to create a taste.

For the history of Venice the reader must also go elsewhere, yet for the sake of clarity a little history has found its way even into these pages. To go to Venice without first knowing her story is a mistake, and doubly foolish because the city has been peculiarly fortunate in her chroniclers and eulogists. Mr. H. F. Brown stands first among the living, as Ruskin among the dead; but Ruskin is for the student patient under chastisement, whereas Mr. Brown's serenely human pages are for all. Of Mr. Howells' *Venetian Life* I have spoken more than once in this book; its truth and vivacity are a proof of how little the central Venice has altered, no matter what changes there may have been in

v

government or how often campanili fall.   The
late Col. Hugh Douglas's *Venice on Foot*, if
conscientiously followed, is such a key to a
treasury of interest as no other city has ever
possessed.   To Mrs. Aubrey Richardson's *Doges
of Venice* I am greatly indebted, and Herr
Baedeker has been here as elsewhere (in the Arab
idiom) my father and my mother.

E. V. L.

June, 1914.

PREFACE TO THE REVISED EDITION, 1923

AN old lady arriving in Venice for the first
time, on her son's yacht, is famous for re-
marking, after a shrewd glance at palaces, domes,
and minarets—some sadly out of the perpendicular
—" This place won't last long."   That she may
happily be proved a false prophet is suggested by
the length of the time which Venice has already
lasted ; but one has to admit that the endurance
is due more to the grace of God and the sound-
ness of the original builders than the modern
Venetians' solicitude.

After an absence of nine years—during which,
one has to remember, a disheartening and im-

poverishing war was fought—I notice many signs
of deterioration and neglect: the palaces on the
Grand Canal in worse repair, the posts before
them rotting and unpainted, the golden horses
of S. Mark's almost black, a general sense of
déshabille and want of pride, which may, of course,
be not unassociated with want of money.

In course of time these wrongs may be righted.
I hope so with all my heart ; although, of course,
a Venice spick and span is as undesirable as un-
thinkable. Meanwhile Venice seems to be more
popular than ever with English and American
travellers, who cheerfully pay the doubled fees
now demanded in Italy at all the public insti-
tutions.

A certain displacement of pictures in the Accademia caused by the war—many being removed
to places of greater safety—is now being cor-
rected, and in this edition I am not able to indicate
the exact position of every work of art. I have,
however, retained the references to them, and I
have enlarged the index to take note of all.

Titian's " Assumption " has now left the Accademia for ever, to resume its original place
over the high altar of the Frari.

Tiepolo's ceiling at the Scalzi was utterly destroyed by a bomb from the air ; otherwise little
damage to the city was done.

Another change is the removal of the collections in the Civic Museum in the Fondaco dei Turchi, on the Grand Canal, to rooms set apart for them in the Royal Palace, which the King has lately made over to the State.

The gondoliers struck me as being more grasping than ever and less restrained under disappointment; but my sympathies are with them as sufferers from the competition of the motor launch, which has largely increased both in numbers and in speed.

Travellers may like to be reminded that in Italy now there is no more tipping in hotels, restaurants, or cafés, a percentage, satisfactory to the waiters, who indeed arranged the matter, being added to the bill. Railway porters, however, still cherish great expectations.

E. V. L.

February, 1923

CONTENTS

CHAPTER X

CHAPTER XI

CHAPTER XII

CHAPTER XIII

CHAPTER XIV

CHAPTER XV

CHAPTER XVI

CHAPTER XVII

CHAPTER XVIII

CHAPTER XIX

CHAPTER XX

CONTENTS

LIST OF ILLUSTRATIONS
IN COLOUR

LIST OF ILLUSTRATIONS
IN MONOTONE

"In like manner I say, that had there bin an offer made unto me before I took my journey to Venice, eyther that foure of the richest manors of Somerset-shire (wherein I was borne) should be gratis bestowed upon me if I never saw Venice, or neither of them if I should see it; although certainly these manors would do me much more good in respect of a state of livelyhood to live in the world than the sight of Venice, yet notwithstanding I will ever say while I live, that the sight of Venice and her resplendent beauty, antiquities, and monuments, hath by many degrees more contented my minde, and satisfied my desires, than those foure Lordships could possibly have done."—THOMAS CORYAT.

A WANDERER IN VENICE

CHAPTER I

THE BRIDE OF THE ADRIATIC

The best approach to Venice—Chioggia—A first view—Another water approach—Padua and Fusina—The railway station—A complete transformation—A Venetian guide-book—A city of a dream.

I HAVE no doubt whatever that, if the diversion can be arranged, the perfect way for the railway traveller to approach Venice for the first time is from Chioggia, in the afternoon.

Chioggia is at the end of a line from Rovigo, and it ought not to be difficult to get there either overnight or in the morning. If overnight, one would spend some very delightful hours in drifting about Chioggia itself, which is a kind of foretaste of Venice, although not like enough to her to impair the surprise. (But nothing can do that. Not all the books or photographs in the world, not Turner, nor Whistler, nor Clara Montalba, can so familiarize the stranger with the idea of Venice that the reality of Venice fails to be sudden and arresting. Venice is so peculiarly herself, so exotic and unbelievable, that so far from ever being ready for her, even her residents, returning, can never be fully prepared.)

But to resume—Chioggia is the end of all things. The

train stops at the station because there is no future for it; the road to the steamer stops at the pier because otherwise it would run into the water. Standing there, looking north, one sees nothing but the still, land-locked lagoon with red and umber and orange-sailed fishing-boats, and tiny islands here and there. But only ten miles away, due north, is Venice. And a steamer leaves several times a day to take you there, gently and loiteringly, in the Venetian manner, in two hours, with pauses at odd little places *en route*. And that is the way to enter Venice, because not only do you approach her by sea, as is right, Venice being the bride of the sea not merely by poetical tradition but as a solemn and wonderful fact, but you see her from afar, and gradually more and more is disclosed, and your first near view, sudden and complete as you skirt the island of S. Giorgio Maggiore, has all the most desired ingredients: the Campanile of S. Marco, S. Marco's domes, the Doges' Palace, S. Theodore on one column and the Lion on the other, the Custom House, S. Maria della Salute, the blue Merceria clock, all the business of the Riva, and a gondola under your very prow.

That is why one should come to Venice from Chioggia.

The other sea approach is from Fusina, at the end of an electric-tram line from Padua. If the Chioggia scheme is too difficult, then the Fusina route should be taken, for it is simplicity itself. All that the traveller has to do is to leave the train at Padua overnight—and he will be very glad to do so, for that last five-hour lap from Milan to Venice is very trying, with all the disentanglement of re-gistered luggage at the end of it before one can get to the hotel—and spend the next morning in exploring Padua's own riches: Giotto's frescoes in the Madonna dell' Arena; Mantegna's in the Eremitani; Donatello's altar in the church of Padua's own sweet Saint Anthony; the same master's glorious equestrian statue of Gattamelata, and so forth; and then in the afternoon take the tram for Fusina. This approach is not so attractive as that from Chioggia, but it is more quiet and fitting than the rush over the viaduct in the train. One is behaving with more propriety than that, for one is doing what, until a few poor decades ago of scientific fuss, every visitor travelling to Venice had to do: one is embarked on the most romantic of voyages: one is crossing the sea to its Queen.

This way one enters Venice by her mercantile shipping gate, where there are chimneys and factories and a vast system of electric wires. Not that the scene is not beautiful; Venice can no more fail to be beautiful, whatever she does, than a Persian kitten can; yet it does not compare with the Chioggia adventure, which not only is perfect visually, but, though brief, is long enough to create a mood of repose for the anticipatory traveller such as Venice deserves.

On the other hand, it must not be forgotten that there are many visitors who want their first impression of this city of their dreams to be abrupt; who want the transition from the rattle of the train to the peace of the gondola to be instantaneous; and these, of course, must enter Venice at the station. If they leave London as most travellers from England do, by the 2 o'clock train and do not break the journey, they will reach Venice on the evening of the next day.

But whether it is by day or by night, this first shock of Venice is not to be forgotten. To step out of the dusty stuffy carriage, jostle one's way through a thousand hotel porters, and be confronted by the sea washing the station steps is terrific! The sea tamed, it is true; the

sea on strange visiting terms with churches and houses;
but the sea none the less; and if one had the pluck to
taste the water one would find it salt. There is probably
no surprise to the eye more complete and alluring than
this first view of the Grand Canal at the Venetian terminus.

But why do I put myself to the trouble of writing this
when it has all been done for me by an earlier hand?   In
the most popular of the little guide books to Venice, published in German, English, and, I think, French, as well as the
original Italian, the impact of the city on the traveller by
rail is described with real feeling and eloquence, and with
a curious intensity only possible when an Italian author
chooses an Italian translator to act as intermediary between
himself and the English reader. The author is Signor A.
Carlo, and the translator, whose independence, in a city
which swarms with Anglo-Saxon visitors and even residents, in refusing to make use of their services in revising
his English, cannot be too much admired, is Signor G. Sarri.

Here is the opening flight of these Two Gentlemen of
Venice: " The traveller, compelled by a monotone rail-
way-carriage, to look for hours at the endless stretching of
the beautifull and sad Venetian plain, feels getting wear,
[? near] this divine Queen of the Seas, whom so many
artists, painters and poets have exalted in every time and
every way; feels, I say, that something new, something
unexpected is really about to happen : something that will
surely leave a deep mark on his imagination, and last
through all his life. I mean that peculiar radiation of
impulsive energy issueing from anything really great,
vibrating and palpitating from afar, fitting the soul to
emotion or enthusiasm. . . ."

Yesterday, or even this morning, in Padua, Verona,
Milan, Chioggia, or wherever it was, whips were cracking,

hoofs clattering, motor horns booming, wheels endangering your life. Farewell now to all !—there is not a wheel in Venice save those that steer rudders, or ring bells; but instead, as you discern in time when the brightness and unfamiliarity of it all no longer bemuse your eyes, here are long black boats by the score, at the foot of the steps, all ready to take you and your luggage anywhere for a sum which, at the end of the journey, no matter how carefully arranged at the start, will be hotly questioned. You are in Venice.

If you go to the National Gallery and look at No. 163 by Canaletto you will see the first thing that meets the gaze as one emerges upon fairyland from the Venice terminus: the copper dome of S. Simeone. The scene was not much different when it was painted, say, *circa* 1740. The iron bridge was not yet, and a church stands where the station now is; but the rest is much the same. And as you wander here and there in this city, in the days to come, that will be one of your dominating impressions— how much of the past remains unharmed. Venice is a city of yesterdays.

One should stay in her midst either long enough really to know something about her or only for three or four days. In the second case all is magical and bewildering, and one carries away, for the mind to rejoice in, no very definite detail, but a vague, confused impression of wonder and un- reality and loveliness. Dickens, in his *Pictures of Italy*, with sure instinct makes Venice a city of a dream, while all the other towns which he describes are treated realistically.

But for no matter how short a time one is in Venice, a large proportion of it should be sacred to idleness. Unless Venice is permitted and encouraged to invite one's soul to loaf, she is visited in vain.

CHAPTER II

S. MARK'S. I : THE EXTERIOR

Rival cathedrals—The lure of S. Mark's—The façade at night—The Doge's device—S. Mark's body—A successful theft—Miracle pictures—Mosaic patterns—The central door—Two problems—The north wall—The fall of Venice—Napoleon—The Austrian occupation—Daniele Manin—Victor Emmanuel—An artist's model—The south wall—The Pietra del Bando—The pillars from Acre.

OF S. Mark's what is one to say? To write about it at all seems indeed more than commonly futile. The wise thing to do is to enter its doors whenever one has the opportunity, if only for five minutes; to sit in it as often as possible, at some point in the gallery for choice; and to read Ruskin.

To Byzantine architecture one may not be very sympathetic; the visitor may come to Venice with the cool gloom of Milan still comforting his soul, or with the profound conviction that Chartres or Cologne represents the final word in ecclesiastical beauty and fitness; but none the less, in time, S. Mark's will win. It will not necessarily displace those earlier loves, but it will establish other ties.

But you must be passive and receptive. No cathedral so demands surrender. You must sink on its bosom.

S. Mark's façade is, I think, more beautiful in the mass than in detail. Seen from the Piazza, from a good distance, say half-way across it, through the red flagstaffs, it

6

is always strange and lovely and unreal. To begin with, there is the remarkable fact that after years of familiarity with this wonderful scene, in painting and coloured photographs, one should really be here at all. The realization of a dream is always amazing.

It is possible—indeed it may be a common experience—to find S. Mark's, as seen for the first time, especially on a Sunday or fête day, when the vast red and green and white flags are streaming before it, a little garish, a little gaudy; too like a coloured photograph; not what one thinks a cathedral ought to be. Should it have all these hues? one asks oneself, and replies no. But the saint does not long permit this scepticism: after a while he sees that the doubter drifts into his vestibule, to be rather taken by the novelty of the mosaics—so much quieter in tone here—and the pavement, with its myriad delicate patterns. And then the traveller dares the church itself and the spell begins to work; and after a little more familiarity, a few more visits to the Piazza, even if only for coffee, the fane has another devotee.

At night the façade behaves very oddly, for it becomes then as flat as a drop scene. Seen from the Piazza when the band plays and the lamps are lit, S. Mark's has no depth whatever. It is just a lovely piece of decoration stretched across the end.

The history of S. Mark's is this. The first patron saint of Venice was S. Theodore, who stands in stone with his crocodile in the Piazzetta, and to whose history we shall come later. In 828, however, it occurred to the astute Doge Giustiniano Partecipazio that both ecclesiastically and commercially Venice would be greatly benefited if a really first-class holy body could be preserved in her midst. Now S. Mark had died in A.D. 57, after grievous imprisonment, during which Christ appeared to him, speaking those words which are incised in the very heart of Venice, " Pax tibi, Marce, evangelista meus "—" Peace be to thee, Mark, my evangelist " ; and he was buried in Alexandria, the place of his martyrdom, by his fellow-Christians.   Why should not the sacred remains be stolen from the Egyptian city and brought to Venice ? Why not ?   The Doge therefore arranged with two adventurers, Rustico of Torcello and Buono of Mala-mocco, to make the attempt; and they were successful. When the body was exhumed such sweetness proceeded from it that all Alexandria marvelled, but did not trace the cause.

The saint seems to have approved of the sacrilege.   At any rate, when his remains were safely on board the Venetian ship, and a man in another ship scoffed at the idea that they were authentic, the Venetian ship instantly and mysteriously made for the one containing this sceptic, stove its side in, and continued to ram it until he took back his doubts.   And later, when. undismayed by this event, one of the sailors on S. Mark's own ship also denied that the body was genuine, he was possessed of a devil until he too changed his mind.

The mosaics on the cathedral façade all bear upon the life of S. Mark.   That over the second door on the left, with a figure in red, oddly like Anatole France, looking down upon the bed, represents S. Mark's death.   In the Accademia are pictures by Tintoretto of the finding of the body of S. Mark by the Venetians, and the transporta-tion of it from Alexandria, under a terrific thunderstorm in which the merchants and their camel are alone undis-mayed.

Arrived in Venice the remains were enclosed in a marble

pillar for greater safety, but only two or three persons knew which pillar, and, these dying, the secret perished. In their dismay all the people grieved, but suddenly the stones opened and revealed the corpse. Thereafter many miracles were performed by it; Venice was visited by pilgrims from all parts of the world; its reputation as a centre of religion grew; and the Doge's foresight and address were justified.

Before, however, S. Mark and his lion could become the protectors of the Republic, S. Theodore had to be deposed. S. Theodore's church, which stood originally on a part of the Piazza (an inscription in the pavement marks the site) now covered by the Campanile and one or two of the flagstaffs, is supposed to have been built in the sixth century. That it was destroyed by fire in the tenth, we know, and it is known too that certain remains of it were incorporated in the present structure of S. Mark's, which dates from the eleventh century, having been preceded by earlier ones.

To my mind not one of the external mosaic pictures is worth study; but some of the mosaic patterns over the doors are among the most lovely things I ever saw. Look at the delicate black and gold in the arch over the extreme right-hand door. Look at the black and gold bosses in that next it. On the other side of the main entrance these bosses have a little colour in them. On the extreme left we find symbolism: a golden horseman, the emblems of the four Evangelists, and so forth, while above is a relief in black stone, netted in: this and the group over the central door being the only external statuary in Venice to which the pigeons have no access.

The carvings over the central door are interesting, although they have a crudity which will shock visitors

fresh from the Baptistery doors at Florence.   As in most
Venetian sculpture symbolism plays an important part,
and one is not always able to translate it.   Here are
arches within arches : one of scriptural incidents—at any
rate Adam and Eve and Cain and Abel are identifiable ;
one of grotesques and animals ; one of uncouth toilers—
a shepherd and woodman and so forth—with God the
Father on the keystone.   What these mean beyond the
broad fact that religion is for all, I cannot say.   Angels
are above, and surmounting the doorway is Christ.
Among all this dark stonework one is conscious now and
then of little pink touches which examination shows to be
the feet of reposing pigeons.

Above is the parapet with the four famous golden horses
in the midst ; above them in the architrave over the
central recess is S. Mark's lion with the open book against
a background of starred blue.   Then angels mounting
to Christ, and on each side pinnacled saints.   It is all
rather barbaric, very much of a medley, and unforgettable
in its total effect.

Two mysteries the façade holds for me.   One is the
black space behind the horses, which seems so cowardly
an evasion of responsibility on the part of artists and
architects for many years, as it was there when Gentile
Bellini painted his Santa Croce miracle—but I must confess that at evening the black glass reflects the sinking sun
very wonderfully ; and the other is the identity of the two
little grotesque figures with a jug, one towards each end of
the parapet over the door.   No book tells me who they
are, and indeed no Venetian seems to know.   They do not
appear to be scriptural.

The north façade of S. Mark's receives less attention
than it should, although one cannot leave Cook's office

S. MARK'S FROM THE PIAZZA.   THE MERCERIA CLOCK ON THE LEFT

without seeing it. The north has a lovely Gothic doorway and much sculpture, including on the west wall of the
transept a rather nice group of sheep, and beneath it a
pretty little saint; while the Evangelists are again here—
S. Luke painting, S. Matthew looking up from his book,
S. John brooding, and S. Mark writing. The doorway
has a quaint interesting relief of the manger, containing
a very large Christ child, in its arch. Pinnacled saints,
with holy men beneath canopies between them, are here,
and on one point the quaintest little crowned Madonna.
At sunset the light on this wall can be very lovely.

At the end of the transept is a tomb built against
the wall, with lions to guard it, and a statue of S. George
high above. The tomb is that of Daniele Manin, and
since we are here I cannot avoid an historical digression,
for this man stands for the rise of the present Venice.
When Lodovico Manin, the last Doge, came to the throne,
in 1788, Venice was, of course, no longer the great power
that she had been; but at any rate she was Venice, the
capital of a republic with the grandest and noblest traditions. She had even just given one more proof of her sea
power by her defeat of the pirates of Algiers. But her
position in Europe had disappeared and a terrible glow
was beginning to tinge the northern sky—none other than
that of the French Revolution, from which was to emerge
a Man of Destiny whose short sharp way with the map of
Europe must disturb the life of frivolity and ease which
the Venetians contrived still to live.

Then came Napoleon's Italian campaign and his defeat
of Lombardy. Venice resisted; but such resistance was
merely a matter of time: the force was all-conquering.
Two events precipitated her fate. One was the massacre of
the French colony in Verona after that city had been

vanquished; another was the attack on a French vessel cruising in Venetian waters on the watch for Austrian men-of-war. The Lido fort fired on her and killed her commander, Langier. It was then that Napoleon declared his intention of being a second Attila to the city of the sea. He followed up his threat with a fleet; but very little force was needed, for Doge Manin gave way almost instantly. The capitulation was indeed more than complete; the Venetians not only gave in but grovelled. The words "Pax tibi, Marce, Evangelista meus" on the lion's book on S. Mark façade were changed to "Rights of Man and of Citizenship," and Napoleon was thanked in a profuse epistle for providing Venice with glorious liberty. Various riots of course accompanied this renunciation of centuries of noble tradition, and under the Tree of Liberty in the Piazza the Ducal insignia and the Libro d'Oro were burned. The tricolour flew from the three flagstaffs, and the two columns in the Piazzetta were covered with inscriptions praising the French. This was in May, 1797.

So much for Venice under Manin, Lodovico. The way is now paved for Manin, Daniele, who was no relation, but a poor Jewish boy to whom a Manin had stood as godfather. Daniele was born in 1804. In 1805 the Peace of Pressburg was signed, and Venice, which had passed to Austria in 1798, was taken from Austria and united to Napoleon's Italian kingdom, with Eugène Beauharnais, the Emperor's step-son, as ruler under the title Prince of Venice. In 1807 Napoleon visited the city and at once decreed a number of improvements on his own practical sensible lines. He laid out the Giardini Pubblici; he examined the ports and improved them; he revised the laws. But not even Napoleon could be everywhere at once or succeed in everything, and in 1813 Austria took advantage of his other troubles to try and recapture the Queen of the Adriatic by force, and when the general Napoleonic collapse came the restitution was formally made, Venice and Lombardy becoming again Austrian and the brother of Francis I their ruler.

All went fairly quietly in Venice until 1847, when, shortly after the fall of the Orleans dynasty in France, Daniele Manin, now an eloquent and burningly patriotic lawyer, dared to petition the Austrian Emperor for justice to the nation whom he had conquered, and as a reply was imprisoned for high treason, together with Niccolò Tommaseo. In 1848, on March 17, the city rose in revolt, the prison was forced, and Manin not only was released but proclaimed President of the Venetian Republic. He was now forty-four, and in the year of struggle that followed proved himself both a great administrator and a great soldier.

He did all that was humanly possible against the Austrians, but events were too much for him ; bigger battalions, combined with famine and cholera, broke the Venetian defence; and in 1849 Austria again ruled the province. All Italy had been similarly in revolt, but her time was not yet. The Austrians continued to rule until Garibaldi and Victor Emmanuel built up the United Italy which we now know. Manin, however, did not live to see that. Forbidden to return to Venice, he retired to Paris a poor and broken man, and there died in 1857.

The myriad Austrians who used to be projected into Venice daily in the summer, by excursion steamers from Trieste, rarely, I imagine, got so far as the Campo dominated by Manin's exuberant statue with the great winged lion, and therefore did not see this fine fellow who lived to preserve his country from them. Nor did they as a rule visit that side of S. Mark's where his tomb stands. But they can hardly have failed to see the monument to Victor Emmanuel on the Riva—with the lion which they had wounded so grievously, symbolizing Italy under the enemy, on the one side, and the same animal, all alert and confident, on the other, flushed with the assurance which 1886 brought, and the sturdy king riding forth to victory above.

The Great War of 1914-18 stopped the daily invasion of Venice by trippers from Trieste, but now that peace reigns the steamers bring them again, although not so often or in such numbers. Any ambition which they once may have had to possess Venice again has probably disappeared for ever.

The little piazzetta on the north side of S. Mark's has a famous well, with two porphyry lions beside it on which small Venetians love to straddle. A bathing-place for pigeons is here too, and I have counted twenty-seven in it at once. Here one day I found an artist at work on the head of an old man—a cunning old rascal with short-cropped grey hair, a wrinkled face packed with craft, and a big pipe. The artist, a tall, bearded man, was painting with vigour, but without, so far as I could discern, any model ; and yet it was obviously a portrait on which he was engaged and no work of invention. After joining the crowd before the easel for a minute or so, I was passing on when a figure emerged from a cool corner where he had been resting and held out his hand for alms. He was a cunning old rascal with short-cropped grey hair, a wrinkled face packed with craft, and a big pipe ; after a moment's perplexity I recognized him as the model, and the idea that the privilege of seeing the picture in the making should carry with it an obligation to the sitter was so comic that I could not repulse him with the grave face that is important on such occasions. Later in the same day I met the artist himself in the waters of the Lido—a form of rencontre that is very common in Venice in the summer. The converse is, however, the more amusing and usually disenchanting: the recognition, in the Piazza, in the evening, in their clothes, of certain of the morning's bathers.

On the south wall of S. Mark's, looking over the Molo and the lagoon, is the famous Madonna before whom two lights burn all night. Not all day too, as I have seen it stated. Above her are two pretty cherubs against a light-blue background, holding the head of Christ: one of the gayest pieces of colour in Venice. Justice is again pin-nacled here, and on her right, on another pinnacle, is a charming angel, upon whom a lion fondlingly climbs. Between and on each side are holy men within canopies, and beneath is much delicate work in sculpture. Below are porphyry insets and veined marbles, and on the para-pet two griffins, one apparently destroying a child and one a lamb. The porphyry stone on the ground at the corner on our left is the Pietra del Bando, from which the laws of the Republic were read to the people. Thomas Coryat, the traveller, who walked from Somerset to Venice in 1608 and wrote the result of his journey in a quaint volume called *Coryat's Crudities*, adds another to the functions of the Pietra del Bando. "On this stone," he says, "are laide for the space of three dayes and three nights the heads of all such as being enemies or traitors to the State, or some notorious offenders, have been ap-prehended out of the citie, and beheaded by those that have been bountifully hired by the Senate for the same purpose." The four affectionate figures, in porphyry, at

the corner of the Doges' Palace doorway, came also from
the East. Nothing definite is known of them, but many
stories are told. The two richly carved isolated columns
were brought from Acre in 1256.

Of these columns old Coryat has a story which I have
found in no other writer. It may be true, and on the
other hand it may have been the invention of some mischievous Venetian wag wishing to get a laugh out of the
inquisitive Somerset pedestrian, whose leg was, I take it,
invitingly pullable. " Near to this stone," he says,
referring to the Pietra del Bando, " is another memorable
thing to be observed. A marvailous faire paire of gallowes made of alabaster, the pillars being wrought with
many curious borders, and workes, which served for no other
purpose but to hang the Duke whensoever he shall happen
to commit any treason against the State. And for that
cause it is erected before the very gate of his Palace to
the end to put him in minde to be faithfull and true to
his country. If not, he seeth the place of punishment at
hand. But this is not a perfect gallowes, because there
are only two pillars without a transverse beame, which
beame (they say) is to be erected when there is any
execution, not else. Betwixt this gallowes malefactors
and condemned men (that are to goe to be executed upon
a scaffold betwixt the two famous pillars before mentioned
at the South end of S. Mark's street, neare the Adriaticque
Sea) are wont to say their prayers, to the Image of the
Virgin Mary, standing on a part of S. Mark's Church right
opposite unto them."

CHAPTER III

S. MARK'S. II: THE INTERIOR

Vandal guides—Emperor and Pope—The Bible in mosaic—The Creation of the world—Cain and Abel—Noah—The story of Joseph—The golden horses—A horseless city—A fiction gross and palpable—A populous church—The French pilgrims—Rain in Venice—S. Mark's Day—The procession—New Testament mosaics—S. Isidoro's chapel—The chapel of the Males—A coign of vantage—The Pala d'oro—Sansovino—S. Mark's treasures—The Baptistery—The good Andrea Dandolo—The vision of Bishop Magnus—The parasites.

LET us now enter the atrium When I first did so, in 1889, I fell at once into the hands of a guide, who, having completed his other services, offered for sale a few pieces of mosaic which he had casually chipped off the wall with his knife somewhere in the gallery. Being young and simple I supposed this the correct thing for guides to do, and was justified in that belief when at the Acropolis, a few weeks later, the terrible Greek who had me in tow ran lightly up a workman's ladder, produced a hammer from his pocket and knocked a beautiful carved leaf from a capital. But S. Mark's has no such vandals to-day. There are guides in plenty, who detach themselves from its portals or appear suddenly between the flagstaffs with promises of assistance; but they are easily repulsed and the mosaics are safe.

Entering the atrium by the central door we come upon history at once. For just inside on the pavement whose tesselations are not less lovely than the ceiling mosaics—indeed I often think more lovely—are the porphyry slabs on which the Emperor Frederick Barbarossa asked pardon of Pope Alexander III, whom he had driven from Rome into an exile which had now brought him to Venice. The story has it that the great Emperor divested himself of his cloak of power and lay full length on these very stones ; the Pope placed his foot on his neck, saying, "I will tread on the asp and the basilisk". The Emperor ventured the remark that he was submitting not to the Pope but to S. Peter. "To both of us," said Alexander. That was on July 24, 1177, and on the walls of the Doges' Palace we shall see pictures of the Pope's sojourn in Venice and subsequent triumph.

The vestibule mosaics are not easy to study, as the best are in the domes immediately overhead. But they are very interesting in their simple directness. Their authors had but one end in view, and that was to tell the story. As thorough illustrations they could not be over-praised. And here let me say that though Baedeker is an important book in Venice, and S. Mark's Square is often red with it, there is one even more useful and necessary, especially in S. Mark's, and that is the Bible. One has not to be a very profound Biblical student to keep pace, in memory, with the Old Masters when they go to the New Testament; but when the Old is the inspiration, as chiefly here, one is continually at fault.

The vestibule mosaics are largely thirteenth century. That is to say, they were being fixed together in these domes and on these walls when England was under the first Edwards, and long indeed before America, which now sends so many travellers to see them—so many in fact that

ONE OF THE NOAH MOSAICS
In the Atrium of S. Mark's

it is almost impossible to be in any show-place without hearing the American accent—was dreamed of.

The series begins in the first dome on the right, with the creation of the world, a design spread over three circles. In the inner one is the origin of all things—or as far back as the artist, wisely untroubled by the question of the creation of the Creator, cared to go. Angels seem always to have been. In the next circle we find the creation of the sun, moon, and stars, birds, beasts, and fishes, and finally of man. The outer circle belongs to Adam and Eve. Adam names the animals; his rib is extracted; Eve, a curiously forbidding woman, rather a Gauguinesque type, results; she is presented to Adam; they eat the fruit; they take to foliage; they are judged; the leaves become real garments; they are driven forth to toil, Adam with an axe and Eve with a distaff.

On the sides is the story of Cain and Abel carried back to an earlier point than we are accustomed to see it. Later, to the altar Cain brings fruit and Abel a lamb; a hand is extended from heaven to the fortunate Abel while Cain sulks on a chair. The two brothers then share a sentry-box in apparent amity, until Cain becomes a murderer.

We next come, on the sides, to the story of Noah and the Tower of Babel. Noah's biography is vivid and detailed. We see him receiving Divine instruction to build the ark, and his workmen busy. He is next among the birds, and himself carries a pair of peacocks to the vessel. Then the beasts are seen, and he carries in a pair of leopards, or perhaps pumas; and then his whole family stand by while two eagles are inserted, and other big birds, such as storks and pelicans, await their turn. On the other side the rains have begun and the world is drowning. Noah sends out the dove and receives it again; the waters suh-side; he builds his altar, and the animals released from the ark gambol on the slopes of Ararat. I reproduce this series. The third series of events in the life of Noah I leave to the visitor to decipher. One of the incidents so captured the Venetian imagination that it is repeated at the eastern corner of the Ducal Palace lagoon façade.

The second dome tells the history of Abraham, and then three domes are given to the best story in the world, the story of Joseph. The first dome treats of his dream, showing him asleep and busy with it, and the result, the pit being a cylinder projecting some feet from the ground. Jacob's grief on seeing the coat of many colours is very dramatic. In the next we find Potiphar's wife, Joseph's downfall, and the two dreaming officials. The third tells of Joseph and Jacob and is full of Egyptian local colour, a group of pyramids occurring twice. On the wall are subsidiary scenes, such as Joseph before Pharaoh, the in-cident of Benjamin's sack with the cup in it, and the scene of the lean kine devouring the fat, which they are doing with tremendous spirit, all beginning simultaneously from behind.

The last dome relates the story of Moses, but it is by an inferior artist and does not compare with the others. The miracle of the manna on the wall is, however, amusing, the manna being rather like melons and the quails as large as pheasants. On the extreme left a cook is at work grilling some on a very open fire. Another inferior mosaic on the north side of the atrium, represents S. Chris-topher with his little Passenger. It is a pity that Titian's delightful version in the Doges' Palace could not have been followed.

The atrium is remarkable not only for its illustrations to

Genesis. Its mosaic patterns are very lovely, and its carved capitals. The staircase to the left of the centre door of the church proper leads to the interior galleries and to the exterior gallery, where the golden horses are. Of the interior galleries I speak later. Let me say here that these noble steeds were originally designed and cast for a triumphal arch, to be driven by Victory, in honour of Nero. Filched from Rome by Constantine, they were carried to his own city as an ornament to the imperial hippodrome. In 1204 the great Doge Enrico Dandolo, having humiliated Constantinople, brought the horses to Venice as a trophy, and they were transferred to the service of the church. There is a picture of them in Windsor Castle, by Canaletto, in which they are set upon four pedestals in front of the Doges' Palace, facing the Old Library; but I think that this represents not a fact but a project. Above the central portal of S. Mark's they stood for nearly six centuries, and then in 1797 a more modern Constantine, one Napoleon, carried them to Paris, to beautify his city. In 1815, however, when there was a redistribution of Napoleonic spoils, back they came to Venice, to their ancient platform, and there they now are, unchanged, except that their golden skins are covered with the autographs of tourists.

One odd thing about them is that they and Colleoni's and Victor Emmanuel's steeds are the only horses which many Venetians have ever seen. As to the horselessness of Venice, the last word, as well as one of the first, in English, was written by our old friend Coryat in the following passage : " For you must consider that neither the Venetian Gentlemen nor any others can ride horses in the streets of Venice as in other Cities and Townes, because their streets being both very narrow and slippery, in regard they are all paved with smooth bricke, and joyning to the water, the horse would quickly fall into the river, and so drowne both himselfe and his rider. Therefore

the Venetians do use Gondolaes in their streets insteede of
horses, I meane their liquid streets: that is, their pleasant
channels.   So that I now finde by mine owne experience
that the speeches of a certaine English Gentleman (with
whom I once discoursed before my travels), a man that
much vaunted of his observations in Italy, are utterly
false.   For when I asked him what principall things he
observed in Venice, he answered me that he noted but little
of the city, because he rode through it in post.   A fiction,
and as grosse and palpable as ever was coyned."

From the horses' gallery there is a most interesting view
of the Piazza and the Piazzetta, and the Old Library
and Loggetta are as well seen from here as anywhere.

Within the church itself two things at once strike us:
the unusual popularity of it, and the friendliness.   Why
an intensely foreign building of great size should exert
this power of welcome I cannot say; but the fact remains
that S. Mark's, for all its Eastern domes and gold and odd
designs and billowy floor, does more to make a stranger
and a Protestant at home than any cathedral I know; and
more people are also under its sway than under that of
any other.   Most of them are sightseers, no doubt, but
they are sightseers from whom mere curiosity has fallen:
they seem to like to be there for its own sake.

The coming and going are incessant, both of worshippers
and tourists, units and companies.   Guides, professional
and amateur, bring in little groups of travellers, and one
hears their monotonous informative voices above the foot-
falls; for, as in all cathedrals, the prevailing sound is of
boots.   In S. Mark's the boots make more noise than in
most of the others because of the unevenness of the pavement, which here and there lures to the trot.   One day
as I sat in my favourite seat, high up in the gallery, by a
mosaic of S. Liberale, a great gathering of French pil-

grims entered, and, seating themselves in the right transept, beneath me, they disposed themselves to listen to an address by the French priest who shepherded them. His nasal eloquence still rings in my ears. A little while after I chanced to be at Padua, and there, in the church of S. Anthony, I found him again, again intoning rhetoric.

S. Mark's is never empty, but when the rain falls—and in Venice rain literally does fall—it is full. Then do the great leaden spouts over the façade pour out their floods, while those in the courtyard of the Doges' Palace expel an even fiercer torrent. But the city's recovery from a deluge is instant.

But the most populous occasion on which I ever saw S. Mark's was on S. Mark's own day—April 25. Then it is solid with people : on account of the procession, which moves from a point in front of the high altar and makes a tour of the church, passing down to the door of the Baptistery, through the atrium, and into the church again by the door close to the Cappella dei Mascoli. There is something in all Roman Catholic ceremonial which for me impairs its impressiveness—perhaps a thought too much mechanism—and I watched this chanting line of choristers, priests, and prelates without emotion, but perfectly willing to believe that the fault lay with me. Three things abide vividly in the memory : the Jewish cast of so many of the large inscrutable faces of the wearers of the white mitres ; a little aged, isolated, ecclesiastic of high rank who muttered irascibly to himself; and a precentor who for a moment unfolded his hands and lowered his eyes to pull out his watch and peep at it. Standing just inside the church and watching the people swarm in their hundreds for this pageantry, I was struck by the comparatively small number who made any entering

salutation. No children did. Perhaps the raptest worshipper was one of Venice's many dwarfs, a tiny, alert man
in blue linen with a fine eloquent face and a great mass of
iron-grey hair.

This was the only occasion on which I saw the Baptistery accessible freely to all and the door into the
Piazzetta open.

One should not look at a guide-book on the first visit
to S. Mark's; nor on the second or third, unless, of course,
one is pressed for time. Let the walls and the floors and
the pillars and the ceiling do their own quiet magical
work first. Later you can gather some of their history.
The church has but one fault which I have discovered, and
that is the circular window to the south. Beautiful as
this is, it is utterly out of place, and whoever cut it
was a vandal.

But indeed S. Mark's ought to have a human appeal, considering the human patience and thought that have gone
to its making and beautifying, inside and out. No other
church has had much more than a tithe of such toil. The
Sixtine Chapel in Rome is wonderful enough, with its
frescoes; but what is the labour on a fresco compared
with that on a mosaic? Before every mosaic there must
be the artist and the glass-maker; and then think of the
labour of translating the artist's picture into this exacting
and difficult medium and absolutely covering every inch
of the building with it! And that is merely decoration;
not structure at all.

There are mosaics here which date from the tenth century; and there are mosaics which are being renewed at
this moment, for the prosperity of the church is continually in the thoughts of the city fathers. The earliest
is that of Christ, the Virgin, and S. Mark, on the inside

wall over the central door. My own favourites are all
among the earlier ones. Indeed, some of the later ones
are almost repulsively flamboyant and self-conscious.
Particularly I like the great scene of Christ's agony high
up on the right wall, with its lovely green and gold
border, touched with red. But all the patterns, especially
in the roof arches, are a delight, especially those with
green in them. I like too the picture of Christ on a
white ass in the right transept, with the children laying
their cloaks in His way. And the naïve scene of Christ's
temptation above it, and the quaint row of disciples beneath it, waiting to have their feet washed.

Of the more modern mosaics the " Annunciation " and
" Adoration of the Magi " are among the most pleasing.

There are some curious and interesting early mosaics in
the chapel of S. Isidoro in the left transept. It is always
dark in this tiny recess, but bit by bit the incidents in the
pictures are revealed. They are very dramatic, and the
principal scene of the saint's torture by being dragged
over the ground by galloping horses is repeated in relief
on the altar. I have failed to find any life of any S. Isidoro
that relates the story. Note the little bronze lions on
each side of the altar—two more for that census of Venetian
lions which I somewhere suggest might be made. The
little chapel on the left of S. Isidoro's is known as the
Cappella dei Mascoli, or males, for hither come the young
wives of Venice to pray that they may bring forth little
gondoliers. That at any rate is one story; another says
that it was the chapel of a confraternity of men to which
no woman might belong. In the mosaic high up on the
left is a most adorably gay little church, and on the altar
are a pretty baby and angels. On a big pillar close to this
chapel is a Madonna with a votive rifle hung by it; but

I have been unable to find its story.   It might be a moving one.

It is not detail, however lovely, for which one seeks S. Mark's, but general impressions, and these are inexhaustible. It is a temple of beauty and mystery in which to loiter long, and, as I have said, just by the S. Liberale in the gallery of the right transept, I made my seat.   From this point one sees under the most favourable conditions the mosaic of the entry into Jerusalem ; the choir; the choir screen with its pillars and saints; the two mysterious pulpits, beneath which children creep and play on great days; and all the miracle of the pavements.   From here one can follow the Mass and listen to the singing, undisturbed by the moving crowd.

S. Mark's is described by Ruskin as an illuminated missal in mosaic.   It is also a treasury of precious stones, for in addition to every known coloured stone that this earth of ours can produce, with which it is built and decorated and floored, it has the wonderful Pala d'oro, that sumptuous altar-piece of gold and silver and enamel which contains some six thousand jewels.   More people, I guess, come to see this than anything else ; but it is worth standing before, if only as a reminder of how far the Church has travelled since a carpenter's son, who despised riches, founded it ; as a reminder, too, as so much of this building is, of the day when Constantinople, where in the eleventh century the Pala d'oro was made, was Christian also.

The fine carved pillars of the high altar's canopy are very beautiful, and time has given them a quality as of ivory. According to a custodian, without whom one cannot enter the choir, the remains of S. Mark still lie beneath the high altar, but this probably is not true.   At the back of the

high altar is a second altar with pillars of alabaster, and
the custodian places his candle behind the central ones to
illustrate their soft lucency, and affirms that they are from
Solomon's own temple. His candle illumines also Sansovino's bronze sacristy door, with its fine reliefs of the
Deposition and the Resurrection, with the heads of
Evangelists and Prophets above them. Six realistic heads
are here too, one of which is Titian's, one Sansovino's himself, and one the head of Aretino, the witty and licentious
writer and gilt-edged parasite—this last a strange selection
for a sacristy door. Sansovino designed also the bronze
figures of the Evangelists on the balustrade of the choir
stalls and the reliefs of the Doge's and Dogaressa's private
pews.

There are two Treasuries in S. Mark's. One can be seen
every day for half a franc; the other is open only on Fri-
days and the entrance fee is, I believe, five francs. I have
not laid out this larger amount; but in the other I have
spent some time and seen various priceless temporal indications of spiritual power. There is a sword of Doge Mocenigo, a wonderful turquoise bowl, a ring for the Adriatic nuptials, and so forth. But I doubt if such details
of S. Mark's are things to write about. One should
go there to see S. Mark's as a whole, just as one goes to
Venice to see Venice.

The Baptistery is near the entrance on the left as you
leave the church. But before entering it, it is interesting to stand in the centre of the aisle with one's back
to the high altar and look through the open door at
the Piazza lying in the sun. The scene is fascinating in
this frame; and one also discovers how very much askew
the façade of S. Mark's must be, for instead of seeing, immediately in front, the centre of the far end of the square,

as most persons would expect, one sees Naya's photograph shop at the corner.

The Baptistery is notable for its mosaic biography of the Baptist, its noble font, and the beautiful mural tomb of Doge Andrea Dandolo.   Andrea, the last Doge to be buried within S. Mark's, was one of the greatest of them all. His short reign of but ten years, 1343 to 1354, when he died aged only forty-six, was much troubled by war with the Genoese ; but he succeeded in completing an alliance against the Turks and in finally suppressing Zara, and he wrote a history of Venice and revised its code of laws. Petrarch, who was his intimate friend, described Andrea as " just, upright, full of zeal and of love for his country . . . erudite . . . wise, affable, and humane ".   His successor was the traitor Marino Faliero.   The tomb of the Doge is one of the most beautiful things in Venice, all black bronze.

It was the good Andrea, not to be confused with old Henry Dandolo, the scourge of the Greeks, to whom we are indebted for the charming story of the origin of certain Venetian churches.   It runs thus in the translation in *St. Mark's Rest* :—

" As head and bishop of the islands, the Bishop Magnus of Altinum went from place to place to give them comfort, saying that they ought to thank God for having escaped from these barbarian cruelties.   And there appeared to him S. Peter, ordering him that in the head of Venice, or truly of the city of Rivoalto, where he should find oxen and sheep feeding, he was to build a church under his (S. Peter's) name.   And thus he did ; building S. Peter's Church in the island of Olivolo [now Castello], where at present is the seat and cathedral church of Venice.

" Afterwards appeared to him the angel Raphael, com-

THE CAMPANILE AND THE PIAZZA FROM COOK'S CORNER

mitting it to him, that at another place, where he should find a number of birds together, he should build him a church : and so he did, which is the church of the Angel Raphael in Dorsoduro.

"Afterwards appeared to him Messer Jesus Christ our Lord, and committed to him that in the midst of the city he should build a church, in the place above which he should see a red cloud rest : and so he did, and it is San Salvador.

"Afterwards appeared to him the most holy Mary the Virgin, very beautiful, and commanded him that where he should see a white cloud rest, he should build a church : which is the church of S. Mary the Beautiful.

"Yet still appeared to him S. John the Baptist, commanding that he should build two churches, one near the other,—the one to be in his name, and the other in the name of his father. Which he did, and they are San Giovanni in Bragora, and San Zaccaria.

"Then appeared to him the apostles of Christ, wishing, they also, to have a church in this new city : and they committed it to him that where he should see twelve cranes in a company, there he should build it."

Of the Baptistery mosaics the most scanned will always be that in which Salome bears in the head. In another the decapitated saint bends down and touches his own head. The scene of Christ's baptism is very quaint, Christ being half-submerged in Jordan's waves, and fish swimming past during the sacred ceremony. Behind the altar, on which is a block of stone from Mount Tabor, is a very spirited relief of S. George killing the dragon.

The adjoining chapel is that named after Cardinal Zeno. who lies in the magnificent central tomb beneath a bronze effigy of himself, while his sacred hat is in crimson mosaic

on each side of the altar.   The tomb and altar alike
are splendid rather than beautiful : its late Renaissance
sculptors, being far removed from Donatello, Mino, and
Desiderio, the last of whom was one of the authors of the
beautiful font in the adjoining Baptistery.   Earlier and
more satisfactory reliefs are those of an angel on the right
of the altar and a Madonna and Child on the left which
date from a time when sculpture was anonymous.   The
mosaics represent the history of S. Mark.

One may walk or sit at will in S. Mark's as long as one
wishes, free and unharassed ; but a ticket is required for
the galleries and a ticket for the choir and treasury ; and
the Baptistery and Zeno chapel can be entered only by
grace of a loafer with a key who expects something in
return for opening it.   The history of this loafer's privilege
I have not obtained, and it would be interesting to learn
by what authority he is there, for he has no uniform and
he accepts any sum you give him.   The post may be
hereditary.

The wise traveller will make a habit of going to S.
Mark's every morning, early, before the crowds arrive.
Only thus can he extract its fullest charm.

CHAPTER IV

THE PIAZZA AND THE CAMPANILE

The heart of Venice—Old-fashioned music—Foreign invaders—The honeymooners—True republicanism—A city of the poor—The black shawls — A brief triumph — Red hair — A band-night incident — The pigeons of the Piazza—The two Procuratie—A royal palace—The Historical Museum — The shopkeepers — Florian's —¡Great names — Venetian restaurants—Little fish—The old campanile—A noble re. solve—The new campanile—The angel vane—The rival campanili—. The welcome lift—The bells—Venice from the Campanile.

S. MARK'S Square, or the Piazza, is more than the centre of Venice : to a large extent it is Venice. Good Venetians when they die flit evermore among its arcades.

No other city has so representative a heart. On the four musical nights here—afternoons in the winter—the Piazza draws like a magnet. That every stranger is here, you may be sure, and most Venetian men. Some sit outside Florian's and the other cafés ; others walk round and round the bandstand ; others pause fascinated beside the musicians. And so it has been for centuries, and will be. New ideas and fashions come slowly into this city, where one does quite naturally what one's father and grandfather did ; and a good instance of such contented conservatism is to be found in the music offered to these contented

31

crowds, for they are still true to Verdi, Wagner, and Rossini, and with reluctance are experiments made among the newer men.

In the daytime the population of the Piazza is more foreign than Venetian. In fact the only Venetians to be seen are waiters, photographers, and guides, the knots of errand boys watching the artists, and, I might add, the pigeons, of which the number seems to me to have enormously increased since 1913. But at night Venice claims it, although the foreigner is there too. It is amusing to sit at a table on the outside edge of Florian's great quadrangle of chairs and try to pick out the nationalities.

The Venetians reach the Square first, smart, knowing, confident, friendly, and cheerful; and then, after their hotel dinners, at about a quarter past nine, the English and the Americans. For if Venice cannot be called almost an American city, S. Mark's Square is unquestionably, in the season, a Main Street. For the most part the English and Americans do not promenade, but sit and talk, the Americans more audibly than the English. But the honeymooners are the best—the solicitous young bridegrooms from Surbiton and Chislehurst in their dinnerjackets and black ties; their slender brides, with pretty wraps on their heads, here probably for the last or the first time, and so determined to appear Continental and tolerant, bless their hearts! They walk round and round, or sit over their coffee, and would be so happy and unselfconscious and clinging were it not for the other English here.

The fine republicanism of Venice is nowhere so apparent as on band nights. Such aristocrats as the city holds (and

judging from the condition of the palaces to-day, there
cannot be many now in residence) either look exactly like
the middle classes or abstain from the Piazza.   The prevailing type is the well-to-do citizen, very rarely with
his women folk, who moves among street urchins at play ;
cigar-end hunters ; soldiers watchful for officers to salute ;
officers sometimes returning and often ignoring salutes ;
groups of slim upright Venetian girls in the stately black
shawls, moving, as they always do, like queens ; little uni-
formed schoolboys in " crocodiles " ; a policeman or two ;
a party from the country ; a workman with his wife and
babies (for though the Venetians adore babies they see no
incongruity in keeping them up till ten o'clock); epauletted
and cockhatted gendarmes ; and at intervals, like ghosts,
officials from the arsenal, often alone, in their spotless
white linen.

Every type of Venetian is seen in the Square, save one—
the gondolier.   Never have I seen a gondolier there, day
or night : not because it is too grand for him, but it is
off his beat.   When he has done his work he prefers
the wine shops of his own sestiere.   No thought of any
want of welcome would deter him, for Venice is republic
to the core.   In fact one might go farther and say that it
is a city of the poor.   Where the poor lived in the great
days when the palaces were occupied by the rich, one
cannot quite understand, since the palace is the staple
building ; but there is no doubt as to where they live now :
they live everywhere.   The number of palaces which are
wholly occupied by one family must be infinitesimal ; the
rest are tenements, anything but model buildings, rookeries.
Venice has no aristocratic quarter as other cities have.
The poor establish themselves either in a palace or as near
it as possible.

3

I have referred to the girls in their black shawls or
scialli. They remain in the memory as one of Venice's
most distinguished possessions. A handsome young private
gondolier in white linen with a coloured scarf, bending
to the oar and thrusting his boat forward with muscular
strokes, is a delight to watch; but he is without mystery.
These girls have grace and mystery too. They are so
foreign, so slender and straight, so sad. Their faces are
capable of animation, but their prevailing expression is
melancholy. Why is this? Is it because they know how
secondary a place woman holds in this city of well-
nourished, self-satisfied men? Is it that they know that
a girl's life is so brief: one day as supple and active as
they are now and the next a crone? For it is one of the
tragedies that the Venetian atmosphere so rapidly ages
women.

But in their prime the Venetian girls in the black shawls
are distinguished indeed, and there was not a little sagacity
in the remark to me by an observer who said that, were
they wise, all women would adopt a uniform. One has
often thought this, in London, when a nurse in blue or
grey passes refreshingly along a pavement made bizarre
by expensive and foolish fashions; one realizes it even
more in Venice.

Most of these girls have dark or black hair. The
famous red hair of Venetian women is rarely seen out of
pictures.

Round and round goes the chattering contented crowd,
while every table at each of the four cafés, Florian's
and the Aurora, the Quadri and the Ortes Rosa, swells the
noise. Now and then the music, or the ordinary murmur
of the Square in the long intervals, is broken by the noisy
rattle of a descending shop shutter, or the hour is struck by

the Merceria clock's bronze giants ; now and then a pigeon crosses the sky and shows luminous where the light strikes its breast ; now and then a feather flutters from a window ledge, great bats flit up and down, and the mosquitoes ping in one's ear. It is an entertainment never failing in interest to the observer, and not the least amusing question that one asks oneself is, Where does every one sleep ?

I shall always remember one band night here, for it was then that I saw a girl and her father whose images will never leave me, I know not why. Every now and then, but seldom indeed, a strange face or form will thus suddenly photograph itself on the memory, when it is only with the utmost concentrated effort, or not at all, that we can call up mental pictures of those near and dear to us. I know nothing of these two ; I saw them only once again, and then in just the same fugitive way ; but if an artist were now to show me a portrait of either, I could point out where his hand was at fault. The band was playing the usual music—*Il Trovatore* or *Aïda* or *Lohengrin*—and the crowd was circulating when an elderly man with a long-pointed grey beard and moustache and the peculiar cast of countenance belonging to them (Don Quixotic) walked past. He wore a straw hat slightly tilted and was smoking a cigar. His arm was passed through that of a tall slender girl of about his own height, and, say, twenty-five, in red. She was leaning towards him and he slightly inclined towards her. They walked faster than Venice, and talked animatedly in English as they passed me, and the world had no one in it but themselves ; and so they disappeared, with long strides and a curious ease of combined movement almost like skilful partners in a dance. Two nights later I saw them again. This time she was in black, and again they sailed through the crowd, a little

leaning towards each other, he again holding her arm, and
again both discussing in English something with such interest that they were conscious of nothing around them.
Sitting outside a café on the Piazza every evening for a
month, one naturally sees many travellers come and go;
but none other in that phantasmagoria left any mark on
my mind.   Why did these?

So much for S. Mark's Square by night.   With thousands of persons, to think of S. Mark's Square by day is
chiefly to think of pigeons.   Many a visitor to Venice who
cannot remember the details of a single painting there can
show you a photograph of herself with pigeons on her
shoulders and arms.   Photographers and dealers in maize
are here all day to effect these pretty conjunctions; but
the Kodak has seriously impaired their profits.   The birds
are smaller than our London monsters and not quite so
brilliantly burnished.   How many there are I have no
idea; but since they are sacred, their numbers must be
ever greater.   Why they are sacred is something of a
mystery.   One story states that the great Enrico Dandolo
had carrier-pigeons with him in the East which conveyed
the grand tidings of victories to Venice; another says that
the same heroic old man was put in possession of valuable
strategic information by means of a carrier-pigeon, and on
returning to Venice proclaimed it a bird to be reverenced.
There was once a custom of loosing a number of pigeons
among the crowd in the Piazza on Palm Sunday.   The
birds being weighted floundered downwards and were
caught and killed for the pot; but such as escaped were
held to have earned their liberty for ever.

At night no doubt the pigeons roost among S. Mark's
statuary and on convenient ledges in the neighbourhood;
by day, when not on the pavement of the Piazza, the bulk

THE PRESENTATION

FROM THE PAINTING BY TITIAN

In the Accademia

of the flock are dotted about among the reliefs of the Atrio, facing S. Mark's.

They have no timidity, but by a kind of honourable understanding they all affect to be startled by the bells at certain hours and the midday gun, and ascend in a grey cloud for a few seconds.

They are never so engaging as when flying double, bird and shadow, against the Campanile.

Their collective cooing fills the air and makes the Piazza's day music.

Venetians crossing the Piazza walk straight on, through the birds, like Moses crossing the Red Sea ; the foreigners pick their way.

What with S. Mark's and the pigeons, the Campanile and coffee, few visitors have any time to inquire as to the other buildings of the Piazza. Nor are they of much interest. Briefly they are the Old Procuratie, which forms the side on which the clock is, the Atrio or Nuova Fabbrica opposite S. Mark's, whose sculptured relief provides the pigeons with their favourite resting place, and the New Procuratie on the Campanile side. The old Procuratie, whose main row of windows I once counted, making either one hundred or a hundred and one, is now offices and, above, residences. Here once abode the nine procurators of Venice who, under the Doge, ruled the city.

The New Procuratie became the Royal Palace. It is the finer building ; over the arches it has good sprawling Michael-Angelesque figures, noble lions' heads, and massive ornamentations.

I don't know for certain, but I should guess that the Royal Palace in Venice was the only abode of a European King that has shops underneath it. I say was, because the King has recently made over several of his palaces to

the nation, among them this one, with the idea of providing additional space for the display of art, decorative
and applied, and thus encouraging its influence. No
doubt His Majesty will pay Venice an occasional visit,
and for this purpose a royal suite will be retained, but
already it has become the historical museum of the city
in place of the old Fondaco dei Turchi, on the Grand
Canal.

Assuming that the collection is what it was, I can
promise the visitor some very interesting moments. Among
the works of art are some amusing scenes of Venetian life
in the eighteenth century by the Hogarth of the Adriatic
—Pietro Longhi. Old Venice may also be reconstructed
with the assistance of drawings by Canaletto. Guardi
has many sketches here, and other heroes of the place are
Canova, the sculptor, and Goldoni, the dramatist. Old
prints abound, and all the usual relics of an historical
museum are numerous, such as coins (you may see the
ducat of Shylock's day), manuscripts, Kings' costumes and
death-masks of Doges.

Among the pictures a quaint and ugly but fascinating
thing, attributed to Carpaccio and said to represent two
courtesans at home, is the most memorable. Why it
should not equally represent two ladies of unimpeachable
character, I cannot see. Ruskin went beyond everything
in his praises, in *St. Mark's Rest*, of this picture. He
suggests that it is the best picture in the world. But
read his amazing words. "I know," he says, "no other
which unites every nameable quality of painter's art in so
intense a degree—breadth with tenderness, brilliancy with
quietness, decision with minuteness, colour with light and
shade: all that is faithfullest in Holland, fancifullest in

Venice, severest in Florence, naturalest in England. Whatever de Hooghe could do in shade, Van Eyck in detail, Giorgione in mass, Titian in colour, Bewick and Landseer in animal life, is here at once; and I know no other picture in the world which can be compared with it."

Beneath these three buildings—the two Procuratie and the Fabbrica Nuova—runs an arcade where the Venetians congregate in wet weather and where the snares for tourists are chiefly laid by the dealers in jewellery, coral, statuary, lace, glass, and mosaic. But the Venetian shopkeepers are not clever : they have not the sense to leave the nibbler alone. One has not been looking in the window for more than two seconds before a silky-voiced youth appears at the door and begins to recommend his wares and invite custom ; and then of course one moves away in terror.

Here, too, under the arcade, are the head-quarters of the cafés, which do most of their business on the pavement of the Square. Of these Florian's is the oldest and best. At certain hours, however, one must cross the Square to either the Ortes Rosa or Quadri, or be roasted. The original Florian was wise in his choice of site, for he has more shady hours than his rivals opposite. In an advertisement of the café in the musical programme it is stated that, " the oldest and most aristocratic establishment of its kind in Venice, it can count among its clients, since 1720, Byron, Goethe, Rousseau, Canova, Dumas, and Moor," meaning by Moor not Othello but Byron's friend and biographer, the Anacreon of Erin. How Florian's early patrons looked one can see in a brilliant little picture by Guardi in the National Gallery, No. 2099. The café boasts that its doors are never shut, day or night; and I have no doubt that this is true, but I have never tested it in the small hours.

Oddly enough there are no restaurants in the Piazza, but many about its borders on the north and west. The visitor to Venice, as a rule, eats in his hotel; and I think he is wise. But wishing to be in Venice rather more thoroughly than that, I once lived in rooms for a month and ate in all the restaurants in turn. Having had this experience, I expect to be believed when I say that the restaurants of Venice are not good. The food is monotonous, and the waiting is leisurely. The waiters are Venetians, and Venetians won't be hurried. They say " Pronto " and take their time. Add to this that the guests receive no welcome, partly because, all the places being understaffed, no one can be spared for that friendly office, and partly because politeness is not a Venetian foible. An immense interval can then elapse before the lista, or bill of fare, is brought, partly because there is no waiter disengaged and partly because there seems to be a law in Venetian restaurants that one menu shall suffice for eight tables.

Then comes the struggle—to find anything new either to eat or drink. The lista contains in print a large number of attractive things, but few are obtainable, for on an Italian menu print is nothing; it is only the not too legible written words that have any relevance. Once a meal is ordered it comes rapidly enough. For the most part Venetian food is Italian food : that is to say, almost wholly veal and paste; but in the matter of fish Venice has her specialities. There are, for example, those little toy octopuses which on my first visit, too many years ago, used to be seen everywhere in baskets at corners, but now have disappeared from the streets. These are known as calamai or calamaretti, and if one has the courage to take the shuddering first step that counts they will be found to be very good. But they fail to look nice. Better still are scampi, a kind of small crawfish, tender and sweet.

To the investigator I recommend the dish called fritto di mare, in which one has a fried jumble of the smaller sea creatures of the lagoon, to the scampi and calamaretti being added fresh sardines (which the fishermen catch with their hand at low tide), shrimps, little soles, little red mullets, and a slice or two of big cuttle fish. A popular large fish is the bronzino, and great steaks of tunny are always in demand too. But considering Venice's peculiar position with regard to the sea and her boasted dominion over it, fish are very dear.

Even more striking is the dearness of fruit, but this, I take it, is due to the distance that it must come, either by rail or water. No restaurant that I discovered—as in the fair land of France and indeed elsewhere in Italy—places wine or grapes free on the table.

As I say, I tried all the Venetian houses, small and large—the Cappello Nero, the Bella Venezia, the Antico Panada, the Bauer-Grünwald (which has now ceased to be, although the hotel remains), the Bonvecchiato, the Cavalletti, the Pilsen ; and the only one to which I felt any desire to return was the Pilsen, which, though large and noisy and intensely Teutonic, was a shade more attentive than the others. But since those days the Luna was opened—half indoors and half out, just at the south-west corner as you leave or enter the great square—and I commend that.

I cannot remember the old campanile with enough vividness to be sure, but my impression is that its brick was a mellower tint than that of the new : nearer

the richness of S. Giorgio Maggiore's, across the water.
Time may do as much for the new campanile, but at
present its colour is not very satisfactory except when the
sun is setting. Indeed, so new is it that one cannot think
of it as having any association whatever with S. Mark's.
If it belongs to anything it is to Venice as a whole. Yet
one ought not to cavil, for it stands so bravely on the
spot where its predecessor fell, and is a very satisfactory
proof that the Venetians, for all the decay of their lovely
city and the disappearance of their marvellous power, are
Venetians still.

The old campanile, after giving various warnings, fell
on July 14, 1902, at half-past nine in the morning. On
the evening of the same day the Town Council met, under
the chairmanship of Count Grimani, the mayor, and without the least hesitation decided that a successor must be
erected : in the fine words of the count : " Dov'era,
com'era " (" Where it was and as it was "). Sympathy
and contributions poured in from the outside world to
strengthen the hands of the Venetians, and on S. Mark's
Day (April 25), 1903, the first stone was laid. On S. Mark's
Day, 1912, the new campanile was declared complete in
every part and blessed in the presence of representatives
of all Italy, while 2479 pigeons, brought hither for the
purpose, carried the tidings to every corner of the
country.

The most remarkable circumstance about the fall of the
campanile is that no one was hurt. The Piazza and
Piazzetta are by no means empty at half-past nine in the
morning, yet these myriad tons of brick and stone sank
bodily to the ground and not a human bruise resulted.
Here its behaviour was better than that of the previous
campanile of S. Giorgio Maggiore, which, when it fell in

1774, killed one monk and injured two others. Nor was
S. Mark's harmed, although its sacristan confesses to have
been dumb for three days from the shock. The falling
golden angel from the top of the campanile was found in
front of the central door as though to protect the church.
Sansovino's Loggetta, it is true, was crushed and buried
beneath the débris, but human energy is indomitable, and
the present state of that lovely building is a testimony to
the skill and tenacity which still inhabit Venetian hands
and breasts.

What I chiefly miss in the new campanile is any aerial
suggestion. It has actual solidity in every inch of it,
apart from the fact that it also conveys the idea of solidity,
as any building must which has taken the place of one so
misguided as to fall down. But its want of this intangible
quality, together with its newness, have displaced it in
my eyes as the king campanile of Venice. In my eyes
the campanile of S. Giorgio Maggiore now reigns supreme,
while I am very much attached also to those of the Frari
and S. Francesco della Vigna. But let S. Mark's campanile take heart : some day Anno Domini will claim
these others too, and then the rivalry will pass. But as
it is, morning, noon, and evening the warm red bricks and
rich green copper top of S. Giorgio Maggiore's bell-tower
draw the gaze first and hold it longest. It is the most
beautiful campanile of all, and its inevitableness is such
that did we not know the truth we should wonder if the
six days of creation had not included an afternoon for the
ordainment of such edifices.

It would need a Hans Andersen to describe the feelings of the other Venetian campaniles when S. Mark's
tall column fell. S. Giorgio's I imagine instantly took
command, but no doubt there were other claimants to the

throne. I rather fancy that the Frari's had something
to say, and S. Pietro in Castello's also, on account of his
age and his early importance ; but who could pay any
serious attention at that time to a tower so pathetically
out of the perpendicular as he now is ?

The new campanile endeavours to reproduce the old
faithfully, and it was found possible to utilize a little of
the old material. The figures of Venice on the east wall
above the belfry canopy and Justice on the west are the
ancient ones pieced together and made whole; the lions
on the north and south sides are new. The golden angel
on the summit is the old one restored, with the novelty,
to her, as to us, of being set on a pivot to act as a vane.
I made this discovery for myself, after being puzzled by
what might have been fancied changes of posture from
day to day, due to optical illusion. One of the shopkeepers
on the Square, who has the campanile before his eye continually, replied, however, when I asked him if the figure
was fixed or movable, " Fixed ". This double duty of the
new campanile angel—to shine in golden glory over the
city and also to tell the wind—must be a little mortifying
to her celestial sister on the campanile of S. Giorgio, who
is immovable. But no doubt she has philosophy enough to
consider subjection to the caprices of the breeze a humilia-
tion.   The Custom House figure is the most trustworthy.

Another change for which one cannot be too grateful
is the lift.   For the modest sum of a few pence one can be
whirled to the belfry in a few seconds at any time of the
day and refresh one's eyes with the city and the lagoon,
the Tyrolese Alps, and the Euganean hills. Of old one
ascended painfully ; but never again. Before the fall there
were five bells, of which only the greatest escaped injury.

The other four were taken to a foundry set up on the
island of Sant' Elena and there fused and recast at the
personal cost of His Holiness, Pope Pius X, who was
Patriarch of Venice. I advise no one to remain in the
belfry when the five are at work. They begin slowly
and with some method ; they proceed to a deafening
cacophony, tolerable only when one is far distant.

There are certain surprises in the view from the campanile. One is that none of the water of the city is visible—
not a gleam—except a few yards of the Grand Canal and
a stretch of the Canale della Giudecca; the houses are
too high for any of the by-ways to be seen. Another
revelation is that the floor pattern of the Piazza has no
relation to its sides. The roofs of Venice we observe to be
neither red nor brown, but something between the two.
Looking first to the north, over the three flagstaffs and
the pigeon feeders and the Merceria clock, we see away
across the lagoon the huge sheds of the dirigibles and (to
the left) the long railway causeway joining Venice to the
mainland as by a thread. Immediately below us in the
north-east are the domes of S. Mark's, surmounted by the
graceful golden balls on their branches, springing from the
leaden roof, and farther off are the rising bulk of SS. Giovanni
e Paolo, with its derivative dome and golden balls, the
leaning tower of S. Maria del Pianto, and beyond this the
cemetery and Murano. Beneath us on the east side is the
Ducal Palace, and we look right into the courtyard and on
to the prison roof. Farther away are the green trees of the
Giardini Pubblici, the leaning tower of S. Pietro di Castello,
and S. Nicholas of the Lido. In the south-east are the Lido's
various hotels and the islands of S. Lazzaro (with the
campanile) and S. Servolo. In the south is the Grand
Canal with a Guardi pattern of gondolas upon it, criss-

crossing like flies; then S. Giorgio's lovely island and the
Giudecca, and beyond these various islands of the lagoon:
La Grazia, S. Clemente, and, in the far distance, Malamocco.   In the south-west the Custom House pushes its
nose into the water, with the vast white mountain of
the Salute behind it.   In the west is the Piazza, immediately below, with its myriad tables and chairs; then the
backs of the S. Moïse statues; and farther away the Frari
and its campanile, the huge telegraph-wire carriers of
the harbour; across the water Fusina, and beyond in the
far distance the jagged Euganean hills.

At sunset the landscape is sharpened and brought nearer.
The deep blue of the real sea, beyond the lagoon, grows
deeper; the great fields of mud (if it is low tide) gleam
and glisten.   And so it will ever be.

CHAPTER V

THE DOGES' PALACE. I: THE INTERIOR

I HAVE to confess to weariness in the Ducal apartments. The rooms are splendid, no doubt, and the pictures are monuments of energy ; but it is the windows that frame the most delectable scenes. In Venice, where the sun usually shines, one's normal wish is to be out, except when, as in S. Mark's, there is the wonder of dimness too. For Venice is not like other historic cities ; Venice, for all her treasures of art, is first and foremost the bride of the Adriatic, and the call of the sea is strong. Art's opportunity is the dull days and rainy.

With the best will to do so, I cannot be much impressed by the glory and power of the Doges. They wear a look, to me, very little removed from Town Councillors : carried out to the highest power, no doubt, but incorrigibly

municipal none the less; and the journey through these
halls of their deliberations is tedious and unenchanting.
That I am wrong I am only too well aware. Does not
Venetian history, with its triumphs and pageantry of
world-power, prove it? And would Titian and Paul
Veronese and Tintoretto have done all this for a Mayor
and Corporation? These are awkward questions. None
the less, there it is, and the Doges' Palace, within, would
impart no thrill to me were it not for Tintoretto's
"Bacchus and Ariadne".

Having paid for our tickets (for only on Sundays and
holidays is the Palace free), we take the Scala d'Oro,
designed by Sansovino, originally intended only for the
feet of the grandees of the Golden Book. The first room
is an ante-room where catalogues are sold; but these are
not needed, for every room, or nearly every room, has
hand-charts of the paintings, and every room has a custodian eager to impart information. Next is the Hall of
the Four Doors, with its famous and typical Titian—
Doge Grimani, fully armed and accompanied by warriors,
ecstatically acknowledging religion, as symbolized by a
woman, a cross, and countless cherubim. Behind her is
S. Mark with an expression of some sternness, and beside
him his lion, roaring.

Doges, it appears,—at any rate the Doges who reigned
during Titian's long life—had no sense of humour, or
they could not have permitted this kind of self-glorifica-
tion in paint. Both here and at the Accademia we shall
see picture after picture in which these purse-proud
Venetian administrators, suspecting no incongruity or
absurdity, are placed, by Titian and Tintoretto, on terms
of perfect intimacy with the hierarchy of heaven. Sometimes they merely fraternize; sometimes they masquerade

BACCHUS AND ARIADNE
FROM THE PAINTING BY TINTORETTO
In the Doges' Palace

as the Three Kings or Wise Men from the East; but always it is into the New Testament that, with the aid of the brush of genius, they force their way.

Modesty can never have been a Venetian characteristic; nor is it now, when Venice is only a museum and show place. All the Venetians—the men, that is,—whom one sees in the Piazza have an air of profound self-satisfaction. And this palace of the Doges is no training-place for humility; for if its walls do not bear witness, glorious and chromatic, to the greatness of a Doge, it is merely because the greatness of the Republic requires the space. In this room, for example, we find Tiepolo allegorizing Venice as the conqueror of the sea.

And now for the jewel of art in the Doges' Palace. It is in the room opposite the door by which we entered—the ante-room of the Sala del Collegio—and it faces us, on the left as we enter: the "Bacchus and Ariadne" of Tintoretto. We have all seen the "Bacchus and Ariadne" of Titian in our National Gallery, that superb, burning, synchronized epitome of the whole legend. Tintoretto has chosen one incident only; Love bringing Bacchus to the arms of Ariadne and at the same moment placing on her head a starry coronal. Even here the eternal pride of Venice comes in, for, made local, it has been construed as Love, or say Destiny, completing the nuptials of the Adriatic (Bacchus) with Venice (Ariadne), and conferring on Venice the crown of supremacy. But that matters nothing. What matters is that the picture is at once Tintoretto's simplest work and his most lovely. One can do nothing but enjoy it in a kind of stupor of satisfaction, so soothing and perfect is it. His "Crucifixion," which we shall see at the Scuola of S. Rocco, must ever be this giant painter's

4

most tremendous achievement; but the picture before us must equally remain his culminating effort in serene, absolute beauty. Three other mythological paintings, companions of the "Bacchus," are here too, of which I like best the "Minerva" and the "Mercury"; but they are far from having the quality of that other. I have an idea that "The Origin of the Milky Way," in the National Gallery, was painted as a ceiling piece to go with these four, but I have no data for the theory, beyond its similarity in size and scheme. The other great picture in this room is Paul Veronese's sumptuous "Rape of Europa".

The Sala del Collegio itself, leading from this room, is full of Doges in all the magnificence of paint, above the tawdriest of wainscotting. Tintoretto gives us Doge Andrea Gritti praying to the Virgin, Doge Francesco Donato witnessing as an honoured guest the nuptials of S. Catherine, Doge Niccolò da Ponte surveying the Virgin in glory, and Doge Alvise Mocenigo condescending to adore his Saviour. Paul Veronese depicts an allegory of the battle of Lepanto in 1571, at which Venice temporarily overcame the Turks. The kneeling white-bearded warrior beside S. Giustina is the victor, afterwards Doge Sebastiano Venier, and Christ looks on in approval. Tintoretto also painted for the Palace a picture of this battle, but it perished in the fire of 1576. It is Veronese who painted the virtues and attributes on the ceiling, one of his most famous works being the woman with a web, who is sometimes called "Industry" and sometimes "Dialectics," so flexible is symbolism. "Fidelity" has a dog with a fine trustful head. To my weary eye the finest of the groups is that of Mars and Neptune, with flying cherubs, which is superbly drawn and coloured. Nothing but a chaise-longue on which to lie supine, at ease, can make the study of these wonderful ceilings anything but a distressing source of fatigue.

The next room is the Sala del Senato, and here again we find a blend of heaven and Venice, with Doges as a common denominator. A " Descent from the Cross " (by Tintoretto) is witnessed by Doge Pietro Lando and Doge Marcantonio Trevisan ; and the same hand gives us Pietro Loredan imploring the aid of the Virgin. In the centre ceiling painting Tintoretto depicts Venice as Queen of the Sea. The other artist here is Palma the younger, whose principal picture represents Doge Leonardo Loredan presiding over an attack by a lion on a bull, typifying the position of the Republic when Pope Julius launched the League of Cambray against it in 1508. The Doge does not look dismayed, but Venice never recovered from the blow.

The room on the right of the throne leads to the chapel, which has several small pictures. A Giovanni Bellini is over the altar, but it is not one of his best. During his long life in Venice Bellini saw ten Doges, and in his capacity as ducal painter painted four of them.

Returning to the Sala delle Quattro Porte (by way of the " Bacchus and Ariadne " room, if we are wise), we make for the Sala del Consiglio dei Dieci, the terrible Council of Ten. All Venetian histories are eloquent upon this secret Tribunal, which, more powerful far than the Doge himself, for five centuries, beginning early in the fourteenth, ruled the city. On the walls are historical paintings which are admirable examples of story-telling, and on the ceiling are Veroneses, original or copied, the best of which depicts an old man with his head on his hand, fine both in drawing and colour. It was in the wall of the next room that the famous Bocca di Leone was placed, into which were dropped those anonymous charges against Venetian citizens which the Council of Ten investigated, and if true, or, very likely, if not true, punished with such swiftness and thoroughness. How a state that offered such easy temptations to anti-social baseness and treachery could expect to prosper one cannot imagine. It suggests that the Venetian knowledge of human nature was defective at the roots.

In the next room the Three Heads of the Council of Ten debated, and here the attendant goes into spasms of delight over a dazzling inlaid floor.

This is all that is shown upstairs, for the piombi, or prison cells in the leaden roof, are now closed.

Downstairs we come to the two Great Halls—first the gigantic Sala del Maggior Consiglio, with Tintoretto's "Paradiso" at one end; historical pictures all around; the portraits of the Doges above; a gorgeous ceiling which, I fear, demands attention; and, mercifully, the little balcony over the lagoon for escape and recovery. But first let us peep into the room on the left, where the re-mains of Guariento's fresco of Paradise, which Tintoretto was to supersede, have been set up : a necessarily somewhat meaningless assemblage of delicate tints and pure drawing. Then the photograph stall, which is in that ancient room of the palace that has the two beautiful windows on a lower level than the rest.

It is melancholy to look round this gigantic sala of the great Council and think of the pictures which were destroyed by the great fire in 1576, when Sebastiano Venier was Doge, among them that rendering of the battle of Lepanto, the Doge's own victory, which Tintoretto painted with such enthusiasm. A list of only a few of the

works of art which from time to time have fallen to the
flames would be tragic reading. Among the artists whose
paintings were lost in the 1576 fire were, in addition to
Tintoretto, Titian, Giovanni and Gentile Bellini, Gentile
da Fabriano and Carpaccio. Sad, too, to think that the
Senators who once thronged here—those grave, astute
gentlemen in furred cloaks whom Tintoretto and Titian
and Moroni and Moretto painted for us—assemble here no
more. Sightseers now claim the palace, and the administrators of Venetian affairs meet in the Municipio, or Town
Hall, on the Grand Canal.

The best thing about the room is the room itself : the
courage of it, in a little place like Venice ! Next, I suppose, all eyes turn to the "Paradiso," and they can do
nothing else if the custodian has made himself one of the
party, as he is apt to do. The custodians of Venice are in
the main silent, pessimistic men. They themselves neither
take interest in art nor understand why you should.
Their attitude to you, if not contempt, is only one remove
from it. But in the Doges' Palace the officials are more
condescending.

The "Paradiso" was one of Tintoretto's last works,
the commission coming to him by the accident of
Veronese's death. Veronese was the artist first chosen,
with a Bassano to assist, but when he died, Tintoretto,
who had been passed over as too old, was permitted
to try. The great man, painting on canvas, at the
Misericordia, which had been turned into a studio for
him, and being assisted by his son Domenico, finished
the "Paradiso" in 1590 ; and it was the delight of Venice.
At first he refused payment for it, and then consented to
take a present, but a smaller one than the Senate wished
to offer.

The scheme of the work is logical and again illustrates his thoughtful thoroughness. At the head of all is Christ with His Mother, about and around them the angelic host led by the archangels—Michael with the scales, Gabriel with lilies, and Raphael, in prayer, each of whom presides, as we have seen, over one corner of the Palace. The next circle contains the greatest Biblical figures, Moses, David, Abraham, Solomon, Noah, the Evangelists (S. Mark prominent with his lion), and the Early Fathers. The rest of the picture is given to saints and martyrs. Not the least interesting figure is the S. Christopher, on the right, low down by the door. At his feet is the painter's daughter, for years his constant companion, who died while he was at work upon this masterpiece.

The ceiling should be examined, if one has the strength, for Veronese's sumptuous allegory of the Apotheosis of Venice. In this work the painter's wife sat for Venice, as she sat also for Europa in the picture which we have just seen in the Ante-Collegio.

On the walls are one-and-twenty representations of scenes in Venetian history devoted to the exploits of the two Doges, Sebastiano Ziani (1172-1178) and Enrico Dandolo (1192-1205). The greatest moment in the career of Ziani was the meeting of Barbarossa and the Pope, Alexander III, at S. Mark's, which has already been described; but his reign was eventful throughout. His first act as Doge was to punish the assassination of his predecessor, Vitale Michiel, who, for what was held to be the bad management of an Eastern campaign which utterly and disastrously failed, and for other reasons, was killed by the mob outside S. Zaccaria. To him succeeded Ziani and the close of the long feud between the Pope and the Emperor. It was the Pope's sojourn in Venice and his pleasure in the

THE CORNER OF THE OLD LIBRARY AND THE DOGES' PALACE

Venetians' hospitality which led to the elaboration of the ceremony of espousing the Adriatic. The Pope gave Ziani a consecrated ring with which to wed his bride, and much splendour was added to the pageant; while Ziani, on his return from a visit to the Pope at the Vatican, where the reconciliation with Barbarossa made it possible for the Pontiff to be at ease again, brought with him various pompous insignia that enormously increased his prestige among simple folk. It was also Ziani who had the columns of S. Theodore and the Lion erected on the Molo, while it was in his reign that the first Rialto bridge was begun. Having been Doge for six years, he retired to the monastery of S. Giorgio and there died some years later, leaving a large fortune to the poor of Venice and the church of S. Mark.

The paintings represent the Pope Alexander III recognized by the Doge when hiding in Venice; the departure of the Papal and Venetian Ambassadors for Pavia to interview the Emperor; the Pope presenting the Doge with a blessed candle; the Ambassadors before the Emperor (by Tintoretto); the Pope presenting the Doge with a sword, on the Molo; the Pope blessing the Doge; the naval battle of Salvatore, in which the Emperor Otto was captured; the Doge presenting Otto to the Pope; the Pope giving Otto his liberty; the Emperor at the Pope's feet in the vestibule of S. Mark's; the arrival of the Pope elsewhere; the Emperor and the Doge at Ancona; the Pope presenting the Doge with gifts in Rome.

Ziani seems to have been a man of address, but the great Enrico Dandolo was something more. He was a superb adventurer. He became Doge in 1193, at the trifling age of eighty-four, with eyes that had long been dimmed, and at once plunged into enterprises which, if not greatly to the good of Venice, proved his own indomitable spirit and resource. It was the time of the Fourth Crusade and the Venetians were asked to supply transports for the French warriors of the Cross to the theatre of war. After much discussion Dandolo replied that they would do so, the terms being that the Venetian vessels should carry 4500 horses, 9000 esquires, and 20,000 foot soldiers, with provisions for nine months, and for this they should be paid 85,000 silver marks. Venice also would participate in the actual fighting to the extent of providing fifty galleys, on condition that half of every conquest, whether by sea or by land, should be hers. Such was the arrangement, and the shipbuilding began at once.

But disaster after disaster occurred. The Christian commander sickened and died ; a number of Crusaders backed out ; others went direct to Palestine. This meant that the Venetians, who had prepared for a mighty host, incurred immense expenses which could not be met. As some reparation it was suggested to the small army of Crusaders who did arrive in the city for deportation that on their way to the Holy Land they should stop at Zara, on the Dalmatian coast, an unruly dependence of the Republic, and assist in chastising it. The objections to this course were grave. One was that the King of Hungary, in whose dominions was Zara, was a Christian and a Crusader himself ; another that the Pope (Innocent III) forbade the project. Old blind Dandolo, however, was adamant. Not only must the Crusaders help the Venetians whom they had so much embarrassed by their broken bond, but he would go too. Calling the people together in S. Mark's, this ancient sightless bravo asked if it was not right that he should depart on this high mission and they answered yes. Descending from the pulpit he knelt at the altar and on his bonnet the Cross was fastened.

Before the expedition left, a messenger came from Alexius, nephew of the usurping King of Constantinople and son of the rightful king, praying the Venetians to sail first for Constantinople and support his father's case, and to deal faithfully with Zara later; but Dandolo said that the rebellious Zara had prior claims, and in spite of Papal threats and even excommunication, he sailed for that place on November 10, 1202. It did not take long to subdue the garrison, but winter setting in, Dandolo decided to encamp there until the spring. The delay was not profitable to the Holy Cause. The French and the Venetians grew quarrelsome, and letters from the Pope warned the French (who held him in a dread not shared by their allies) that they must leave Zara and proceed with the Crusade instantly, or expect to suffer his wrath.

Then arrived the Prince Alexius once more, with definite promises of money and men for the Crusades if the allies would come at once and win back for him the Constantinople throne. Dandolo, who saw immense Venetian advantage here, agreed, and carrying with it most of the French, the fleet sailed for the Golden Horn. Dandolo, I might remark, was now ninety-four, and it should not be forgotten that it was when he was an emissary of the Republic at Constantinople years before that he had been deprived forcibly of his sight. He was a soldier, a statesman, and (as all good Doges were) a merchant, but he was humanly mindful of past injustices too. Hence perhaps much of his eagerness to turn aside for Byzantium.

The plan was for the French to attack on the land; the Venetians on the sea. Blind though he had become, Dandolo's memory of the harbour and fortifications enabled him to arrange the naval attack with the greatest skill, and he carried all before him, himself standing on the prow of a vessel waving the banner of S. Mark. The French on land had a less rapid victory, but they won, none the less, and the ex-king Isaac was liberated and crowned once more, with his son. Both, however, instantly took to tyranny and luxurious excess, and when the time came for the promises of reward to be fulfilled nothing was done. This led to the mortification and anger of the allies, who declared that unless they were paid they would take Constantinople for themselves. War was inevitable. Meanwhile the Greeks, hating alike Venetians, French, and the Pope, proclaimed a new king, who at once killed Alexius; and the allies prepared for battle by signing a treaty, drawn up by the wily nonagenarian, in which in the event of victory Venice took literally the lion's share of the spoils.

The fighting then began. At first the Greeks were too strong, and a feeling grew among the allies that withdrawal was best; but Dandolo refused; they fought on, and Constantinople was theirs. Unhappily the victors then lost all control, and every kind of horror followed, including the wanton destruction of works of art beautiful beyond dreams. Such visible trophies of the conquest as were saved and brought back to Venice are now to be seen in S. Mark's. The four bronze horses were Dandolo's spoils, the Pala d'oro, probably the four carved columns of the high altar, and countless stone pillars and ornaments that have been worked into the structure.

The terms of the treaty were carried out faithfully, and the French paid the Venetians their original debt. Baldwin, Count of Flanders, the head of the Crusade, was named Emperor and crowned; Venice acquired large tracts of land, including the Ionian Islands ; and Dandolo became " Doge of Venice, Dalmatia, and Croatia, and Lord of one-fourth and one-eighth of the Roman Empire".

The painters have chosen from Dandolo's career the following scenes : Dandolo and the Crusaders pledging themselves in S. Mark's ; the capture of Zara ; the request of Alexius for help ; the first capture of Constantinople by Dandolo, who set the banner on the wall ; the second capture of Constantinople ; the election of Baldwin as Emperor ; the crowning of Baldwin by Dandolo.

I said at the beginning of this précis of a gigantic campaign that it was not of great profit to Venice ; nor was it. All her life she had better have listened to the Little Venice party, but particularly then, for only misfortune resulted. Dandolo, however, remains a terrific figure. He died in Constantinople in 1205 and was buried in S. Sofia. Doge Andrea Dandolo, whose tomb we saw in the Baptistery, was a descendant who came to the throne some hundred and forty years later.

Mention of Andrea Dandolo brings us to the portraits of Doges around the walls of this great hall, where the other Dandolo will also be found ; for in the place adjoining Andrea's head is a black square. Once the portrait of the Doge who succeeded Andrea was here too, but it was blacked out. Marino Faliero, for he it was, became Doge in 1354 when his age was seventy-six, having been both a soldier and a diplomatist. He found himself at once involved in the war with Genoa, and almost immediately came the battle of Sapienza, when the Genoese took five thousand prisoners, including the admiral, Niccolò Pisani. This blow was a very serious one for the Venetians, involving as it did great loss of life, and there was a growing feeling that they were badly governed. The

Doge, who was but a figure-head of the Council of Ten, secretly thinking so too, plotted for the overthrow of the Council and the establishment of himself in supreme power. The Arsenal men were to form his chief army in the revolt; the false alarm of a Genoese attack was to get the populace together; and then the blow was to be struck and Faliero proclaimed prince. But the plot miscarried through one of the conspirators warning a friend to keep indoors; the ringleaders were caught and hanged or exiled; and the Doge, after confessing his guilt, was beheaded in the courtyard of this palace. His coffin may be seen in the Museo Civico, and of his unhappy story Byron made a drama.

One of Faliero's party was Calendario, an architect, employed on the part of the Doges' Palace in which we are now standing. He was hanged or strangled between the two red columns in the upper arches of the Piazzetta façade.

The first Doge to be represented here is Antenorio Obelerio (804-810), but he had had predecessors, the first in fact dating from 697. Of Obelerio little good is known. He married a foreigner whom some believe to have been an illegitimate daughter of Charlemagne, and her influence was bad. His brother Beato shared his throne, and in the end probably chased him from it. Beato was Doge when Rialto became the seat of government, Malamocco having gone over to the Franks under Pepin. But of Beato no account is here taken, Obelerio's successor being Angelo Partecipazio (810-827), who was also the first occupant of the first Ducal Palace, on the site of a portion of the present one. It was his son Giustiniano, sharing the throne with his father, who hit upon the brilliant idea of stealing the body of S. Mark from Alexandria and of preserving it in

Venice, thus establishing that city not only as a religious
centre but also as a place of pilgrimage and renown.   As
Mrs. Richardson remarks in her admirable survey of the
Doges : " Was it not well that the government of the Doge
Giustiniano and his successors throughout the age should
become the special concern of a Saint-Evangelist in whose
name all national acts might be undertaken and accomplished ; all national desires and plans—as distinct from
and dominant over purely ecclesiastical ones—be sanctified
and made righteous ? "   The success of the scheme of
theft I have related in an earlier chapter ; and how
this foresight was justified, history tells.   It is odd that
Venice does not make more acclamation of Giustiniano (or
Partecipazio II).   To his brother Giovanni, who early had
shown regrettable sympathy with the Franks and had been
banished accordingly, Giustiniano bequeathed the Doge-
ship (as was then possible), and it was in his reign (829-
836) that S. Mark's was begun.

The last Doge in this room is Girolamo Priuli (1559-
1567), of whom nothing of account is remembered save
that it was he who invited Tintoretto to work in the palace
and on one of the ceilings.   You may see his portrait in
one of the rooms, from Tintoretto's brush, in the company
of Venice, Justice, S. Mark and the Lion.

Of the others of the six-and-seventy Doges around the
room I do not here speak.   The names of such as are
important will be found elsewhere throughout this book,
as we stand beside their tombs or glide past their palaces.

Before leaving the Hall one should, as I have said, walk
to the balcony, the door of which the custodian opens for
each visitor with a mercenary hand.   It should of course
be free to all ; and Venice would do well to appoint some
official (if such could be found) to enforce such liberties.

Immediately below is all the movement of the Molo; then the edge of the lagoon with its myriad gondolas; then the sparkling water, with all its busy activities and swaying gondoliers; and away beyond it the lovely island of S. Giorgio. A fairer prospect the earth cannot show.

The first Doge in the Sala dello Scrutinio is Pietro Loredan (1567-1570) and the last of all Lodovico Manin (1788-1797) who fell before the inroads of Napoleon. "Take it away," he said to his servant, handing him the linen cap worn beneath the ducal corno, "we shall not need it any more." He retired into piety and left his fortune to good works.

This room, also a fine and spacious hall but smaller than the Sala del Maggior Consiglio, has historical pictures, and a "Last Judgment," by Palma the younger, which immensely interests the custodian by reason of a little human touch which may or may not be true. On the left of the picture, in the Infernal regions, low down, will be seen a large semi-nude female sinner in torment; on the right, in heaven, the same person is seen again, in bliss. According to the custodian this lady was the painter's innamorata, and he set her in both places as a reward for her varying moods. The other pictures represent the capture of Zara by Marco Giustiniani in 1346. Zara, I may mention, had very badly the habit of capture: this was the eighth time it had fallen. Tintoretto is the painter, and it is one of his best historical works. The great sea-fight picture on the right wall represents another battle of Lepanto, a later engagement than Venier's; the painter is Andrea Vicentino, who has depicted himself as the figure in the water; while in another naval battle scene, in the Dardanelles, the painter, Pietro Liberi, is the fat naked slave with a poniard. For the rest the

S. CHRISTOPHER
FROM THE FRESCO BY TITIAN
In the Doges' Palace

guide-book should be consulted. The balcony of the room, which juts over the Piazzetta, is rarely accessible ; but if it is open one should tarry there for the fine view of Sansovino's Old Library.

It is on the wall of one of the staircases in what is called the Archæological Museum that we find the charming fresco of S. Christopher which Titian made for Doge Andrea Gritti. It is a very pleasing rendering, and the Christ Child never rode more gaily or trustfully on the friendly saint. With true patriotism Titian has placed the incident in a shallow of the lagoon and the Doges' Palace is seen in the distance. I give a reproduction.

The antique section of the Archæological Museum is not of general interest. It consists chiefly of Greek and Roman sculpture collected by Cardinal Grimani or dug from time to time from the soil of Venetian provinces. Here are a few beautiful or precious relics and much that is indifferent. In the absence of a Hermaphrodite, the most popular possession is (as ever) a group of Leda and the Swan. I noted among the more attractive pieces a Roman altar with lovers (Baedeker calls them satyrs) ; and a very beautiful Pietà by Giovanni Bellini, painted under the influence of Dürer, should be sought and found.

The Bridge of Sighs, a little way upon which one may venture, is more interesting in romantic fancy than in fact, and its chief merit is to span very gracefully the gulf between the Palace and the Prison. With the terrible cells of the Doges' Palace, to which we are about to descend, it has no connexion. When Byron says, in the famous line beginning the fourth canto of " Childe Harold,"

I stood in Venice, on the Bridge of Sighs,

he probably meant that he stood in Venice on the Bridge of Straw (Ponte di Paglia) and contemplated the Bridge of

Sighs. Because one does not stand on the Bridge of Sighs but in it, for it is merely dark passages lit by gratings. But to stand on the Ponte di Paglia on the Riva and gaze up the sombre Rio del Palazzo with the famous arch set high over it, is one of the first duties of all visitors to Venice and a very memorable experience. On a morning in September, 1922, I found it impossible by reason of the crowds assembled, the magnet being a company of cinema actors at the gates of the prison.

Lastly, the visitor is led to the horrible cells, upon which and the damp sinister rooms where the place of execution and oubliette were situated, a saturnine custodian says all that is necessary. Let me, however, quote a warning from the little Venetian guide-book : " Every. body to whom are pointed out the prisons to which Carmagnola, Jacopo Foscari, Antonio Foscarini, etc., were confined, will easily understand that such indications cannot be true at all ".

CHAPTER VI

THE DOGES' PALACE. II: THE EXTERIOR

The colour of Venice—Sunny Gothic—A magical edifice—The evolution of a palace—A fascinating balcony—The carved capitals—A responsible column—The *Porta della Carta*—The lions of Venice—The Giants' Stairs —Antonio Rizzo—A closed arcade—Casanova—The bronze wells—A wonderful courtyard—Anonymous accusations—A Venetian Valhalla.

"THAT house," said an American on a Lido steamboat, pointing to the Doges' Palace, " is a wonder in its way."

Its way is unique. The soft gentle pink of its south and west façades remains in the memory as long and as firmly as the kaleidoscopic hues of S. Mark's. This pink is, I believe, the colour of Venice.

Whether or not the Doges' Palace as seen from S. Giorgio Maggiore, with its seventeen massive arches below, its thirty-four slender arches above, above them its row of quatrefoiled circles, and above them its patterned pink wall with its little balcony and fine windows, the whole surmounted by a gay fringe of dazzling white stone— whether or not this is the most beautiful building in the world is a question for individual decision; but it would, I think, puzzle anyone to name a more beautiful one, or one half so charming. There is nothing within it so entrancing as its exterior—always with the exception of Tintoretto's " Bacchus and Ariadne ".

The Ducal Palace is Gothic made sprightly and sunny :

Gothic without a hint of solidity or gloom. So light and
fresh is the effect, chiefly the result of the double row of
arches and especially of the upper row, but not a little
due to the zig-zagging of the brickwork and the vivid
cheerfulness of the coping fringe, that one has difficulty
in believing that the palace is of any age at all or that it
will really be there to-morrow. The other buildings in
the neighbourhood—the Prison, the Mint, the Library,
the Campanile : these are rooted. But the Doges' Palace
might float away at any moment. Aladdin's lamp set it
there : another rub and why should it not vanish ?

The palace as we see it now has been in existence from
the middle of the sixteenth century. Certain internal
changes and rebuildings have occurred, but its façades
on the Piazzetta and lagoon, the Giants' Stairs, the courtyard, were then as now. But before that time constant
structural modification was in progress. The original
palace ran beside the Rio del Palazzo from S. Mark's
towers to the Ponte di Paglia, with a wing along the lagoon. Its width was equal to that from the present Noah
or Vine corner by the Ponte di Paglia to the fifth column
from that corner. Its wing extended to the Piazzetta.
A wall and moat protected it, the extent of its ramparts
being practically identical with the extent of the present
building. This, the first, palace was erected in the ninth
century, after the seat of government was changed from
Malamocco to Venice proper.

Various conflagrations, in addition to the growing
needs of the State, led to rebuilding and enlargement.
The first wing was added in the twelfth century, when
the basement and first floor of the portion from the Porta
della Carta to the thick seventh column from the Adam
and Eve group, under the medallion of Venice, on the

THE PONTE DI PAGLIA AND THE BRIDGE OF SIGHS, WITH A CORNER OF
THE DOGES PALACE AND THE PRISON

Piazzetta façade, was set up, but not in the style which we now know. That was copied three centuries later from the Riva or lagoon façade. In 1301 the hall above the original portion on the Rio del Palazzo side, now called the Sala del Senato, was added and the lagoon wing was rebuilt, the lower arches, which are there to-day, being then established. A few years later, a still greater hall being needed, the present Sala del Maggior Consiglio was erected, and this was ready for use in 1423. The lagoon façade as we see it now, with its slender arches above the sturdy arches, thus dates from the beginning of the fifteenth century, and this design gave the key to the builders of later Venice, as a voyage of the Grand Canal will prove.

It was the great Doge Tommaso Mocenigo (1413-1423) who urged upon the Senate the necessity of completing the palace. In 1424 the work was begun. Progress was slow and was hindered by the usual fire, but gradually the splendid stone wall on the Rio del Palazzo side went up, and the right end of the lagoon façade, and the Giants' Stairs, and the Piazzetta façade, reproducing the lagoon façade. The elaborately decorated façades of the courtyard came later, and by 1550 the palace was finished. The irregularity of the windows on the lagoon façade is explained by this piecemeal structure. The four plain windows and the very graceful balcony belong to the Sala del Maggior Consiglio. The two ornate windows on the right were added when the palace was brought into line with this portion, and they are lower because the room they light is on a level lower than the great Council Hall's. The two ugly little square windows (Bonington in his picture in the Louvre makes them three) probably also were added then.

When the elegant spired cupolas at each corner of the

palace roof were built, I do not know, but they look like
a happy afterthought.   The small balcony overlooking the
lagoon, which is gained from the Sala del Maggior Consiglio, and which in Canaletto and Guardi's eighteenth-
century pictures always, as now, has a few people on it,
was built in 1404.   It is to be seen rightly only from the
water or through glasses.   The Madonna in the circle is
charming.   She has one child in her arms and two at her
knees, and her lap is a favourite resting-place for pigeons.
In the morning when the day is fine the green bronze
of the sword and crown of Justice (or, as some say, Mars),
who surmounts all, is beautiful against the blue of the sky.

The Piazzetta façade balcony was built early in the
sixteenth century, but the statue of S. George is a recent
addition, Canova being the sculptor.

Now let us examine the carved capitals of the columns
of the Ducal Palace arcade, for these are extremely interesting and transform it into something like an encyclopedia
in stone.   Much thought has gone to them, the old Venetians' love of symbols being gratified often to our perplexity.
We will begin at the end by the Porta della Carta, under
the group representing the Judgment of Solomon—the
Venetians' platonic affection for the idea of Justice being
here again displayed.   This group, though primitive, the
work of two sculptors from Fiesole early in the fifteenth
century, has a beauty of its own which grows increasingly
attractive as one returns and returns to the Piazzetta.
Above the group is the Angel Gabriel ; below it, on the
richly foliated capital of this sturdy corner column, which
bears so much weight and splendour, is Justice herself,
facing Sansovino's Loggetta : a little stone lady with scales
and sword of bronze.   Here also is Aristotle giving the law
to some bearded men ; while other figures represent Solon,

another jurist, Scipio the chaste, Numa Pompilius building a church, Moses receiving the tables of the law, and Trajan on horseback administering justice to a widow. All are named in Latin.

The second capital has cherubs with fruit and birds and no lettering.

The third has cranes and no lettering.

The fourth is allegorical, representing, but without much psychology, named virtues and vices, such as misery, cheerfulness, folly, chastity, honesty, falsehood, injustice, abstinence.

The fifth has figures and no lettering. A cobbler faces the campanile. It is above this fifth column that we notice in the upper row of arches two columns of reddish stain. It was between these that malefactors were strangled.

The sixth has symbolical figures which I do not understand. Ruskin suggests that they typify the degradation of human instincts. A knight in armour is here. A musician seated on a fish faces the Old Library. There is no lettering, and as is the case throughout the figures on the wall side are difficult to discern.

The seventh represents the vices, and names them: luxury, gluttony, pride, anger, avarice, idleness, vanity, envy.

The eighth represents the virtues and names them: hope, faith, fortitude, temperance, humility, charity, justice, prudence.

The ninth has virtues and vices, named and mixed: modesty, discord, patience, constancy, infidelity, despair, obedience, liberality.

The tenth has named fruits.

Ruskin thinks that the eleventh may illustrate various phases of idleness. It has no lettering.

The twelfth has the months and their employments, divided thus: January (indoors) and February, March blowing his pipes, April with a lamb and May, June (the month of cherries), July with a sheaf of corn and August, September (the vintage), October and November, and December, pig-sticking.

The thirteenth, on a stouter column than the others, because it has a heavier duty, namely, to bear the party wall of the great Council Hall, depicts the life of man. There is no lettering. The scenes represent love (apparently at first sight), courtship, the marriage bed, and so forth, the birth of the baby, his growth and his death. Many years ago this column was shown to me by the captain of a tramp steamer, as the most interesting thing in Venice; and there are others who share his opinion. Above it on the façade is the medallion of the Queen of the Adriatic ruling her domains.

The fourteenth capital represents national types, named : Persian, Latin, Tartar, Turk, Hungarian, Greek, Goth, and Egyptian.

The fifteenth is more elaborate and ingenious. It represents the ages of man and his place in the stellar system. Thus, infancy is governed by the moon, childhood by Mercury, youth by the sun, and so forth.

The sixteenth depicts various craftsmen : the smith, the mason, the goldsmith, the carpenter, the notary, the cobbler, the manservant, the husbandman. Over this are traces of a medallion, probably of porphyry, now removed.

The seventeenth has the heads of animals : lion, bear, wolf, and so forth, including the griffin, each with its prey.

The eighteenth has eight stone-carving saints, some

THE ADAM AND EVE CORNER OF THE DOGES' PALACE

with a piece of coloured marble, all named, and all at work : S. Simplicius, S. Symphorian, who sculps a figure, S. Claudius, and others.

And now we are at the brave corner column which unconcernedly assumes a responsibility that can hardly be surpassed in the world. For if it were to falter all would go. Down would topple two of the loveliest façades that man ever constructed or the centuries ever caressed into greater beauty. This corner of the palace has an ever-increasing fascination for me, and at all hours of the day and night this strong column below and the slenderer one above it hold the light—whether of sun or moon or artifice—with a peculiar grace.

The design of this capital is, fittingly enough, cosmic. It represents the signs of the Zodiac with the addition, on the facet opposite the Dogana, of Christ blessing a child. Facing S. Giorgio are Aquarius and Capricornus, facing the Lido are Pisces and Sagittarius. Elsewhere are Justice on the Bull, the Moon in a boat with a Crab, and a Virgin reading to the Twins.

Above this capital, on the corner of the building itself, are the famous Adam and Eve, presiding over the keystone of the structure as over the human race. It is a naïve group, as the photograph shows, beneath the most tactful of trees, and it has no details of beauty ; and yet, like its companions, the Judgment of Solomon and the Sin of Ham, it has a curious charm—due not a little perhaps to the softening effect of the winds and the rains. High above our first parents is the Angel Michael.

The first capital after the corner (we are now proceeding down the Riva) has Tubal Cain the musician, Solomon, Priscian the grammarian, Aristotle the logician, Euclid the geometrician, and so forth, all named and all characteristically employed.

The second has heads of, I suppose, types. Ruskin suggests that the best looking is a Venetian and the others the Venetians' inferiors drawn from the rest of the world.

The third has youths and women with symbols, signifying I know not what. All are corpulent enough to suggest gluttony. This is repeated in No. 11 on the Piazzetta side.

The fourth has various animals and no lettering.

The fifth has lions' heads and no lettering.

The sixth has virtues and vices and is repeated in the fourth on the Piazzetta.

The seventh has cranes, and is repeated in the third on the Piazzetta.

The eighth has vices again and is repeated in the seventh on the Piazzetta. Above it are traces of a medallion over three triangles.

The ninth has virtues and is repeated in the eighth on the Piazzetta.

The tenth has symbolical figures, and is repeated in the sixth on the Piazzetta.

The eleventh has vices and virtues and is repeated in the ninth on the Piazzetta.

The twelfth has female heads and no lettering.

The thirteenth has named rulers : Octavius, Titus, Trajan, Priam, Darius, and so forth, all crowned and ruling.

The fourteenth has children and no lettering.

The fifteenth has heads, male and female, and no lettering. Above it was once another medallion and three triangles.

The sixteenth has pelicans and no lettering.

The seventeenth and last has children with symbols and no lettering.

Above this, on the corner by the bridge, is the group representing the Sin of Ham. Noah's two sons are very attractive figures. Above the Noah group is the Angel Raphael.

The gateway of the palace—the Porta della Carta—was designed by Giovanni and Bartolommeo Bon, father and son, in the fourteen thirties and forties. Francesco Foscari (1423-1457) being then Doge, it is he who kneels to the lion on the relief above, and again on the balcony of the Piazzetta façade. At the summit of the portal is Justice once more, with two attendant lions, cherubs climbing to her, and live pigeons for ever nestling among them. I counted thirty-five lions' heads in the border of the window and thirty-five in the border of the door, and these, with Foscari's one and Justice's two, and those on the shields on each side of the window, make seventy-five lions for this gateway alone. Then there are lions' heads between the circular upper arches all along each façade of the palace.

It would be amusing to have an exact census of the lions of Venice, both winged and without wings. On the Grand Canal alone there must be a hundred of the little pensive watchers that sit on the balustrades peering down. As to which is the best lion, opinions must, of course, differ, the range being so vast : between, say, the lion on the Molo column and Daniele Manin's flamboyant sentinel at the foot of the statue in his Campo. Some would choose Carpaccio's painted lion in this palace ; others might say that the lion over the Giants' Stairs is as satisfying as any ; others might prefer that fine one on the Palazzo dei Camerlenghi by the Rialto bridge, and the Merceria clock tower's lion would not want adherents.

pigeons come much to the little drinking place in the pavement here but go rather to that larger one opposite Cook's office.

Everything that an architect can need to know—and more—may be learned in this courtyard, which would be yet more wonderful if it had not its two brick walls. Many styles meet and mingle here: Gothic and Renaissance, stately and fanciful, sombre and gay. Every capital is different. Round arches are here and pointed; invented patterns and marble with symmetrical natural veining which is perhaps more beautiful. Every inch has been thought out and worked upon with devotion and the highest technical skill; and the antiseptic air of Venice and cleansing sun have preserved its details as though it were under glass.

In the walls beneath the arcade on the Piazzetta side may be seen various ancient letter-boxes for the reception of those accusations against citizens, usually anonymous, in which the Venetians seem ever to have rejoiced. One is for charges of evading taxation, another for those who adulterate bread, and so forth.

The upper gallery running round the courtyard has been converted into a Venetian—almost an Italian— Valhalla. Here are busts of the greatest men, and of one woman, Catherine Cornaro, who gave Cyprus to the Republic and whom Titian painted. Among the first busts that I noted—ascending the stairs close to the Porta della Carta—was that of Ugo Foscolo, the poet, patriot, and miscellaneous writer, who spent the last years of his life in London and became a contributor to English periodicals. One of his most popular works in Italy was his translation of Sterne's *Sentimental Journey*. He died at Turnham Green in 1827, but his remains, many

S. TRIFONIO AND THE BASILISK

FROM THE PAINTING BY CARPACCIO

At S. Giorgio degli Schiavoni

years after, were moved to Santa Croce in Florence. Others are Carlo Zeno, the soldier; Goldoni, the dramatist; Paolo Sarpi, the monkish diplomatist; Galileo Galilei, the astronomer and mathematician; the two Cabots, the explorers, and Marco Polo, their predecessor; Niccolò Tommaseo, the patriot and associate of Daniele Manin, looking very like a blend of Walt Whitman and Tennyson; Dante; a small selection of Doges, of whom the great Andrea Dandolo is the most striking; Tintoretto, Giovanni Bellini, Titian, and Paul Veronese; Tiepolo, a big-faced man in a wig whom the inscription credits with having "renewed the glory" of the two last named; Canova, the sculptor; Daniele Manin, rather like John Bright; Lazzaro Mocenigo, commander in chief of the Venetian forces, rather like Buffalo Bill; and flanking the entrance to the palace Vittorio Pisani and Carlo Zeno, the two patriots and warriors who together saved the Republic in the Chioggian war with the Genoese in the fourteenth century.

This collection of great men makes no effort to be complete, but it is rather surprising not to find such very loyal sons of Venice as Canaletto, Guardi and Longhi among the artists, and Giorgione is of course a grievous omission.

CHAPTER VII

THE PIAZZETTA

The two columns—An ingenious engineer—S. Mark's lion—S. Theodore of Heraclea—The Old Library—Jacopo Sansovino—The Venetian Brunelleschi—Vasari's life—A Venetian library—Early printed books— The Grimani breviary—A pageant of the Seasons—The Loggetta— Coryat again—The view from the Molo—The gondolier—Alessandro and Ferdinando—The danger of the traghetto—Indomitable talkers— The fair and the fare—A proud father—The rampino.

THE Piazzetta is more remarkable in its architectural riches than the Piazza. S. Mark's main façade is of course beyond words wonderful; but after this the Piazza has only the Merceria clock and the Old and the New Procuratie, whereas the Piazzetta has S. Mark's small façade, the Porta della Carta and lovely west façade of the Doges' Palace, the columns bearing S. Mark's lion and S. Theodore, Sansovino's Old Library and Loggetta; while the Campanile is common to both. The Piazzetta has a café too, although it is not on an equality either with Florian's or the Quadri, and on three nights a week a band plays.

The famous Piazzetta columns, with S. Theodore and his crocodile (or dragon) on one and the lion of S. Mark on the other, which have become as much a symbol of Venice as the façade of S. Mark's itself, were brought from Syria after the conquest of Tyre. Three were brought in all, but one fell into the water and was never recovered.

78

The others lay on the quay here for half a century waiting
to be set up, a task beyond human skill until an engineer
from Lombardy volunteered to do it on condition that
he was to have any request granted. His request was to
be allowed the right of establishing a gaming-table between
the columns; and the authorities had to comply, although
gambling was hateful to them. A few centuries later the
gallows were placed here too. Now there is neither
gambling nor hanging; but all day long loafers sit on the
steps of the columns and discuss pronto and subito and
cinque and all the other topics of Venetian conversation.

I wonder how many visitors to Venice, asked whether
S. Theodore on his column faces the lagoon or the
Merceria clock, would give the right answer. His face
is turned towards the clock; his back to the lagoon.
The lion, which looks towards the Lido and is of
bronze with white agates for his eyes, has known many
vicissitudes. Where he came from originally, no one
knows, but it is extremely probable that he began as a
pagan and was pressed into the service of the Evangelist
much later. Napoleon took him to Paris, together with
the bronze horses, and while there he was broken. He
came back in 1815 and was restored, and twenty years
ago he was restored again. S. Theodore was also strength-
ened at the same time, being moved into the Doges'
Palace courtyard for that purpose.

There are several saints named Theodore, but the pro-
tector and patron of the Venetians in the early days before
Mark's body was stolen from Alexandria, is S. Theodore
of Heraclea. S. Theodore, surnamed Stratelates, or general
of the army, was a famous soldier and the governor of
the country of the Mariandyni, whose capital was Heraclea.
Accepting and professing the Christian faith, he was

beheaded by the Emperor Licinius on February 7, 319.
On June 8 in the same year his remains were translated
to Euchaia, the burial-place of the family, and the town
at once became so famous as a shrine that its name was
changed to Theodoropolis. As late as 970 the patronage
of the Saint gave the Emperor John I a victory over the
Saracens, and in gratitude the emperor rebuilt the church
where Theodore's relics were preserved. Subsequently
they were moved to Mesembria and then to Constantinople, from which city the great Doge Dandolo brought
them to Venice. They now repose in S. Salvatore beneath
an altar.

The west side of the Piazzetta consists of the quiet and
beautiful façade of Sansovino's Old Library. To see it
properly one should sit down at ease under the Doge's
arcade or mount to the quadriga gallery of S. Mark's.
Its proportions seem to me perfect, but Baedeker's description of it as the most magnificent secular edifice in Italy
seems odd with the Ducal Palace so near. They do not,
however, conflict, for the Ducal Palace is so gay and light,
and this so serious and stately. The cherubs with their
garlands are a relaxation, like a smile on a grave face ;
yet the total effect is rather calm thoughtfulness than
sternness. The living statues on the coping help to lighten
the structure, and if one steps back along the Riva one
sees a brilliant column of white stone—a chimney perhaps
—which is another inspiriting touch. In the early morning, with the sun on them, these statues are the whitest
things imaginable.

The end building, the Zecca, or mint, is also Sansovino's,
as are the fascinating little Loggetta beneath the campanile, together with much of its statuary, the giants at the
head of Rizzo's staircase opposite, and the chancel bronzes

in S. Mark's, so that altogether this is peculiarly the place to inquire into what manner of man the Brunelleschi of Venice was. For Jacopo Sansovino stands to Venice much as that great architect to Florence. He found it lacking certain essential things, and, supplying them, made it far more beautiful and impressive; and whatever he did seems inevitable and right.

Vasari wrote a very full life of Sansovino, not included among his other Lives but separately published. In this we learn that Jacopo was born in Florence in 1477, the son of a mattress-maker named Tatti; but apparently 1486 is the right date. Appreciating his natural bent towards art, his mother had him secretly taught to draw, hoping that he might become a great sculptor like Michael Angelo, and he was put as apprentice to the sculptor Andrea Contucci of Monte Sansovino, who had recently set up in Florence and was at work on two figures for San Giovanni; and Jacopo so attached himself to the older man that he became known as Sansovino too. Another of his friends as a youth was Andrea del Sarto.

From Florence he passed to Rome, where he came under the patronage of the Pope Julius II, of Bramante, the architect, and of Perugino, the painter, and learned much by his studies there. Returning to Florence, he became one of the most desired of sculptors and executed that superb modern-antique, the Bacchus in the Bargello. Taking to architecture, he continued his successful progress, chiefly again in Rome, but when the sack of that city occurred in 1527 he fled and to the great good fortune of Venice took refuge here. The Doge, Andrea Gritti, welcomed so distinguished a fugitive and at once set him to work on the restoration of S. Mark's cupolas, and this

6

task he completed with such skill that he was made a Senior Procurator and given a fine house and salary.

As a Procurator he seems to have been tactful and active, and Vasari gives various examples of his reforming zeal by which the annual income of the Procuranzia was increased by two thousand ducats. When, however, one of the arches of Sansovino's beautiful library fell, owing to a subsidence of the foundations, neither his eminent position nor ability prevented the authorities from throwing him into prison as a bad workman; nor was he liberated, for all his powerful friends, without a heavy fine. He built also several fine palaces, the mint, and various churches, but still kept time for his early love, sculpture, as his perfect little Loggetta, and the giants on the Staircase, and such a tomb as that in S. Salvatore, show.

This is Vasari's description of the man : "Jacopo Sansovino, as to his person, was of the middle height, but rather slender than otherwise, and his carriage was remarkably upright ; he was fair, with a red beard, and in his youth was of a goodly presence, wherefore he did not fail to be loved, and that by dames of no small importance. In his age he had an exceedingly venerable appearance ; with his beautiful white beard, he still retained the carriage of his youth : he was strong and healthy even to his ninety-third year, and could see the smallest object, at whatever distance, without glasses, even then. When writing, he sat with his head up, not supporting himself in any manner, as it is usual for men to do. He liked to be handsomely dressed, and was singularly nice in his person. The society of ladies was acceptable to Sansovino, even to the extremity of age, and he always enjoyed conversing with or of them. He had not been particularly healthy in his youth, yet in his old age he suffered from no malady

S. JEROME IN HIS CELL

FROM THE PAINTING BY CARPACCIO

At S. Giorgio degli Schiavoni

whatever, in-so-much that, for a period of fifty years, he would never consult any physician even when he did feel himself indisposed. Nay, when he was once attacked by apoplexy, he would still have nothing to do with physic, but cured himself by keeping in bed for two months in a dark and well-warmed chamber. His digestion was so good that he could eat all things without distinction: during the summer he lived almost entirely on fruits, and in the very extremity of his age would frequently eat three cucumbers and half a lemon at one time.

" With respect to the qualities of his mind, Sansovino was very prudent; he foresaw readily the coming events, and sagaciously compared the present with the past. Attentive to his duties, he shunned no labour in the fulfilment of the same, and never neglected his business for his pleasure. He spoke well and largely on such subjects as he understood, giving appropriate illustrations of his thoughts with infinite grace of manner. This rendered him acceptable to high and low alike, as well as to his own friends. In his greatest age his memory continued excellent; he remembered all the events of his childhood, and could minutely refer to the sack of Rome and all the other occurrences, fortunate or otherwise, of his youth and early manhood. He was very courageous, and delighted from his boyhood in contending with those who were greater than himself, affirming that he who struggles with the great may become greater, but he who disputes with the little must become less. He esteemed honour above all else in the world, and was so upright a man of his word, that no temptation could induce him to break it, of which he gave frequent proof to his lords, who, for that as well as other qualities, considered him rather as a father or brother than as their agent or steward, honouring in him an excellence that was no pretence, but his true nature."

Sansovino died in 1570, and he was buried at San Gimignano, in a church that he himself had built. In 1807, this church being demolished, his remains were transferred to the Seminario della Salute in Venice, where they now are.

Adjoining the Old Library is the Mint, now S. Mark's Library, which may be both seen and used by strangers. It is not exactly a British Museum Reading-room, for there are but twelve tables with six seats at each, but judging by its usually empty state, it more than suffices for the scholarly needs of Venice. Upstairs you are shown various treasures brought together by Cardinal Bessarione : MSS., autographs, illuminated books, and incunabula. A fourteenth-century Dante lies open, with coloured pictures : the poet very short on one page and very tall on the next, and Virgil, at his side, very like Christ. A *Relazione della Morte de Anna Regina de Francia*, a fifteenth-century work, has a curious picture of the queen's burial. The first book ever printed in Venice is here : Cicero's *Epistolæ*, 1469, from the press of Johannes di Spira, which was followed by an edition of Pliny the Younger. A fine Venetian *Hypnerotomachia*, 1499, is here, and a very beautiful Herodotus with lovely type from the press of Gregorius of Venice in 1494. Old bindings may be seen too, among them a lavish Byzantine example with enamels and mosaics. The exhibited autographs include Titian's hand, large and forcible ; Leopardi's, very neat ; Goldoni's, delicate and self-conscious ; Galileo's, much in earnest ; and a poem by Tasso with myriad afterthoughts.

But the one idea of the custodian is to get you to admire

the famous Grimani Breviary, which, if you are pleasing
in your manner, will be shown to you in the original as
well as in a coloured reproduction. What the Fouquet
Missal is to Chantilly, the Grimani Breviary is to the
Old Library: with the difference that Fouquet's delicious
miniatures are on the wall and these in a book, which is
displayed, if displayed at all, in a case and at a respect-
ful distance from the observer. The Grimani Breviary
dates from the early sixteenth century and is the work
of some ingenious and masterly Flemish miniaturist with
a fine sense of the open air and the movement of
the seasons. January reveals a rich man at his table,
dining alone, with his servitors and dogs about him;
February's scene is white with snow—a small farm with
the wife at the spinning-wheel, seen through the door, and
various indications of cold, without; March shows the re-
vival of field labours; April, a love scene among lords and
ladies; May, a courtly festival; June, haymaking outside
a fascinating city; July, sheep-shearing and reaping;
August, the departure for the chase; September, grape-
picking for the vintage; October, sowing seeds in a field near
another fascinating city—a busy scene of various activities;
November, beating oak-trees to bring down acorns for the
pigs; and December, a boar hunt—the death. And all
most gaily coloured, with the signs of the Zodiac added.

The little building under the campanile is Sansovino's
Loggetta, which he seems to have set there as a proof of
his wonderful catholicity—to demonstrate that he was not
only severe as in the Old Library, and Titanic as in the
Giants, but that he had his gentler, sweeter thoughts too.
The Loggetta was destroyed by the fall of the campanile;
but it has risen from its ruins with a freshness and vivacity

that are bewildering. It is possible indeed to think of its revivification as being even more of a miracle than the new campanile : for the new campanile was a straightforward building feat, whereas to reconstruct Sansovino's charm and delicacy required peculiar and very unusual gifts. Yet there it is : not what it was, of course, for the softening quality of old age has left it, yet very beautiful, and in a niche within a wonderful restoration of Sansovino's group of the Madonna and Child with S. John. The reliefs outside have been pieced together too, and though here and there a nose has gone, the effect remains admirable. The glory of Venice is the subject of all.

The most superb of the external bronzes is the " Mercury " on the left of the façade. To the patience and genius of Signor Giacomo Boni is the restored statuary of the Loggetta due ; Cav. Munaretti was responsible for the bronzes, and Signor Moretti for the building. All honour to them !

Old Coryat's enthusiasm for the Loggetta is very hearty. " There is," he says, " adjoyned unto this tower [the campanile] a most glorious little roome that is very worthy to be spoken of, namely the Logetto, which is a place where some of the Procurators of Saint Markes doe use to sit in judgement, and discusse matters of controversies. This place is indeed but little, yet of that singular and incomparable beauty, being made all of Corinthian worke, that I never saw the like before for the quantity thereof."

Where the Piazzetta especially gains over the Piazza is in its lagoon view. From its shore you look directly over the water to the church and island of S. Giorgio Maggiore, which are beautiful from every point and at every hour, so happily do dome and white façade, red campanile and green roof, windowed houses and little white towers, compose. But then, in Venice everything composes : an artist has but to paint what he sees. From the Piazzetta's shore you look diagonally to the right to the Dogana and the vast Salute and all the masts in the Giudecca canal ; diagonally to the left is the Lido with a mile of dancing water between us and it.

The shore of the Piazzetta, or more correctly the Molo, is of course the spot where the gondolas most do congregate, apparently inextricably wedged between the twisted trees of this marine forest, although when the time comes— that is, when the gondolier is at last secured—easily enough detached. For there is a bewildering rule which seems to prevent the gondolier who hails you from being your oarsman, and if you think that the gondolier whom you hail is the one who is going to row you, you are greatly mistaken. It is always another. The wise traveller in Venice having chanced upon a good gondolier takes his name and number and makes further arrangements with him. This being done, on arriving at the Molo he asks if his man is there, and the name—let us say Alessandro —is passed up and down like a bucket at a fire. If Alessandro chances to be there and available, all is well ; but if not, to acquire a substitute, even among so many obviously disengaged mariners, is no joke.

Some gondoliers even start cheerfully, and most become human in time, but not all.

A gondolier with a grudge can be a most dismal companion, for he talks to himself. What he says, you cannot comprehend, for it is muttered and acutely foreign, but there is no doubt whatever that it is criticism detrimental to you, to some other equally objectionable person, or to the world at large.

The gondolier does not differ noticeably from any other man whose business it is to convey his fellow-creatures from one spot to another. The continual practice of assisting richer people than oneself to do things that oneself never does except for a livelihood would seem to engender a sardonic cast of mind. Where the gondolier chiefly differs from, say, the London cabman, is in his gift of speech. Cabmen can be caustic, sceptical, critical, censorious, but they do occasionally stop for breath. There is no need for a gondolier ever to do so either by day or night ; while when he is not talking he is accompanying every movement by a grunt.

It is this habit of talking and bickering which should make one very careful in choosing a lodging. Never let it be near a traghetto ; for at traghetti there is talk incessant, day and night : argument, abuse, and raillery. The prevailing tone is that of men with a grievance. The only sound you never hear there is laughter.

The passion for bickering belongs to watermen, although loquacity is shared by the whole city. The right to the back answer is one which the Venetian cherishes as jealously, I should say, as any ; so much so that the gondolier whom your generosity struck dumb would be an unhappy man in spite of his windfall.

The gondolier assimilates to the cabman also in his liking to be overpaid. The English and Americans have been overpaying him for so many years that to receive now an exact fare from foreigners fills him with dismay. From Venetians, who, however, do not much use gondolas except as ferry boats, he expects it ; but not from us, especially if there is a lady on board, for she is always his ally (as he knows) when it comes to pay time. A cabman

THE DOGANA (WITH S. GIORGIO MAGGIORE JUST VISIBLE)

who sits on a box and whips his horse, or a chauffeur who turns a wheel, is that and nothing more; but a gondolier is a romantic figure, and a gondola is a romantic craft, and the poor fellow has had to do it all himself, and did you hear how he was panting, and do look at those dark eyes! And there you are! Writing, however, strictly for unattended male passengers, or for strong-minded ladies, let me say that every gondola has its tariff, in several languages, on board. If one goes by this and makes an additional tip, one is always in the right and the gondolier knows it.

One of the prettiest sights that I remember in Venice was, one Sunday morning, a gondolier in his shirt sleeves, carefully dressed in his best, with a very long cigar and a very black moustache and a flashing gold ring, lolling back in his own gondola while his small son, aged about nine, was rowing him up the Grand Canal. Occasionally a word of praise or caution was uttered, but for the most part they went along silently, the father receiving more warmth from the consciousness of successful paternity than we from the sun itself.

Gondoliers can have pride: but there is no pride about a rampino, the old scaramouch who hooks the gondola at the steps. Since he too was once a gondolier this is odd. But pride and he are strangers now. His hat is ever in his hand for a copper, and the transference of your still burning cigar-end to his lips is one of the most natural actions in the world.

Cigar, did I say? Alas! unless you are a smuggler or a millionaire equal to the tobacco tax at the douane, you will enjoy no cigar south of Switzerland. If the bare-headed young men with crimped hair and walking sticks who have filled the streets of Italy of late, intent upon reform—the Fascisti—find time heavy on their hands, they might bend their energies towards getting Havana leaf at a reasonable cost into their lovely land.

CHAPTER VIII

THE GRAND CANAL. I: FROM THE DOGANA TO THE PALAZZO REZZONICO, LOOKING TO THE LEFT

The river of Venice—Canal steamers—Motor boats—The great architects —Venetian nobility to-day—A desirable enactment—The custom house vane—The Seminario and Giorgione—S. Maria della Salute—Tintoretto's "Marriage in Cana"—The lost blue curtain—San Gregorio— The Palazzo Dario—Porphyry—The story of S. Vio—Delectable homes —Browning in Venice—S. Maria della Carità.

TO me the Grand Canal is the river of Venice—its Thames, its Seine, its Arno. I think of it as "the river". The rest are canals. And yet as a matter of fact to the Venetians the rest are rivers—Rio this and Rio that—and this the canal.

During a stay in Venice of however short a time one is so often on the Grand Canal that a knowledge of its palaces should come early. For a trifling sum one may travel its whole length in a steamboat, and then make the return journey, and there is no more interesting hour's voyage in the world. The guide-books, as a rule, describe both banks from the same starting-point, which is usually the Molo. This seems to me to be a mistake, for two reasons. One is that even in a leisurely gondola " all' ora " one cannot keep pace with literature bearing on both sides at once, and the other is that since one enters Venice at the railway station it is interesting to begin forthwith to learn something of the city from that point and one ought not to be asked to read backwards to do this. In this book therefore the left bank, from the custom house to the railway station, is described first, and then the other side returning from the station to the Molo.

The Grand Canal has for long had its steamers, and when they were installed there was a desperate outcry, led by Ruskin. Later a similar outcry was made against motor-boats, with, I think, more reason, but wholly in vain. But the steamer is useful and practically unnoticeable except when it whistles. None the less it was an interesting experience in April, 1914, to be living on the Grand Canal during a steamer strike which lasted for several days. It gave one the quieter Venice of the past and incidentally turned the gondoliers into plutocrats.

But there is a great difference between the steamers and the motor-boat. The steamer does not leave the Grand Canal except to enter the lagoon; and therefore the injustice that it does to the gondolier is limited to depriving him of his Grand Canal and Lido fares. The motor-boat can supersede the gondola on the small canals too. It may be urged that the gondolier has only to become an engineer and his position will be as secure. That may be true; but we all know how insidious is the deteriorating influence of petrol on the human character. The gondolier even now is not always a model of courtesy and content; what will he be when the poison of machinery is in him?

But there are graver reasons why the motor-boat should be viewed by the city fathers with suspicion. One is purely æsthetic, yet not the less weighty for that, since the prosperity of Venice in her decay resides in her romantic beauty and associations. The symbol of these is the gondola and gondolier, indivisible, and the only conditions under which they can be preserved are quietude and leisure. The motor-boat, which is always in a hurry and which as it multiplies will multiply hooters and whistles, must necessarily destroy the last vestige of Venetian calm. A second reason is that a small motor-boat makes a bigger wash than a crowded Grand Canal steamer, and this wash, continually increasing as the number of boats increases, must weaken and undermine the foundations of the houses on each side of the canals through which they pass. The erosive action of water is irresistible. No natural law is sterner than that which decrees that restless water shall prevail.

Enjoyment of voyages up and down the Grand Canal is immensely increased by some knowledge of architecture ; but that subject is so vast that in such a *hors d'œuvre* to the Venetian banquet as the present book nothing of value can be said. Let it not be forgotten that Ruskin gave years of his life to the study. The most I can do is to name the architects of the most famous of the palaces and draw the reader's attention to the frequency with which the lovely Ducal gallery pattern recurs, like a theme in a fugue, until one comes to think the symbol of the city not the winged lion but a row of Gothic curved and pointed arches surmounted by circles containing equilateral crosses. The greatest names in Venetian architecture are Polifilo, who wrote the *Hypnerotomachia*, the two Bons, Rizzo, Sansovino, the Lombardis, Scarpagnino, Leopardi, Palladio, Sammicheli, and Longhena.

In the following notes I have tried to mention the place of practically every rio and every calle so that the identification of the buildings may be the more simple. The names of the palaces usually given are those by which the Venetians know them ; but many, if not most, have changed ownership more than once since those names were fixed.

Although for the most part the palaces of the Grand Canal have declined from their original status as the homes of the nobility and aristocracy and are now hotels, antiquity stores, offices, and tenements, it not seldom happens that the modern representative of the great family retains the top floor for an annual Venetian sojourn, living for the rest of the year in the country.

I wish it could be made compulsory for the posts before the palaces to be renewed or repainted every year.

And so begins the voyage. The white stone building which forms the thin end of the wedge dividing the Grand Canal from the Canale della Giudecca is the Dogana or Customs House, and the cape is called the Punta della Salute. The figure on the gilded ball, which from certain points has almost as much lightness as Gian Bologna's famous Mercury, represents Fortune and turns with the wind. The next building (with a green and shady garden on the Zattere side) is the Seminario Patriarcale, a great bare schoolhouse, in which a few pictures are preserved, and, downstairs, a collection of ancient sculpture. Among the pictures is a much damaged classical scene supposed to represent Apollo and Daphne in a romantic landscape. Giorgione's name is often associated with it; I know not with what accuracy, but Signor Paoli, who has written so well upon Venice, is convinced, and the figure of Apollo is certainly free and fair as from a master's hand. Another picture, a Madonna and Child with two companions, is called a Leonardo da Vinci; but Baedeker gives it to Marco d'Oggiano. There is also a Filippino Lippi, which one likes to find in Venice, where the prevailing art is so different from his. One of the most charming things here is a little relief of the manger: as pretty a rendering as one could wish for. Downstairs is the tomb of the great Jacopo Sansovino.

And now rises the imposing church of S. Maria della Salute which, although younger than most of the Venetian churches, has taken the next place to S. Mark's as an ecclesiastical symbol of the city. To me it is a building attractive only when seen in its place as a Venetian detail; although it must always have the impressiveness of size and accumulation and the beauty that white stone in such an air as this can hardly escape. Seen from the Grand Canal or from a window opposite, it is pretentious and an interloper, particularly if the slender and distinguished Gothic windows of the apse of S. Gregorio are also visible; seen from any distant enough spot, its dome and towers fall with equal naturalness into the majestic Venetian pageant of full light, or the fairy Venetian mirage of the crepuscle.

The church was decreed in 1630 as a thankoffering to the Virgin for staying the plague of that year. Hence the name—S. Mary of Salvation. It was designed by Baldassare Longhena, a Venetian architect who worked during the first half of the seventeenth century and whose masterpiece this is.

Within, the Salute is notable for possessing Tintoretto's "Marriage in Cana," one of the few pictures painted by him in which he allowed himself an interval (so to speak) of perfect calm. It is, as it was bound to be in his hands and no doubt was in reality, a busy scene. The guests are all animated; the servitors are bustling about; a number of spectators talk together at the back; a woman in the foreground holds out a vessel to the men opposite to show them the remarkable change which the water has undergone. But it is in the centre of his picture (which is reproduced on the opposite page) that the painter has achieved one of his pleasantest effects, for here is a row of pretty women sitting side by side at the banqueting table, with a soft light upon them, who make together one of the most charming of those rare oases of pure sweetness in all Tintoretto's work. The chief light is theirs and they shine most graciously in it.

Among other pictures are a S. Sebastian by Basaiti, with a good landscape ; a glowing altar-piece by Titian, in his Giorgionesque manner, representing S. Mark and four saints ; a " Descent of the Holy Ghost," by the same hand but under no such influence ; and a spirited if rather theatrical " Nativity of the Virgin " by Luca Giordano. In the outer sacristy the kneeling figure of Doge Agostino Barbarigo should be looked for.

The Salute in Guardi's day seems to have had the most entrancing light blue curtains at its main entrance, if we may take the artist as our authority. See No. 2098 in the National Gallery, and also No. 503 at the Wallace collection. But now only a tiny side door is opened.

A steamboat station, used almost wholly by visitors, is here, and then a canal, and then the fourteenth-century abbey of S. Gregorio, whose cloisters now form an antiquity store and whose severe and simple apse is such a rebuke to Longhena's Renaissance floridity. Next is a delightful little house with one of the old cup-chimneys, forming one of the most desirable residences in Venice. It has a glazed loggia looking down to the Riva. We next come to a brand-new spacious building divided into apartments, then a tiny house, and then the rather squalid Palazzo Martinengo. The calle and traghetto of S. Gregorio, and two or three old palaces and the new building which now holds Salviati's glass business, follow. After the Rio del Formase is a

THE MARRIAGE AT CANA
FROM THE PAINTING BY TINTORETTO
In the Church of S. Maria della Salute

common little house, and then the Palazzo Volkoff, once
Eleonora Duse's Venetian home.

Next is the splendid fifteenth-century Palazzo Dario,
to my eyes perhaps the most satisfying of all, with
its rich colouring, leaning walls, ancient chimneys and
porphyry decorations. Readers of Henri de Régnier's
Venetian novel *La Peur de l'Amour* may like to know
that much of it was written in this palace. We shall see
porphyry all along the Canal on both sides, always enrich-
ing in its effect. This stone is a red or purple volcanic
rock which comes from Egypt, on the west coast of the
Red Sea. The Romans first detected its beauty and made
great use of it to decorate their buildings.

Another rio, the Torreselle, some wine stores, and then
the foundations of what was to have been the Palazzo
Venier, which never was built. Instead there are walls and
a very delectable garden—a riot of lovely wistaria in the
spring—into which fortunate people are assisted from
gondolas by superior men-servants. A dull house comes
next; then a *stoffe* factory; and then the Mula Palace,
with fine dark blue poles before it surmounted by a
Doge's cap, and good Gothic windows. Again we find
trade where once was aristocracy, for the next palace, which
is now a glass-works' show-room, was once the home of
Pietro Barbarigo, Patriarch of Venice.

The tiny church of S. Vio, now closed, which gives the
name to the Campo and Rio opposite which we now are,
has a pretty history attached to it. It seems that one of
the most devoted worshippers in this minute temple was
the little Contessa Tagliapietra, whose home was on the
other side of the Grand Canal. Her one pleasure was to
retire to this church and make her devotions: a habit
which so exasperated her father that one day he issued a

decree to the gondoliers forbidding them to ferry her across. On arriving at the traghetto and learning this decision, the girl calmly walked over the water, sustained by her piety and virtue.

The next palace, at the corner, is the Palazzo Loredan. Adjoining it is the comfortable Balbi Valier, with a pleasant garden where the Palazzo Paradiso once stood; and then the great and splendid Contarini del Zaffo, or Manzoni, with its good ironwork and medallions and a charming loggia at the side. Robert Browning tried to buy this palace for his son. Indeed he thought he had bought it; but there was a hitch. He describes it in a letter as " the most beautiful house in Venice ". The next, the Brandolin Rota, which adjoins it, was, as a hotel, under the name Albergo dell' Universo, Browning's first Venetian home. Later he moved to the Zattere and after that to the Palazzo Rezzonico, to which we are soon coming, where he died.

Next we reach the church, convent and Scuola of S. Maria della Carità, opposite the iron bridge, which under rearrangement and restoration now forms the Accademia, or Gallery of Fine Arts, famous throughout the world for its Titians, Tintorettos, Bellinis, and Carpaccios. The church, which dates from the fifteenth century, is a most beautiful brown brick building with delicate corbelling under the eaves. Once there was a campanile too, but it fell into the Grand Canal many a long year ago, causing a tidal wave which flung gondolas clean out of the water. We shall return to the Accademia in later chapters: here it is enough to say that the lion on the top of the entrance wall is the most foolish in Venice, turned, as it has been, into a lady's hack.

The first house after the Accademia is negligible—

newish and dull with an enclosed garden; the next is the Querini; the next the dull Mocenigo Gambara; and then we come to the solid Bloomsbury-blackened stone Palazzo Contarini degli Scrigni and its neighbours of the same ownership. Then the Rio S. Trovaso, with a pretty garden visible a little way up, and then a gay new little home, very attractive, with a strip of garden, and next it the fifteenth-century Loredan. A tiny calle, and then the low Dolfin. Then the Rio Malpaga and after it a very delectable new residence with a terrace. A calle and traghetto, with a wall shrine at the corner, come next, and two dull Contarini palaces, one of which has declined very sadly, and then the Rio S. Barnaba and the majestic sombre Rezzonico.

This for long was the home of Robert Browning, and here, as a tablet on the side wall states, he died. "Browning, Browning," exclaim the gondoliers as they point to it; but what the word means to them I cannot say.

CHAPTER IX

THE GRAND CANAL. II: BROWNING AND WAGNER

The Palazzo Rezzonico—Mr. and Mrs. Browning—Browning's Venetian routine—In praise of Goldoni—Browning's death—A funeral service—Love of Italy—The Giustiniani family—A last resource—Wagner in Venice—*Tristan und Isolde*—Plays and Music—The Austrians in power—The gondoliers' chorus—The Foscari Palace.

THE Rezzonico palace and one of the Giustiniani palaces which are its neighbours have such interesting artistic associations that they demand a chapter to themselves.

Browning is more intimately associated with Florence and Asolo than with Venice; but he enjoyed his later Venetian days to the full. His first visit here in 1851, with his wife, was however marred by illness. Mrs. Browning loved the city, as her letters tell. "I have been," she wrote, "between heaven and earth since our arrival at Venice. The heaven of it is ineffable. Never had I touched the skirts of so celestial a place. The beauty of the architecture, the silver trails of water up between all that gorgeous colour and carving, the enchanting silence, the moonlight, the music, the gondolas—I mix it all up together, and maintain that nothing is like it, nothing equal to it, not a second Venice in the world."

Browning left Florence for ever after his wife's death, and to Venice he came again in 1878, with his sister, and thereafter for some years they returned regularly. Until 1881 their home was at the Brandolin Rota. After that they stayed with Mrs. Arthur Bronson, to whom he dedicated *Asolando*, his last book, and who has written a record of his habits in the city of the sea. She tells us that he delighted in walking and was a great frequenter of old curiosity shops. His especial triumph was to discover a calle so narrow that he could not put up an umbrella in it. Every morning he visited the Giardini Pubblici to feed certain of the animals; and on every disengaged afternoon he went over to the Lido, to walk there, or, as Byron had done, to ride. On being asked by his gondolier where he would like to be rowed, he always said, "Towards the Lido," and after his failure to acquire the Palazzo Manzoni he thought seriously for a while of buying an unfinished Lido villa which had been begun for Victor Emmanuel. Browning's desire was to see sunsets from it.

Mrs. Bronson tells us that the poet delighted in the seagulls, which in stormy weather come into the city waters. He used to wonder that no books referred to them. "They are more interesting," he said, "than the doves of St. Mark." Venice did not inspire the poet to much verse. There is of course that poignant little drama entitled "In a Gondola," but not much else, and for some reason the collected works omit the sonnet in honour of Goldoni which was written for the ceremonies attaching to the erection of the dramatist's statue near the Rialto. Mrs. Orr tells us that this sonnet, which had been promised for an album in praise of Goldoni, was forgotten until the messenger from the editor arrived for the copy. Browning wrote it while the boy waited. The day was November 27, 1883.

Goldoni—good, gay, sunniest of souls—
  Glassing half Venice in that verse of thine—
  What though it just reflect the shade and shine
Of common life, nor render, as it rolls,
Grandeur and gloom ?   Sufficient for thy shoals
  Was Carnival : Parini's depths enshrine
  Secrets unsuited to that opaline
Surface of things which laughs along thy scrolls.
There throng the people : how they come and go,
  Lisp the soft language, flaunt the bright garb,—see,—
On Piazza, Calle, under Portico
  And over Bridge !   Dear king of Comedy,
Be honoured !   Thou that did'st love Venice so,
  Venice, and we who love her, all love thee.

The Rezzonico is the house most intimately associated
with Browning in the public mind, although most of his
Venetian life was spent elsewhere. It was here, on his last
visit to his son, that the poet died. He had not been very
well for some time, but he insisted on taking his daily walk
on the Lido even although it was foggy. The fog struck
in—it was November—and the poet gradually grew weaker
until on December 12, 1889, the end came. At first he had
lain in the left-hand corner room on the ground floor ; he
died in the corresponding room on the top floor, where
there was more light.

Browning was buried in Westminster Abbey, but a
funeral service was held first in Venice. In his son's
words, " a public funeral was offered by the Municipality,
which in a modified form was gratefully accepted. A
private service, conducted by the British Chaplain, was
held in one of the halls of the Rezzonico. It was attended
by the Syndic of Venice and the chief City authorities,
as well as by officers of the Army and Navy. Municipal
Guards lined the entrance of the Palace, and a Guard of
Honour, consisting of City firemen in full dress, stood

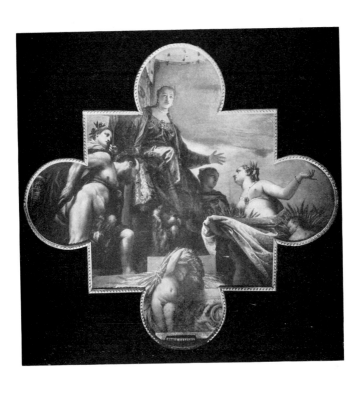

VENICE WITH HERCULES AND CERES
FROM THE PAINTING BY VERONESE
In the Accademia

flanking the coffin during the service, which was attended
by friends and many residents.   The subsequent passage to
the mortuary island of San Michele was organized by the
City, and when the service had been performed the coffin
was carried by firemen to the massive and highly decorated
funeral barge, on which it was guarded during the transit
by four ' Uscieri ' in gala dress, two sergeants of the
Municipal Guard, and two firemen bearing torches.   The
remainder of these followed in their boats.   The funeral
barge was slowly towed by a steam launch of the Royal
Navy.   The chief officers of the Municipality, the family,
and many others in a crowd of gondolas, completed the
procession.   San Michele was reached as the sun was setting,
when the firemen again received their burden and bore it
to the principal mortuary chapel."

Later the municipality of Venice fixed the memorial
tablet to the wall of the palace.   The quotation, from the
poet, cut under his name, runs thus :—

> Open my heart and you will see
> Graved inside of it, Italy.

The tablet is a graceful recognition of the devotion of
Browning and his wife to their adopted country.   Did the
authorities, I wonder, know that Browning's love of their
city led him always to wear on his watch-chain a coin
struck by Manin in 1848 commemorating the overthrow of
Austrian power in Venice ?

The Rezzonico was built by Longhena, the architect
of the Salute.   Carlo Rezzonico, afterwards Pope Clement
XIII, lived here.   The Emperor Joseph II stayed here.
So much for fact.   I like far more to remember the
Christmas dinner eaten here—only, alas, in fancy, yet with
all proper circumstance—by Browning and a Scandinavian
dramatist named Ibsen, brought together for the purpose

by the assiduous Sir Edmund Gosse, as related with such skill and mischief by Mr. Max Beerbohm.

Next the Rezzonico is the commonplace Nani; then a tiny calle; and then an antiquity store, one of the three adjoining palaces of the great Giustiniani family, in the second of which once lived Richard Wagner.

But first a word as to the Giustiniani's great feat, in the twelfth century, of giving every male member to the Republic. It happened that in 1171 nearly all the Venetians in Constantinople were massacred. An expedition was quickly despatched to demand satisfaction for such a deed, but, while anchored at Scio, the plague broke out and practically demolished this too, among those who perished being the Giustiniani to a man. In order that the family might persist, the sole surviving son, a monk named Niccolò, was temporarily released from his vows to be espoused to the daughter of the Doge, Vitale Michiel. Sufficient sons having been born to them, the father returned to his monastery and the mother sought a convent for herself.

In the first of the three Giustiniani palaces Mr. Howells, moving from the Casa Falier across the way, wrote his *Venetian Life*. In the next Wagner wrote part of *Tristan and Isolda*.

Needing solitude for this task, the composer came to Venice in the autumn of 1858, and put up first at Danieli's. Needing a more private abode he came here. From his *Autobiography* I take the story. " I heard that one of the three Giustiniani palaces, situated not far from the Palazzo Foscari, was at present very little patronized by visitors, on account of its situation, which in the winter is somewhat unfavourable. I found some very spacious and imposing apartments there, all of which they told me would remain uninhabited. I here engaged a large stately room with a spacious bedroom adjoining. I had my luggage quickly transferred there, and on the evening of the 30th August I said to myself, 'At last I am living in Venice'.

"My leading idea was that I could work here undisturbed. I immediately wrote to Zürich asking for my Erard 'Grand' and my bed to be sent on to me, as, with regard to the latter, I felt that I should find out what cold meant in Venice. In addition to this, the grey-washed walls of my large room soon annoyed me, as they were so little suited to the ceiling, which was covered with a fresco which I thought was rather tasteful. I decided to have the walls of the large room covered with hangings of a dark-red shade, even if they were of quite common quality. This immediately caused much trouble; but it seemed to me that it was well worth surmounting, when I gazed down from my balcony with growing satisfaction on the wonderful canal, and said to myself that here I would complete *Tristan*."

The composer's life was very simple. "I worked," he says, "till two o'clock, then I got into the gondola that was always in waiting, and was taken along the solemn Grand Canal to the bright Piazzetta, the peculiar charm of which always had a cheerful effect on me. After this I made for my restaurant in the Piazza San Marco, and when I had finished my meal I walked alone or with Karl along the Riva to the Giardini Pubblici, the only pleasure-ground in Venice where there are any trees, and at nightfall I came back in the gondola down the canal, then more sombre and silent, till I reached the spot where I could see my solitary lamp shining from the night-shrouded façade of the old Palazzo Giustiniani.

"After I had worked a little longer Karl, heralded by the swish of the gondola, would come in regularly at eight o'clock for a few hours' chat over our tea. Very rarely did I vary this routine by a visit to one of the theatres. When I did, I preferred the performances at the Camploi Theatre, where Goldoni's pieces were very well played; but I seldom went to the opera, and when I did go it was merely out of curiosity. More frequently, when bad weather deprived us of our walk, we patronized the popular drama at the Malibran Theatre, where the performances were given in the day-time. The admission cost us six kreutzers. The audiences were excellent, the majority being in their shirt-sleeves, and the pieces given were generally of the ultra-melodramatic type. However, one day to my great astonishment and intense delight I saw there *Le Baruffe Chioggiote*, the grotesque comedy that had appealed so strongly to Goethe in his days at this very theatre. So true to nature was this performance that it surpassed anything of the kind I have ever witnessed."

Wagner's impressions of Venice, where, some twenty-four years later, he was to end his anxious and marvellous life, seem to me so interesting that I quote a little more: "There was little else that attracted my attention in the oppressed and degenerate life of the Venetian people, and the only impression I derived from the exquisite ruin of this wonderful city as far as human interest is concerned was that of a watering-place kept up for the benefit of visitors. Strangely enough, it was the thoroughly German element of good military music, to which so much attention is paid in the Austrian army, that brought me into touch with public life in Venice. The conductors in the two Austrian regiments quartered there began playing overtures of mine, *Rienzi* and *Tannhäuser* for instance, and invited me to attend their practices in their barracks. There I also met the whole staff of officers, and was treated by them with great respect. These bands played on alternate evenings amid brilliant illuminations in the middle of the Piazza San Marco, whose acoustic properties for this class of production were really excellent. I was often suddenly startled towards the end of my meal by the sound of my own overtures; then as I sat at the restaurant window giving myself up to impressions of the music, I did not know which dazzled me most, the incomparable Piazza magnificently illuminated and filled with countless numbers of moving people, or the music that seemed to be borne away in rustling glory to the winds. Only one thing was wanting that might certainly have been expected from an Italian audience: the people were gathered round the band in thousands listening most intently, but no two hands ever forgot themselves so far as to applaud, as the least sign of approbation of Austrian military music would have been looked upon as treason to the Italian Fatherland. All public life in Venice also suffered by this extraordinary rift between the general public and the authorities; this was peculiarly apparent in the relations of the population to the Austrian officers, who floated about publicly in Venice like oil on water. The populace, too, behaved with no less reserve, or one might even say hostility, to the clergy, who were for the most part of Italian origin. I saw a procession of clerics in their vestments passing along the Piazza San Marco accompanied by the people with unconcealed derision.

" It was very difficult for Ritter to induce me to interrupt my daily arrangements even to visit a gallery or a church, though, whenever we had to pass through the town, the exceedingly varied architectonic peculiarities and beauties always delighted me afresh. But the frequent

gondola trips towards the Lido constituted my chief
enjoyment during practically the whole of my stay in
Venice. It was more especially on our homeward journeys
at sunset that I was always over-powered by unique impressions. During the first part of our stay in the September
of that year we saw on one of these occasions the marvellous apparition of the great comet, which at that time
was at its highest brilliancy, and was generally said to
portend an imminent catastrophe.

" The singing of a popular choral society, trained by
an official of the Venetian arsenal, seemed like a real
lagoon idyll. They generally sang only three-part naturally harmonized folk-songs. It was new to me not to hear
the higher voice rise above the compass of the alto, that
is to say, without touching the soprano, thereby imparting
to the sound of the chorus a manly youthfulness hitherto
unknown to me. On fine evenings they glided down the
Grand Canal in a large illuminated gondola, stopping
before a few palaces as if to serenade (when requested and
paid for doing so, be it understood), and generally attracted
a number of other gondolas in their wake.

" During one sleepless night, when I felt impelled to go
out on to my balcony in the small hours, I heard for the
first time the famous old folk-song of the *gondolieri*. I
seemed to hear the first call, in the stillness of the night,
proceeding from the Rialto, about a mile away like a
rough lament, and answered in the same tone from a yet
further distance in another direction. This melancholy
dialogue, which was repeated at longer intervals, affected
me so much that I could not fix the very simple musical
component parts in my memory. However on a subsequent
occasion I was told that this folk-song was of great poetic
interest. As I was returning home late one night on the

gloomy canal, the moon appeared suddenly and illuminated the marvellous palaces and the tall figure of my gondolier towering above the stern of the gondola, slowly moving his huge sweep. Suddenly he uttered a deep wail, not unlike the cry of an animal; the cry gradually gained in strength, and formed itself, after a long-drawn ' Oh !' into the simple musical exclamation ' Venezia!' This was followed by other sounds of which I have no distinct recollection, as I was so much moved at the time. Such were the impressions that to me appeared the most characteristic of Venice during my stay there, and they remained with me until the completion of the second act of *Tristan*, and possibly even suggested to me the long-drawn wail of the shepherd's horn at the beginning of the third act."

Later we shall see the palace where Wagner died, which also is on the Grand Canal.

Now comes the great and splendid Foscari Palace, once also a Giustiniani home and once also the lodging of a king of France—Henry III, certain of whose sumptuous Venetian experiences we saw depicted on the walls of the Doges' Palace. The Foscari is very splendid with its golden borders to the windows, its rich reliefs and pretty effects of red brickwork, and more than most it brings to mind the lost aristocratic glories of Venice. To-day it is a commercial school, with a courtyard at the back full of weeds. The fine lamp at its corner must give as useful a light as any in Venice.

CHAPTER X

THE GRAND CANAL. III: FROM THE RIO FOSCARI TO S. SIMEONE, LOOKING TO THE LEFT

Napoleon *s'amuse*—Paul Veronese—The Layard collection—The Palazzo Papadopoli — The Rialto Bridge — The keystone — Carpaccio — The " Uncle " of Venice—Modern painting—English artists in Venice—The Civic Museum—Pictures and curiosities—Carnival costumes—Carpaccio and Ruskin—Historical scenes—A pleasant garden.

THE big palace on the other side of the Rio Foscari, next the shabby brown, deserted house which, with its view down the Canal, might be made so desirable, is the Balbi, and it has the distinction that Napoleon stood in one of its windows to see a Grand Canal regatta, the races in which ended at this point. Next it is the Angaran, and then a nice little place with lions guarding the terrace gate, at the corner of the Rio della Frescada, one of the prettiest of the side canals. Next we come to another large and solid but very dull house, the Civran (afterwards Grimani) ; then the forsaken Dandolo, and we are at the steamboat station of S. Toma, where the passengers for the Frari and S. Rocco land.

Hereabouts the houses are very uninteresting. Two more and a traghetto and the Rio S. Toma; then the Palazzo Giustiniani, a rich Venetian red, with a glimpse of a courtyard; then the ugliest building in the canal, also red, like the back of a block of flats; and after passing

the little Gothic Tiepolo palace, and the larger Palazzo
Tiepolo adjoining it, we are at the fine fifteenth-century
Pisani Moretta, with a double row of rich Gothic
windows. Here once hung Veronese's "Family of Darius,"
now No. 294 in our National Gallery, and, according to
Ruskin, "the most precious" of the painter's works. The
story goes that Veronese being driven to make use of
the Pisani villa at Este as a temporary home, painted the
picture while there and left it behind him with a message
that he hoped it would pay for his board and lodging.
The Pisani family sold it to the National Gallery in
1857.

The next palace is the Barbarigo della Terrazza, with
a better façade on the Rio S. Polo: once famous for its
splendours, which included seventeen Titians that went to
Russia, and are now—where? and then the Rio S. Polo
and the red Capello Palace, where the late Sir Henry
Layard made his home and gathered about him those
pictures which now, like the Darius, belong to our National
Gallery. Next is the Vendramin, with porphyry enrich-
ment, and then the Querini, and then the Barnardo, once
a splendid palace but now business offices, with its Gothic
arches filled with glass. The Rio della Madonnetta here
intervenes; then come two Donà palaces, the first dating
from the twelfth century. A traghetto is here and a pretty
calle, and soon we come to one of the palaces which are
shown to visitors, the Papadopoli, once the Coccina-Tiepolo.

My advice to those who visit such palaces as are shown
to the public is not to go alone. The rigours of ceremonial can be tempered to a party, and the efficient and
discreet French major-domo is less formidable to several
visitors than to one. The principal attraction of the
Papadopoli Palace is two carnival pictures by Tiepolo.

The Rio dei Meloni, where is the Palazzo Albrizzi to which Byron used to resort as a lion, runs by the Papadopoli. At the other corner is the Businello, a nice solid building with two rows of round window-arches. Then the tall decayed Rampinelli and, followed by a calle, the Ramo Barzizza, and next the Mengaldo, with a very choice doorway and arches. Then the yellow Avogadro, now an antiquity dealer's and tenements, with a fondamenta and the S. Silvestro pier. A new building, and we reach the fine red palace adjoining the Casa Petrarca, with its ramping garden.

These two palaces, which have a sottoportico beneath them leading to S. Silvestro, stand on the site of the palace of the Patriarchs of Grado, who had supreme ecclesiastical power here until the fifteenth century, when the Patriarchate of Venice was founded with a residence near S. Pietro in Castello.

From this point a fondamenta runs all the way to the Rialto bridge. The buildings are not of any particular interest, until we come to the last one, with the two arches under it and the fine relief of a lion on the façade : once the head-quarters of the tithe collectors.

People have come mostly to speak of the Rialto as though it was the bridge only. But it is the district, of which the bridge is the centre. No longer do wealthy shipowners and merchants foregather hereabouts ; for none exist. Venice has ceased to fetch and carry for the world, and all her energies are now confined within her own borders. Enough to live and be as happy as may be !

In beauty the Rialto falls far short of most of the bridges of Venice. Its hard angle superimposed on the great arch is unpleasing to an eye accustomed in this city to easy fluid curves. Seen from immediately below,

DOORWAY OF S. MARIA DELLA SALUTE

the arch is noble ; from any greater distance it is lost in the
over-structure, angle and curve conflicting.   Carpaccio's
Santa Croce picture in the Accademia shows us what the
immediate forerunner of the present bridge was like.   It
had a drawbridge in the middle to prevent escape or pursuit
that way during brawls.

Ruskin is very enthusiastic over the conceit which
placed the Spirito Santo on the keystone of the bridge,
the flight, as he thinks, producing an effect of lightness.
He is pleased too with the two angels, and especially that
one on the right, whose foot is placed with horizontal firm-
ness.   On each side of the bridge is a shrine.   But Venice
does not do the Rialto justice.   I am quite sure that when
Antonio da Ponte designed it towards the end of the
sixteenth century (it was being built on the site of an
earlier wooden bridge during the lifetime of the author of
The Merchant of Venice) he had no idea that the time
would come when all the beautiful top arches would be
boarded up.   But boarded up they are, for the convenience
of the hucksters within them, and in the middle there are
even coloured posters, and one has here a very striking
proof of the modern Venetian's want of pride in his city.

The first palace beyond the bridge, now a decaying
congeries of offices, has very rich decorative stonework,
foliation and festoons.   It was once the head-quarters of
the Camerlenghi, the procurators-fiscal of Venice.   Then
come the long fruit and vegetable markets, and then the
new fish market, one of the most successful of new Venetian
buildings, with its springing arches below and its loggia
above and its iron lamp at the right corner and bronze
fisherman at the left.

A fondamenta runs right away from the Rialto bridge
to a point just beyond the new fish market, with some

8

nice houses on it, over shops, the one on the left of the
fish market having very charming windows. The first
palace of any importance is the dull red one on the other
side of the Calle dei Botteri, the Donà. Then a decayed palace and the Calle del Campanile where the
fondamenta ends. Here is the very attractive Palazzo
Morosini, or Brandolin, which dates from the fourteenth
century. Next is a dull house, and then a small one
with little lions on the balustrades, and then the Rio S.
Cassiano. Next is a tiny and very ancient palace with an
inscription stating that the Venetian painter Favretto
worked there ; then a calle, and the Palazzo Corner della
Regina is before us. The Queen of Cyprus was born
here ; other proud and commanding Corners were splendid
here ; and now it is a pawnshop !

The Calle della Regina, two rather nice, neglected
houses (the little pink one quite charming), and we come
to the Rio Pesaro and the splendid Palazzo Pesaro, one
of the great works of Longhena. Note its fluted pillars
and rich stonework. This palace we may enter, for it is
now the Tate Gallery of Venice, housing, below, a changing
exhibition of contemporary art, and, above, a permanent
collection, to which additions are constantly being made,
of modern Italian painting. Foreign artists are admitted
too, and my eyes were gladdened by the work of several
honoured English hands, a melon-seller by Mr. Brangwyn,
a lady in pink by Mr. Lavery, and a fisherman by Mr.
Cayley Robinson. A number of Whistler's Venetian
etchings may also be seen here, and much characteristic
work by Mr. Pennell. Here too are the " Burghers of
Calais " and the "Thinker" of Rodin, while a nude by
Fantin Latour should be sought for. One of the most
interesting pictures so far as subject goes represents the
bridge of boats to the Redentore on a recent All Souls' day.

THE PALAZZO PESARO (ORFEI), CAMPO S. BENEDETTO

I have been absolutely alone in this building, save for the custodians. The Venetian can live very easily without picture galleries, ancient or modern.

The Rio della Pergola washes the other side of the Pesaro palace, and then come two or three houses, once Foscarini homes, given up to antiquity dealers, and then the florid white stone façade of the church of S. Stae (or S. Eustachio) with a delightful little Venetian-red annexe on the left. There is a campo and steamboat station here too. The next palace has pretty little Gothic windows, and then a small brown house stands in its garden on the site of a burnt Contarini palace. A good red-brick fifteenth-century palace, now a wine store, is next, and then the Tron, now an institution, with a garden and well-head seen through the open door. Great scenes have been witnessed in this building, for the Trons were a famous and powerful Venetian family, supplying more than one Doge, and here in 1775 was entertained the Emperor Joseph II.

Then the Rio Tron and then the Palazzo Battagia, with two rich coats of arms in relief, which is also by Longhena, but I hope that it was not he who placed the columns on the roof. The tiny Calle del Megio, and we reach the venerable piece of decay which once was the granary of the Venetian Republic—one of the most dignified and attractive buildings on the canal, with its old brick and coping of pointed arches. The Rio del Megio divides the granary from the old Fondaco dei Turchi, once, after a long and distinguished life as a palace, the head-quarters of the Turks in Venice, and until lately the Civic Museum.

There is a calle and a traghetto next the Fondaco, and then a disreputable but picturesque brown house with a fondamenta, and then the home of the Teodoro Correr who formed the nucleus of the Civic Museum, which I have described in an earlier chapter, and left it to Venice.   His house is now deserted and miserable.   A police station comes next ; then a decayed house ; and then the Palazzo Giovanelli, boarded up and forlorn, but not the one which contains the famous Giorgione.   And here, at the nice garden on the other side of the Rio S. Giovanni Decollato, I think, we may cease to identify the buildings, for nothing else is important.

Beyond S. Simeone, however, at the corner of the Rio della Croce, is a large and shady garden belonging to the Papadopoli family which may be visited on application. It is a very pleasant place.

S. JOHN CHRYSOSTOM WITH SAINTS
FROM THE PAINTING BY PIOMBO
In the Church of S. Giovanni Crisostomo

CHAPTER XI

THE GRAND CANAL. IV: FROM THE STATION TO THE MOCENIGO PALACE, LOOKING TO THE LEFT

The Scalzi—The Labia Palace—The missing cicerone—Tiepolo and Cleopatra—S. Marcuola and Titian—A maker of oars—The death of Wagner—Frescoes on palaces—The Cà d'Oro—Baron Franchetti—S. Sebastian—The Palazzo Michiel dalle Colonne—A merry tapestry—A cardinal's nursery—The Palazzo Lion—The Fondaco dei Tedeschi— Canova, Titian, and Byron.

BEGINNING at the Railway Station and going towards the Ducal Palace, the first building is the church of the Scalzi, by the iron bridge. The church is a very ornate structure famous for its marbles and reliefs, which counterfeit drapery and take the place of altar pictures; but these are an acquired taste. On the ceiling the brave Tiepolo sprawled a vigorous illustration of the spiriting away of the house of the Virgin to Loreto, near Ancona, but a bomb from an Austrian aeroplane in the War ruined it; and here I might note that the damage done to Venice was very slight, considering how vulnerable she was. Whether the reason is to be found in the vigilance of the defensive air force, in the infirmity of the enemy aim, or in the Austrians' very natural wish not to destroy a city of such beauty which they hoped might soon be theirs, I cannot state. It doesn't matter. The blessed fact is that the War is over, and here is Venice with all her campanili standing.

Next come a row of shops, and, at the corner, the Lido

hotels' motor-launch office, and then several negligible
decayed palaces. The first of any importance is the tall
seventeenth-century incomplete Flangini with Michael
Angelesque figures over the door. Then the Scuola dei
Morti with its *memento mori* on the wall, and then S.
Geremia : outside, a fine mass of yellow brick with a commanding campanile ; inside, all Palladian coolness. Against
the church a little house has been built, and at the corner
of the Grand Canal and the Cannaregio is the figure of
the Virgin. The great palace a little way down the canal
which branches off here—the Cannaregio—is the Labia,
interesting chiefly as containing the masterpiece of Tiepolo,
unless one agrees with Symonds that his picture of S. Agnes
in SS. Apostoli is his greatest effort.

But first to get in, for the Labia, once so sumptuous,
is now the home of a hundred poor families, and the
daughter of the concierge whose duty it is to display the
frescoes prefers play to work. For twenty minutes I waited
in the gloomy, deserted hall while her father shuffled off
in one direction and her mother in another, both calling " Emma ! Emma !" with increasing degrees of fury.
Small boys and girls joined in the hunt until the neighbourhood had no other sound. At last the little slovenly
Emma was discovered, and having been well rated she
fetched the key and led me up the grand staircase.
Tiepolo chose two scenes from the life of Cleopatra, and
there is no doubt that he could draw. In one the voluptuous queen is dissolving a pearl in a goblet of wine ; in
the other she and her infatuated Roman are about to em-
bark in a splendid galley. The model for the wanton
queen is said to have been a gondolier's daughter named
Cristina in whom the painter found all the graces that his
brush required.

The frescoes, still in fair preservation, are masterly and aristocratic; but they have left on my mind no very distinct impression. Tiepolo, however, is always a giant, and always brilliant.

Crossing the mouth of the Cannaregio we come to the Querini Palace, now yellow, plain, and ugly. A little campiello, a tiny ugly house and a calle, and we are opposite the Palazzo Contarini, or Lobbia. It is a huge place, now in part empty, with a pretty cable design at the corner. Next, a shady green garden and an attractive little house with a tiny roof loggia and terrace; then a yellow stucco house with a little portico under it, and then the Palazzo Gritti, now decayed and commonplace. A little house with a dog in relief on it and a pretty colonnade and fondamenta, and then the Palazzo Martinengo, or Mandelli, with that very rare thing in Venice, a public clock on the roof, and a garden.

And so we reach the shabby S. Marcuola, her campo, traghetto, and steamer station. S. Marcuola, whose façade, having never been finished, is most ragged and miserable, is a poor man's church, visited by strangers for its early Titian and a "Last Supper" by Tintoretto. The Titian, which is dark and grimy, is quite pleasing, the infant Christ, who stands between S. Andrew and S. Catherine on a little pedestal, being very real and Venetian. There are, however, who deny Titian's authorship; Mr. Ricketts, for example, gives the picture to Francesco Vecellio, the painter's son. Tintoretto's "Last Supper," on the left of the high altar, is more convivial than is usual: there is plenty of food; a woman and children are coming in; a dog begs; Judas is noticeable. Opposite this picture is a rather interesting dark canvas blending seraphim and Italian architecture. Beside the church used to be the

shop of a maker of oars, who might be seen very conscientiously running his eye along a new one.

A neat and smiling little house comes next, with an
inscription stating that it was once the home of the architect Pellegrino Orefice; then a little house with pretty
windows; then the Rio di S. Marcuola; and after a
small and ugly little house with a courtyard that might
be made very attractive, we come to the rich crumbling
red wall of the garden of the Palazzo Vendramin Calergi,
which is notable as architecture, being one of the works of
Pietro Lombardi, in 1481, and also as having once
housed the noble Loredan family, who produced more
than one Doge.   Many years later the Duchesse de
Berry lived here; and, more interesting still, here died
Richard Wagner.

We have seen Wagner's earlier residence in Venice, in
1858-59; to this palace he came in the autumn of 1882, an
old and feeble man. He was well enough to conduct a private
performance of his Symphony in C at the Liceo Martello
on Christmas Eve.   He died quietly on the February 13th
following, and was buried at Bayreuth. In D'Annunzio's
Venetian novel *Il Fuoco*, called, in its English translation,
The Flame of Life, is most curiously woven the personality
of Wagner, his ideals and theories, and his life and death
in this city. It was D'Annunzio who composed the tablet
on the wall.

The palace has an imposing but forbidding taçade, and a
new kind of lion peers over the balcony.   On the façade is
the motto " Non nobis, Domine ". Another garden spreads
before the new wing on the right, and a fine acacia-tree is
over the gateway.   Next is the Palazzo Marcello, and here
too the Duchesse de Berry lived for a while.   The next, with
the little prophet's chamber on the façade and a fine Gothic

THE DREAM OF S. URSULA
FROM THE PAINTING BY CARPACCIO
In the Accademia

window and balcony, is the fifteenth-century Erizzo.   Then
the Piovene, with fluted window pillars and marble decorations; then the Emo, with a fine view down the canal
from its balcony.   A traghetto is here, and then the
Palazzo Molin, now a business house, and the Rio della
Maddalena.   The palace adjoining the Rio is the Barbaro, with an ancient relief on it representing little people
being blessed by the Madonna; and then the Barbarigo,
with remains of frescoes still to be seen, of which one of a
goat and infant is pretty.   It was the custom once to
decorate all façades in this way, but these are now almost
the only ones that remain.

Now comes a very poor series of houses to the next rio,
the Rio di Noale, the last being the Gussoni, or Grimani,
with a nice courtyard seen through the door.   It was once
decorated with frescoes by Tintoretto.   Looking along the
Rio di Noale we see the Misericordia, and only a few yards
up on the left is the Palazzo Giovanelli where Giorgione's
"Tempest" may be seen.   At the other corner is the pretty
little Palazzo Lezze with a terrace and much greenery, and
then the massive but commonplace Boldù palace, adjoining
a decayed building on whose fondamenta are piled gondola
coverings belonging to the traghetto.   A fine carved
column is at the corner of the calle, and next it the Palazzo
Bonhomo, with two arches of a colonnade, a shrine and
fondamenta.   Then a nice house with a tumbled garden,
and in spring purple wistaria and red Judas-trees, and then
the Rio S. Felice and the immense but unimpressive Palazzo
Fontana, built possibly by no less an architect than the
great Sansovino.   A massive head is over the door, and Pope
Clement XIII was born here.   A little green garden adjoins—the Giardinetto Infantile—and next is a boarded-up
dolls' house, and next the Miani or Palazzo Coletti, with

two busts on it, and then the Cà d'Oro, that exquisite riot of Gothic richness.

The history of the Cà d'Oro—or golden house, so called from the prevalence of gold in its ornamentation—is melancholy. It was built by the two Bons, or Buons, of the Doges' Palace, for Pietro Contarini in 1425. It passed through various hands, always, one imagines, declining in condition, until at the end of the eighteenth century it was a dramatic academy, and in the middle of the last century the dancer Taglioni lived in it and not only made it squalid but sold certain of its treasures. Of the famous internal marble staircase, for example, no trace remains. Then, after probably more careless tenants, came Baron Franchetti with his wealth and zeal to restore such of its glories as he might, and he has now presented the palace to the city in perpetuity, and it will bear his honoured name.

Let no one think to know all its beauty until he has penetrated to the little chapel and stood before Mantegna's S. Sebastian, that great simple work of art by an intellectual master. This noble painting, possibly the last from his brush, was found in Mantegna's studio after his death. Notice the smoking candle-wick at the foot, and the motto which says that everything that is not of God is as smoke evanescent.

We are now exactly opposite the new Fish Market on the other bank. Next on our side comes the garden of the Palazzo Pesaro, now the Paraguay consulate; then the Sagredo, an extremely ancient Gothic building with a beautiful window and balcony, now badly served by paint and stucco and shutters; and then another traghetto at the Campo S. Sofia, with a vine ramping over its shelter. Stucco again injures the Palazzo Foscari, which has a

pretty relief of the Madonna and Child; then we come to
a calle and the Cà d'Oro steamboat station.

An ugly yellow building comes next and then the fine
but dingy Palazzo Michiel dalle Colonne with brown posts,
all faded, and ten columns, the owner of which permits
visitors to see it in his absence. It is the first palace since
the Scalzi, except the Cà d'Oro, that seems to be in rightful
hands. The principal attraction is its tapestry, some of
which is most charming, particularly a pattern of plump and
impish cherubs among vines and grapes, which the cicerone
baldly attributes to Rubens, but Baedeker to one of his
pupils. Whoever the designer, he had an agreeable and
robust fancy and a sure hand. The palace seems to have
more rooms than its walls can contain, all possessing costly
accessories and no real beauty. The bedroom of Cardinal
Gregorio Barbarigo is shown: his elaborate cradle with a
stork presiding over it, surely a case of *trop de zèle*; pretty
yellow painted furniture; and a few pictures, including a
fine horseback portrait by Moretto, a Cima, a Giovanni
Bellini, and the usual Longhis. But it is the riotous little
spirits of the vintage that remain in the mind.

After the Michiel dalle Colonne is a little newish house
and the Gothic Palazzo Michiel da Brusà, with nice ironwork; and then the comfortable-looking Mangilli Valmarana and the Rio dei SS. Apostoli with a view of the
campanile along it. Next a dull white building with flush
windows, and next that the fine and ancient Palazzo da
Mosto. This house has many old sculptured slabs worked
into the façade, and it seems a great pity that it should
so have fallen from its proper state. An ugly modern
iron balcony has been set beneath its Gothic windows.
Adjoining is a house which also has pretty Gothic windows, and then the dull and neglected Palazzo Mocenigo.

Then comes the Rio S. Gio. Crisostomo, and next it a house newly faced, and then the fascinating remains of the twelfth-century Palazzo Lion, consisting of an exposed staircase and a very attractive courtyard with round and pointed arches. It is now a rookery. Washing is hung in the loggia at the top, and ragged children lean from the windows.

Next, a pretty little house which might be made very livable in, facing the fruit market, and then the hideous modern Sernagiotto, dating from 1847 and therefore more than negligible. A green little house with a sottoportico under it, and then a little red-brick prison and the ugly Civran palace is reached. Next, the Perducci, now a busy statuary store, and next it the Cà Ruzzini, all spick and span, and the Rio dell' Olio o del Fontego, through which come the fruit barges from Malamocco on their way to the market just across the Grand Canal. And now we touch very interesting history again, for the next great building, with the motor-boats before it, now the central Post Office, is the very Fondaco dei Tedeschi, the head-quarters of German merchants in Venice, on whose walls Giorgione and Titian painted the famous frescoes and in which Tintoretto held a sinecure post. Giorgione's frescoes faced the Canal ; Titian's the Rialto.

And so we reach the Rialto bridge, on this side of which are no shrines, but a lion is on the keystone, and on each side is a holy man. After the Rialto bridge there is nothing of any moment for many yards, save a house with a high narrow archway which may be seen in Mr. Morley's picture, until we reach Sansovino's Palazzo Manin, now the Bank of Italy, a fine building and the home of the last Doge. The three steamboat stations

THE RIALTO BRIDGE FROM THE PALAZZO DEI DIECI SAVII

hereabouts are for passengers for S. Marco and the Lido, for Mestre, and for the railway station, respectively. The palace next the Ponte Manin, over the Rio San Salvatore, is the Bembo, with very fine windows. Then the Calle Bembo, and then various offices on the fondamenta, under chiefly red façades. At the next calle is a traghetto and then the Palazzo Loredan, a Byzantine building of the eleventh or twelfth century, since restored. It has lovely arches. This and the next palace, the Farsetti, now form the Town Hall of Venice: hence the splendid blue posts and golden lions. In the vestibule are posted up the notices of engagements, with full particulars of the contracting parties—the celibi and the nubili. It was in the Farsetti that Canova acquired his earliest knowledge of sculpture, for he was allowed as a boy to copy the casts collected there.

Another calle, the Cavalli, and then a comfortable-looking house with a roof garden, opposite which the fondamenta comes to an end. Fenimore Cooper, the novelist, made this palace his home for a while. The pretty little Palazzo Valmarana comes next, and then the gigantic, sombre Grimani with its stone as dark as a Bath or Bloomsbury mansion, which now is Venice's Court of Appeal. The architect was the famous Michele Sammicheli, who also designed the Lido's forts. Then the Rio di S. Luca and the Palazzo Contarini, with two reliefs of horses on the façade. Next a very tiny pretty little Tron Palace ; then a second Tron, and then the dreary Martinengo, now the Bank of Naples. In its heyday Titian was a frequent visitor here, its owner, Martino d'Anna, a Flemish merchant, being an intimate friend, and Pordenone painted its walls.

Another calle and traghetto and we come to a very

commonplace house, and then, after a business office and another calle, to the Palazzo Benzon, famous a hundred years ago for its literary and artistic receptions. In this house Byron has often been; hither he brought Moore. It is spacious but tawdry, and its plate-glass gives one a shock. Then the Rio Michiel and then the Tornielli, very dull, the Curti, decayed, and the Rio dell' Albero. After the rio, the fine blackened Corner Spinelli with porphyry insets.

At the steamboat station of S. Angelo are new buildings —one a very pretty red brick and stone, one with a loggia —standing on the site of the Teatro S. Angelo. After the Rio S. Angelo we come to a palace which I always admire : red-brick and massive, with good Gothic windows and a bold relief of cupids at the top. It is the Garzoni.

A calle and traghetto next, a shed with a shrine on its wall, a little neat modern house and the Palazzo Corner with its common new glass, and we are abreast the three Mocenigo palaces, only the first of which takes any pride in itself. In the middle one Byron settled in 1818 and wrote *Beppo* and began *Don Juan* and did not a little mischief.

CHAPTER XII

THE GRAND CANAL. V: BYRON IN VENICE

The beautiful Marianna—Rum-punch—The Palazzo Albrizzi—A play at the Fenice—The sick *Ballerina*—The gondola—Praise of Italy—*Beppo*—*Childe Harold*—Riding on the Lido—The inquisitive English—Shelley in Venice—*Julian and Maddalo*—The view from the Lido—The madhouse—The Ducal prisons.

THE name of Byron is so intimately associated with Venice that I think a brief account of his life there (so far as it can be told) might be found interesting.

It was suggested by Madame de Flanhault that Byron was drawn to Venice not only by its romantic character, but because, since he could go everywhere by water, his lameness would attract less attention than elsewhere. Be that as it may, he arrived in Venice late in 1816, being then twenty-eight. He lodged first in the Frezzeria, and at once set to work upon employments so dissimilar as acquiring a knowledge of the Armenian language in the monastery on the island of San Lazzaro and making love to the wife of his landlord. But let his own gay pen tell the story. He is writing to Tom Moore on November 17, 1816: "It is my intention to remain at Venice during the winter, probably, as it has always been (next to the East) the greenest island of my imagination. It has not disappointed me; though its evident decay would, perhaps, have that effect upon others. But I have been familiar with ruins too long to dislike desolation. Besides, I have fallen in love, which, next to falling into the canal (which would be of no use, as I can swim), is the best or the worst thing I could do. I have got some extremely good apartments in the house of a ' Merchant of Venice,' who is a good deal occupied with business, and has a wife in her twenty-second year. Marianna (that is her name) is in her appearance altogether like an antelope. She has the large, black oriental eyes, with that peculiar expression in them which is seen rarely among *Europeans* —even the Italians—and which many of the Turkish women give themselves by tinging the eyelid, an art not known out of that country, I believe. This expression she has *naturally*—and something more than this. In short——— " The rest of this amour, and one strange scene to which it led, very like an incident in an Italian comedy, is no concern of this book. For those who wish to know more, it is to be found, in prose, in the Letters, and, in verse, in *Beppo*.

On this his first visit to Venice, Byron was a private individual. He was sociable in a quiet way, attending one or two salons, but he was not splendid. And he seems really to have thrown himself with his customary vigour into his Armenian studies ; but of those I speak elsewhere. They were for the day : in the evening, he tells Moore, " I do one of many nothings—either at the theatres, or some of the conversaziones, which are like our routs, or rather worse, for the women sit in a semi-circle by the lady of the mansion, and the men stand about the room. To be sure, there is one improvement upon ours—instead of lemonade with their ices, they hand about stiff *rum- punch—punch*, by my palate ; and this they think *English*. I would not disabuse them of so agreeable an error,—' no, not for " Venice " '."

The chief houses to which he went were the Palazzo Benzon and the Palazzo Albrizzi. Moore when in Venice a little later also paid his respects to the Countess Albrizzi. "These assemblies," he wrote home, "which, at a distance, sounded so full of splendour and gallantry to me, turned into something much worse than one of Lydia White's conversaziones."

Here is one of Byron's rattling descriptions of a Venetian night. The date is December 27, 1816, and it is written to his publisher, Murray: "As the news of Venice must be very interesting to you, I will regale you with it. Yesterday being the feast of St. Stephen, every mouth was put in motion. There was nothing but fiddling and playing on the virginals, and all kinds of conceits and divertisements, on every canal of this aquatic city.

"I dined with the Countess Albrizzi and a Paduan and Venetian party, and afterwards went to the opera, at the Fenice theatre (which opens for the Carnival on that day) —the finest, by the way, I have ever seen; it beats our theatres hollow in beauty and scenery, and those of Milan and Brescia bow before it. The opera and its Syrens were much like all other operas and women, but the subject of the said opera was something edifying; it turned—the plot and conduct thereof—upon a fact narrated by Livy of a hundred and fifty married ladies having *poisoned* a hundred and fifty husbands in the good old times. The bachelors of Rome believed this extraordinary mortality to be merely the common effect of matrimony or a pestilence; but the surviving Benedicts, being all seized with the cholic, examined into the matter, and found that their possets had been drugged; the consequence of which was much scandal and several suits at law.

"This is really and truly the subject of the Musical

9

piece at the Fenice; and you can't conceive what pretty things are sung and recitativoed about the *horreda straga*. The conclusion was a lady's head about to be chopped off by a Lictor, but (I am sorry to say) he left it on, and she got up and sang a trio with the two Consuls, the Senate in the background being chorus.

"The ballet was distinguished by nothing remarkable, except that the principal she-dancer went into convulsions because she was not applauded on her first appearance; and the manager came forward to ask if there was 'ever a physician in the theatre'. There was a Greek one in my box, whom I wished very much to volunteer his services, being sure that in this case these would have been the last convulsions which would have troubled the *Ballerina*; but he would not.

"The crowd was enormous; and in coming out, having a lady under my arm, I was obliged in making way, almost to 'beat a Venetian and traduce the state,' being compelled to regale a person with an English punch in the guts which sent him as far back as the squeeze and the passage would admit. He did not ask for another; but with great signs of disapprobation and dismay, appealed to his compatriots, who laughed at him."

Byron's first intention was to write nothing in Venice; but fortunately the idea of *Beppo* came to him, and that masterpiece of gay recklessness and high-spirited imprudence sprang into life. The desk at which he wrote is still preserved in the Palazzo Mocenigo. From *Beppo* I quote elsewhere some stanzas relating to Giorgione; and here are two which bear upon the "hansom of Venice," written when that vehicle was as fresh to Byron as it is to some of us :—

Didst ever see a Gondola?   For fear
   You should not, I'll describe it you exactly :
'Tis a long covered boat that's common here,
   Carved at the prow, built lightly, but compactly,
Rowed by two rowers, each call'd " Gondolier,"
   It glides along the water looking blackly,
Just like a coffin clapt in a canoe,
Where none can make out what you say or do.

And up and down the long canals they go,
   And under the Rialto shoot along,
By night and day, all paces, swift or slow,
   And round the theatres, a sable throng,
They wait in their dusk livery of woe,—
   But not to them do woeful things belong,
For sometimes they contain a deal of fun,
   Like mourning coaches when the funeral's done.

Those useful ciceroni in Venice, the Signori Carlo and
Sarri, seem to have had Byron's description in mind.
"She is all black," they write of the gondola, "everything
giving her a somewhat mysterious air, which awakens in
one's mind a thousand various thoughts about what has
happened, happens, or may happen beneath the little
felze."

It is pleasant to think that, no matter upon what other
Italian experiences the sentiments were founded, the praise
of Italy in the following stanzas was written in a room in
the Mocenigo Palace, looking over the Grand Canal upon
a prospect very similar to that which we see to-day :—

With all its sinful doings, I must say,
   That Italy's a pleasant place to me,
Who love to see the Sun shine every day,
   And vines (not nailed to walls) from tree to tree,
Festooned, much like the back scene of a play,
   Or melodrama, which people flock to see,
When the first act is ended by a dance
In vineyards copied from the South of France.

I like on Autumn evenings to ride out,
  Without being forced to bid my groom be sure
My cloak is round his middle strapped about,
  Because the skies are not the most secure ;
I know too that, if stopped upon my route,
  Where the green alleys windingly allure,
Reeling with *grapes* red wagons choke the way,—
In England 'twould be dung, dust or a dray.

I also like to dine on becaficas,
  To see the Sun set, sure he'll rise to-morrow,
Not through a misty morning twinkling weak as
  A drunken man's dead eye in maudlin sorrow,
But with all Heaven t'himself ; the day will break as
  Beauteous as cloudless, nor be forced to borrow
That sort of farthing candlelight which glimmers
Where reeking London's smoky cauldron simmers.

I love the language, that soft bastard Latin
  Which melts like kisses from a female mouth,
And sounds as if it should be writ on satin,
  With syllables which breathe of the sweet South,
And gentle liquids gliding all so pat in,
  That not a single accent seems uncouth,
Like our harsh northern whistling, grunting guttural,
Which were obliged to hiss, and spit and sputter all.

I like the women too (forgive my folly !),
  From the rich peasant cheek of ruddy bronze,
And large black eyes that flash on you a volley
  Of rays that say a thousand things at once,
To the high Dama's brow, more melancholy,
  But clear, and with a wild and liquid glance,
Heart on her lips, and soul within her eyes,
Soft as her clime, and sunny as her skies.

Byron's next visit to Venice was in 1818, and it was
then that he set up state and became a Venetian lion.
He had now his gondolas, his horses on the Lido, a box
at the Opera, many servants. But his gaiety had left
him. Neither in his letters nor his verse did he recapture

the fun which we find in *Beppo*. To this second period belong such graver Venetian work (either inspired here or written here) as the opening stanzas of the fourth canto of *Childe Harold*. The first line takes the reader into the very heart of the city and is one of the best-known single lines in all poetry. Familiar as the stanzas are, it would be ridiculous to write of Byron in Venice without quoting them again :—

> I stood in Venice, on the " Bridge of Sighs ";
>   A Palace and a prison on each hand :
> I saw from out the wave her structures rise
>   As from the stroke of the Enchanter's wand :
> A thousand Years their cloudy wings expand
>   Around me, and a dying Glory smiles
> O'er the far times, when many a subject land
>   Looked to the wingéd Lion's marble piles,
>   Where Venice sate in state, throned on her hundred isles.
>
> She looks a sea Cybele, fresh from Ocean,
>   Rising with her tiara of proud towers
> At airy distance, with majestic motion,
>   A ruler of the waters and their powers :
> And such she was ;—her daughters had their dowers
>   From spoils of nations, and the exhaustless East
> Poured in her lap all gems in sparkling showers,
>   In purple was she robed, and of her feast
>   Monarchs partook, and deemed their dignity increased.

Byron wrote also, in 1818, an "Ode on Venice," a regret for its decay, in spirit not unlike the succeeding *Childe Harold* stanzas which I do not here quote. Here too he planned *Marino Faliero*, talking it over with his guest, "Monk" Lewis. Another Venetian play of Byron's was *The Two Foscari*, and both prove that he attacked the old chronicles to some purpose and with all his brilliant thoroughness. None the less he made a few blunders, as when in *The Two Foscari* there is an allusion to the Bridge of Sighs, which was not, as it happens, built for more than a century after the date of the play.

No city, however alluring, could be Byron's home for long, and this second sojourn in Venice was not made any simpler by the presence of his daughter Ada. In 1819 he was away again and never returned. No one so little liked the idea of being rooted as he; at a blow the home was broken.

The best account of Byron at this time is that which his friend Hoppner, the British Consul, a son of the painter, wrote to Murray. Hoppner not only saw Byron regularly at night, but used to ride with him on the Lido. " The spot," he says, " where we usually mounted our horses had been a Jewish cemetery ; but the French, during their occupation of Venice, had thrown down the enclosure, and levelled all the tombstones with the ground, in order that they might not interfere with the fortifications upon the Lido, under the guns of which it was situated. To this place, as it was known to be that where he alighted from his gondola and met his horses, the curious amongst our country-people, who were anxious to obtain a glimpse of him, used to resort ; and it was amusing in the extreme to witness the excessive coolness with which ladies, as well as gentlemen, would advance within a very few paces of him, eyeing him, some with their glasses, as they would have done a statue in a museum, or the wild beasts at Exeter 'Change. However flattering this might be to a man's vanity, Lord Byron, though he bore it very patiently, expressed himself, as I believe he really was, excessively annoyed at it.

" The curiosity that was expressed by all classes of travellers to see him, and the eagerness with which they endeavoured to pick up any anecdotes of his mode of life, were carried to a length which will hardly be credited. It formed the chief subject of their inquiries of the gondoliers who conveyed them from *terra firma* to the floating city ; and these people who are generally loquacious, were not at all backward in administering to the taste and humours of their passengers, relating to them the most extravagant and often unfounded stories. They took care to point out the house where he lived, and to give such hints of his movements as might afford them an opportunity of seeing him.

" Many of the English visitors, under pretext of seeing his house, in which there were no paintings of any consequence, nor, besides himself, anything worthy of notice, contrived to obtain admittance through the cupidity of his servants, and with the most barefaced impudence forced their way even into his bed-room, in the hopes of seeing him. Hence arose, in a great measure, his bitterness towards them, which he has expressed in a note to one of his poems, on the occasion of some unfounded remark made upon him by an anonymous traveller in Italy ; and it certainly appears well calculated to foster that cynicism which prevails in his latter works more particularly, and which, as well as the misanthropical expressions that occur in those which first raised his reputation, I do not believe to have been his natural feeling. Of this I am certain, that I never witnessed greater kindness than in Lord Byron."

Byron's note to which Hoppner alludes is in *Marino Faliero*. The conclusion of it is as follows : " The fact is, I hold in utter abhorrence any contact with the travelling English, as my friend the Consul General Hoppner and the Countess Benzoni (in whose house the Conversazione mostly frequented by them is held), could amply testify, were it worth while. I was persecuted by these tourists even to my riding ground at Lido, and reduced to the most disagreeable circuits to avoid them. At Madame Benzoni's I repeatedly refused to be introduced to them; of a thousand such presentations pressed upon me, I accepted two, and both were to Irish women."

Shelley visited Byron at the Mocenigo Palace in 1818 on a matter concerning Byron's daughter Allegra and Claire Clairmont, whom the other poet brought with him. They reached Venice by gondola from Padua, having the fortune to be rowed by a gondolier who had been in Byron's employ and who at once and voluntarily began to talk of him, his luxury and extravagance. At the inn the waiter, also unprovoked, enlarged on the same alluring theme. Shelley's letter describing Byron's Venetian home is torn at its most interesting passage and we are therefore without anything as amusing and vivid as the same correspondent's account of his lordship's Ravenna ménage. Byron took him for a ride on the Lido, the memory of which formed the opening lines of *Julian and Maddalo*. Thus :—

I rode one evening with Count Maddalo
Upon the bank of land which breaks the flow
Of Adria towards Venice : a bare strand
Of hillocks, heaped from ever-shifting sand,
Matted with thistles and amphibious weeds,
Such as from earth's embrace the salt ooze breeds,
Is this ; an uninhabited sea-side,
Which the lone fisher, when his nets are dried,
Abandons ; and no other object breaks
The waste, but one dwarf tree and some few stakes
Broken and unrepaired, and the tide makes
A narrow space of level sand thereon,
Where 'twas our wont to ride while day went down.
This ride was my delight. I love all waste
And solitary places ; where we taste

THE BAPTISM OF CHRIST
FROM THE PAINTING BY CIMA
In the Church of S. Giovanni in Bragora

> The pleasure of believing what we see
> Is boundless, as we wish our souls to be:
> And such was this wide ocean, and this shore
> More barren than its billows; and yet more
> Than all, with a remembered friend I love
> To ride as then I rode;—for the winds drove
> The living spray along the sunny air
> Into our faces; the blue heavens were bare,
> Stripped to their depths by the awakening north;
> And, from the waves, sound like delight broke forth
> Harmonizing with solitude, and sent
> Into our hearts aërial merriment.

When the ride was over and the two poets were returning in Byron's (or Count Maddalo's) gondola, there was such an evening view as one often has, over Venice, and beyond, to the mountains. Shelley describes it :—

> Paved with the image of the sky . . . the hoar
> And aëry Alps towards the North appeared
> Through mist, an heaven-sustaining bulwark reared
> Between the East and West; and half the sky
> Was roofed with clouds of rich emblazonry
> Dark purple at the zenith, which still grew
> Down the steep West into a wondrous hue
> Brighter than burning gold, even to the rent
> Where the swift sun yet paused in his descent
> Among the many-folded hills : they were
> Those famous Euganean hills, which bear,
> As seen from Lido thro' the harbour piles,
> The likeness of a clump of peaked isles—
> And then—as if the Earth and Sea had been
> Dissolved into one lake of fire, were seen
> Those mountains towering as from waves of flame
> Around the vaporous sun, from which there came
> The inmost purple spirit of light, and made
> Their very peaks transparent.

Browning never tired, says Mrs. Bronson, of this evening view from the Lido, and always held that these lines by Shelley were the best description of it.

The poem goes on to describe a visit to the madhouse of S. Clemente and the reflections that arose from it. Towards the close Shelley says :—

> If I had been an unconnected man
> I, from this moment, should have formed some plan
> Never to leave sweet Venice,—for to me
> It was delight to ride by the lone sea ;
> And then, the town is silent—one may write
> Or read in gondolas by day or night,
> Having the little brazen lamp alight,
> Unseen, uninterrupted ; books are there,
> Pictures, and casts from all those statues fair
> Which were twin-born with poetry, and all
> We seek in towns, with little to recall
> Regrets for the green country.

Later in 1818 Mrs. Shelley joined her husband in Venice, but it was a tragic visit, for their daughter Clara died almost immediately after they arrived. She is buried on the Lido.

In a letter to Peacock, Shelley thus describes the city : "Venice is a wonderfully fine city. The approach to it over the laguna, with its domes and turrets glittering in a long line over the blue waves, is one of the finest architectural delusions in the world. It seems to have—and literally it has—its foundations in the sea. The silent streets are paved with water, and you hear nothing but the dashing of the oars, and the occasional cries of the gondolieri. I heard nothing of Tasso. The gondolas themselves are things of a most romantic and picturesque appearance ; I can only compare them to moths of which a coffin might have been the chrysalis. They are hung with black, and painted black, and carpeted with grey ; they curl at the prow and stern, and at the former there is a nondescript beak of shining steel, which glitters at the end of its long black mass.

"The Doge's Palace, with its library, is a fine monument of aristocratic power. I saw the dungeons, where these scoundrels used to torment their victims. They are of three kinds—one adjoining the place of trial, where the prisoners destined to immediate execution were kept. I could not descend into them, because the day on which I visited it was festa. Another under the leads of the palace, where the sufferers were roasted to death or madness by the ardours of an Italian sun: and others called the Pozzi—or wells, deep underneath, and communicating with those on the roof by secret passages—where the prisoners were confined sometimes half-up to their middles in stinking water. When the French came here, they found only one old man in the dungeons, and he could not speak."

CHAPTER XIII

THE GRAND CANAL. VI: FROM THE MOCENIGO PALACE TO THE MOLO, LOOKING TO THE LEFT

W. D. Howells—A gondoliers' quarrel—Mr. Sargent's Diploma picture —The Barbarigo family—Ruskin's sherry—Palace hotels—The Venetian balcony.

THE next palace, with mural inscriptions, also belonged to the Mocenigo, and here Giordano Bruno was staying as a guest when he was betrayed by his host and burned as a heretic. Then comes the dark and narrow Calle Mocenigo Casa Vecchia. Next is the great massive palace, with the square and round porphyry medallions, of the Contarini dalle Figure; the next, with the little inquisitive lions, is the Lezze. After three more, one of which is in a superb position at the corner, opposite the Foscari, and the third has a fondamenta and arcade, we come to the great Moro-Lin, now an antiquity store. Another little modest place between narrow calli, and the plain eighteenth-century Grassi confronts us. The Campo of S. Samuele, with its traghetto, church, and charming campanile, now opens out. The church has had an ugly brown house built against it. Then the Malipiero, with its tropical garden and pretty marble rail, and then two more renovated houses with very ordinary façades, the unfinished stonework on the side of the second of which, with the steps and sottoportico, was to have been a palace for the Duke of Milan, but was discontinued.

Next the Rio del Duca is the pretty little Palazzo Falier, from one of whose windows Mr. Howells used to look when he was gathering material for his *Venetian Life*. Mr. Howells lived there in the early eighteen-sixties, when a member of the American Consulate in Venice. As to how he performed his consular duties, such as they were, I have no notion; but we cannot be too grateful to his country for appointing him to the post, since it provided him with the experiences which make the most attractive Anglo-Saxon book on Venice that has yet been written. It is now more than half a century since *Venetian Life* was published, but it is still true.

It was not at the Palazzo Falier that Mr. Howells enjoyed the ministrations of that most entertaining handmaiden Giovanna; but it was from here that he heard that quarrel between two gondoliers which he describes so vividly and which stands for every quarrel of every gondolier for all time. I take the liberty of quoting it here, because one gondolier's quarrel is essential to every book that hopes to suggest Venice to its readers, and I have none of my own worth recording. "Two large boats, attempting to enter the small canal opposite at the same time, had struck together with a violence that shook the boatmen to their inmost souls. One barge was laden with lime, and belonged to a plasterer of the city; the other was full of fuel, and commanded by a virulent rustic. These rival captains advanced toward the bows of their boats, with murderous looks,

Con la test' alta e con rabbiosa fame,
Sì che parea che l'aer ne temesse,

and there stamped furiously, and beat the wind with hands of deathful challenge, while I looked on with that noble interest which the enlightened mind always feels in people about to punch each other's heads.

"But the storm burst in words.

"'Figure of a pig!' shrieked the Venetian, 'you have ruined my boat for ever!'

"'Thou liest, son of an ugly old dog!' returned the countryman, 'and it was my right to enter the canal first.'

"They then, after this exchange of insult, abandoned the main subject of dispute, and took up the quarrel laterally and in detail. Reciprocally questioning the reputation of all their female relatives to the third and fourth cousins, they defied each other as the offspring of assassins and prostitutes. As the peace-making tide gradually drifted their boats asunder, their anger rose, and they danced back and forth and hurled opprobrium with a foamy volubility that quite left my powers of comprehension behind. At last the townsman, executing a *pas seul* of uncommon violence, stooped and picked up a bit of stone lime, while the countryman, taking shelter at the stern of his boat, there attended the shot. To my infinite disappointment it was not fired. The Venetian seemed to have touched the climax of his passion in the mere demonstration of hostility, and gently gathering up his oar gave the countryman the right of way. The courage of the latter rose as the strange danger passed, and as far as he could be heard, he continued to exult in the wildest excesses of insult: 'Ah-heigh! brutal executioner! Ah, hideous headsman!' Da capo. I now know that these people never intended to do more than quarrel, and no doubt they parted as well pleased as if they had actually carried broken heads from the encounter. But at the time I felt affronted and trifled with by the result, for my disappointments arising out of the dramatic manner of the Italians had not yet been frequent enough to teach me to expect nothing from it."

I too have seen the beginning of many quarrels, chiefly on the water. But I have seen only two Venetians use their fists—and they were infants in arms. For the rest, except at traghetti and at the corners of canals, the Venetians are good-humoured and blessed with an easy smiling tolerance. Venice is the best place in the world, and they are in Venice, and there you are! Why lose one's temper?

Next the Casa Falier is a calle, and then the great Giustinian Lolin Palace. Taglioni lived here for a while too. After another calle, the Giustinian, a dull house with a garden, we are at the Iron Bridge and the Campo S. Vitale, a small poor-people's church, with a Venetian-red house against it, and inside, but difficult to see, yet worth seeing, a fine picture by Carpaccio of a saint on horseback. Opposite is the Accademia.

The magnificent palace in good repair that comes next is the Cavalli, with a row of bronze dragons on the façade. This is the home of the Franchetti family, who have done so much for modern Venice, conspicuously, as we have seen, at the Cà d'Oro. Then the Rio dell' Orso o Cavana, and the Palazzo Barbaro, a beautiful room in which will be familiar to all visitors to the Diploma Gallery at Burlington House, for it is the subject of one of Mr. Sargent's most astounding feats of dexterity. When this picture was painted the palace was the Venetian home of an American; and once no less a personage than Isabella d'Este lived here very shortly after America was discovered. The older of the two Barbaro palaces is fourteenth century, the other, sixteenth. They will have peculiar interest to anyone who has read *La Vie d'un Patricien de Venise au XVI Siècle*, by Yriarte, for that fascinating work deals with Marcantonio Barbaro, who married one of the Giustiniani and lived here.

Nothing of importance before the next rio, the beautiful Rio del Santissimo o di Stefano; nor after this, until the calle and traghetto: merely two neglected houses, one with a fondamenta. And then a pension arises, next to which is one of the most coveted abodes in the whole canal—the little alluring house and garden that belong to Prince Hohenlohe. The majestic palace now before us is one of Sansovino's buildings, the Palazzo Corner della Cà Grande, now the Prefecture of Venice. Opposite it is the beautiful Dario palace and the Venier garden. Next is the Rio S. Maurizio and then two dingy Barbarigo palaces, once the home of a family very famous in Venetian annals. Marco Barbarigo was the first Doge to be crowned at the head of the Giants' Stairs; it was while his brother Agostino was Doge (1486-1501) that Venice acquired Cyprus, and its queen, Caterina Corner, visited this city to abdicate her throne. Cardinal Barbarigo, famous not only for his piety but for refusing to become Pope, was born in this house.

Then the Rio S. Maria Zobenigo o dei Furlani and a palace, adjoining the steamboat station. Another inferior palace, and a traghetto, with vine leaves over its shelter, and looking up the campo we see the church of S. Maria del Giglio, also called S. Zobenigo, with all its holy statues. Ruskin (who later moved to the Zattere) did most of his work on *The Stones of Venice* in the house which is now the Palazzo Swift, an annexe of

MADONNA AND SLEEPING CHILD
FROM THE PAINTING BY GIOVANNI BELLINI
In the Accademia

the Grand Hotel, a little way up this campo.   Here
he lived happily with his young wife and toiled at the
minutiæ of his great book ; here too he entertained
David Roberts and other artists with his father's excellent
sherry, which they described as " like the best painting, at
once tender and expressive ".

And now the hotels begin, almost all of them in houses
built centuries ago for noble families.   Thus the first
Grand Hotel block is fourteenth century—the Palazzo
Gritti.   The next Grand Hotel block is the Palazzo Fini
and is seventeenth century, and the third is the Manolesso-
Ferro, built in the fourteenth century and restored in the
nineteenth.   Then comes the charming fourteenth-century
Contarini-Fasan Palace, known as the house of Desdemona,
which requires more attention.   The upper part seems to
be as it was : the water floor, or sea storey, has evidently
been badly botched.   Its glorious possession is, however, its
balconies, particularly the lower.

Of the Grand Canal balconies, the most beautiful of
which is, I think, that which belongs to this little palace,
no one has written more prettily than that early commen-
tator, Coryat.   " Again," he says, " I noted another thing
in these Venetian Palaces that I have very seldome seen in
England, and it is very little used in any other country
that I could perceive in my travels, saving only in Venice
and other Italian cities.   Somewhere above the middle of
the front of the building, or (as I have observed in many
of their Palaces) a little beneath the toppe of the front
they have right opposite to their windows, a very pleasant
little tarrasse, that jutteth or butteth out from the maine
building, the edge whereof is decked with many pretty
little turned pillars, either of marble or free stone to leane
over.   These kind of tarrasses or little galleries of pleasure

10

Suetonius calleth Meniana.   They give great grace to the whole edifice, and serve only for this purpose, that people may from that place as from a most delectable prospect contemplate and view the parts of the City round about them in the coole evening."—No modern description could improve on the thoroughness of that.

Next is the pretty Barozzi Wedmann Palace, with its pointed windows, said to be designed by Longhena, who built the great Salute church opposite, and then the Palazzo Michiel.   For the rest, I may say that the Britannia was the Palazzo Tiepolo ; the Grand Hotel de l'Europe was yet another Giustiniani palace; while the Grand Canal Hotel was the Vallaresso ; and here is the steamboat station, called S. Marco, for the square rather than the church.   The last house of all before the gardens is the office of the Harbour Master, and it must once have been very graceful before the arches were filled in ; the little pavilion at the corner of the gardens belongs to the yacht club called the Bucintoro, whose boats are to be seen moored between here and the Molo, and whose members are, with those of sculling clubs on the Zattere and elsewhere, the only adult Venetians to use their waters for pleasure.   As for the Royal Palace, it is quite un- worthy and a blot on the Venetian panorama as seen from the Customs House or S. Giorgio Maggiore, or as one sees it from the little Zattere steamboat as the Riva opens up on rounding the Punta di Dogana.   Amid architecture that is almost or quite magical it is just a common utili- tarian façade.   But that it was once better can be seen in one of the Guardis at the National Gallery, No. 2099. The gardens and promenade before it are a favourite resort of Venetian nursemaids who are hardly bigger than their infant charges   The quay here is a very pleasing spot on which to loiter and watch the canal and look across at the eternal, if changing, beauty of S. Giorgio Maggiore.

Finally we have Sansovino's mint, now S. Mark's Library, and then the corner of the matchless Old Library, and the Molo with all its life beneath the two famous columns.

And now that we have completed the voyage of the Grand Canal, each way, let me remind the reader that although the largest palaces were situated there, they are not always the best. All over Venice are others as well worth study. Every little canal has one or two; some have many. Every campo has one or two and some have many. My notebook is full of references to lovely builders' work in squalid surroundings; just as one example take the delicious white marble balconies and windows in a deserted palace a few yards above the Ponte di Polo on the left.

CHAPTER XIV

ISLAND AFTERNOONS' ENTERTAINMENTS. I: MURANO, BURANO, AND TORCELLO

THE cheap way to Murano is by the ordinary steamer from the Fondamenta Nuova. This side of Venice is poor and squalid, but there is more fun here than any where else, for on Sundays the boys borrow any kind of craft that can be obtained and hold merry little regattas, which even those sardonic officials, the captains of the steamboats, respect : stopping or easing down so as to interfere with no event. But one should go to Murano by gondola, and go in the afternoon.

Starting anywhere near the Molo, this means that the route will be by the Rio del Palazzo, under the Ponte di Paglia and the Bridge of Sighs, between the Doges' Palace and the prison ; up the winding Rio di S. Maria Formosa, and then into the Rio dei Mendicanti with a glimpse of the superb Colleoni statue and SS. Giovanni e Paolo and the lions on the Scuola of S. Mark ; under the bridge with a pretty Madonna on it ; and so up the Rio dei Mendicanti, passing on the left a wineyard with two graceful round

148

arches in it and then a pleasant garden with a pergola, and then a busy squero with men always at work on gondolas new or old. And so beneath a high bridge to the open lagoon, with the gay walls and sombre cypresses of the cemetery immediately in front and the island of Murano beyond.

Many persons stop at the Campo Santo, but there is not much profit in so doing unless one is a Robert Blair or an Old Mortality. Its cypresses are more beautiful from the water than close at hand, and the Venetian tombstones dazzle. Moreover, there are no seats, and the custodian insists upon abstracting one's walking-stick. I made fruitless efforts to be directed to the English section, where among many graves of our countrymen is that of the historical novelist, G. P. R. James.

Murano is interesting in art as being the home of that early school of painting in which the Vivarini were the greatest names, which supplied altar-pieces for all the Venetian churches until the Bellini arrived from Padua with more acceptable methods. The invaders brought in an element of worldly splendour hitherto lacking. From the concentrated saintliness of the Vivarini to the sumptuous assurance of Titian is a far cry, yet how few the years that intervened ! To-day there are no painters in Murano ; nothing indeed but gardeners and glass-blowers, and the island is associated purely with the glass industry. Which is the most interesting furnace, I know not, for I have always fallen to the first of all, close to the landing stage, and spent there several amusing half-hours, albeit hotter than the innermost pit. Nothing ever changes there : one sees the same artificers and the same routine ; the same flames rage ; glass is the same mystery, beyond all conjuring, so ductile and malleable here, so brittle and rigid everywhere else. There you sit, or stand, some score of visitors, while the wizards round the furnace busily and incredibly convert molten blobs of anything (you would have said) but glass into delicate carafes and sparkling vases. Meanwhile the sweat streams from them in rivulets, a small Aquarius ever and anon fetches tumblers of water from a tap outside or glasses of red wine, and a soft voice at your ear, in whatever language you happen to be, supplies a commentary on the proceedings. Beware of listening to it with too much interest, for it is this voice which, when the glass-blowing flags, is proposing to sell you something. The "entrance" may be "free," but the exit rarely is so.

Let me describe a particular feat. After a few minutes, in sauntered a little lean detached man with a pointed beard and a long cigar, who casually took from a workman in the foreground a hollow iron rod, at the end of which was a more than commonly large lump of the glowing mass. This he whirled a little, by a rotatory movement of the rod between the palms of his hands, and then again dipped it into the heart of the flames, fetching it out more fiery than ever and much augmented. This too he whirled, blowing down the pipe first (but without taking his cigar from his mouth) again and again, until the solid lump was a great glistening globe. The artist—for if ever there was an artist it is he—carried on this exhausting task with perfect nonchalance, talking and joking with the others the while, but never relaxing the concentration of his hands, until there came a moment when the globe was broken from the original rod and fixed in some magical way to another. Again it went into the furnace, now merely for heat and not for any accretion of glass, and coming out, behold it was a bowl; and so, with repeated visits to the flames, on each return wider and shallower, it eventually was finished as an exact replica of the beautiful greeny-blue flower-dish on a neighbouring table. The artist, still smoking, then sauntered out again for fresh air, and was seen no more for a while.

But one should not be satisfied with the sight of the fashioning of a bowl or goblet, however interesting the process may be; but entering the gondola again should insist upon visiting both S. Pietro Martire and S. Donato, even if the gondolier, as is most probable, will affirm that both are closed.

The first named is on the left of the canal by which we enter Murano, and which for a while is bordered by glass factories as close together as doctors in Harley Street. The church architecturally is nothing; its value is in its pictures, especially a Bellini and a Basaiti, and, in 1913, a sacristan who rejoiced in a simple keenness which is a rarity in Venice. He rejoiced also in his church and in your pleasure in it. He displayed first the Bellini—a Madonna with the strong protective Bellini hands about the child, above them bodiless cherubim flying, and on the right a delectable city with square towers. The Basaiti is chiefly notable for what, were it cleaned, would be a lovely landscape. Before both the sacristan was ecstatic, but on his native heath, in the sacristy itself, he was even more contented. It is an odd room, with carvings all around it in which sacred and profane subjects are most curiously mingled : here John the Baptist in the chief scenes of his life, even to imprisonment in a wooden cage, into which the sacristan slipped a delighted expository hand, and there Nero, Prometheus, Bacchus, and Seneca without a nose.

Re-entering the gondola, escorted to it by hordes of young Muranesi, we move on to the Grand Canal of the island, a noble expanse of water. After turning first to the right and then to the left, and resisting an invitation to enter the glass museum, we disembark, beside a beautiful bridge, at the cathedral, which rises serenely from the soil of its spacious campo.

The exterior of S. Donato is almost more foreign looking than that of S. Mark's, although within S. Mark's is the more exotic. The outside wall of S. Donato's apse, which is the first thing that the traveller sees, is its most beautiful architectural possession and utterly different from anything in Venice: an upper and a lower series of lovely, lonely arches, empty and meaningless in this Saharan campo, the fire of enthusiasm which flamed in their original builders having died away, and this corner of the island being almost depopulated, for Murano gathers now about its glass-works on the other side of its Grand Canal. Hence the impression of desertion is even more complete than at Torcello, where one almost necessarily visits the cathedral in companies twenty to fifty strong.

At the door, to which we are guided by boys who know that cigarettes are thrown away at such points, is the sacristan, who, in 1913, was an aged gentleman in a velvet cap with a fuller and truer pride in his fane than any of his brothers in Venice yonder. With reason too, for this basilica is so old as to make many Venetian churches mere mushrooms, and even S. Mark's itself an imitation in the matter of inlaid pavement. Speaking slowly, with the perfection of enunciation, and burgeoning with satisfaction, the old fellow moved about the floor as he had done so many thousand times, pointing out this beauty and that, above and below, without the faintest trace of mechanism. In course of time, when he was fully persuaded that I was not only English but worthy of his

THE RIO TORRESELLE AND BACK OF THE PALAZZA DARIO

secret, it came out that he had the priceless privilege of knowing Signor "Rooskin" in the flesh, and from his pocket he drew a copy of *The Stones of Venice*, once the property of one Constance Boyle, but now his own. This he fondled, for though the only words in his own chapters that he can understand are "Murano" and "Donato," yet did not his friend the great Signor Rooskin write it, and what is more, spend many, many days in careful examination of everything here before he wrote it? For that is what most appealed to the old gentleman: the recognition of his S. Donato as being worthy of such a study.

The floor is very beautiful, and there is a faded series of saints by one of the Vivarini of Murano, behind the altar, on which the eye rests very comfortably—chiefly perhaps on the panels which are only painted curtains; but the most memorable feature of the cathedral is the ancient Byzantine mosaic of the Madonna—a Greek Madonna—in the hollow of the apse: a long slender figure in blue against a gold background who holds her hands rather in protest than welcome, and is fascinating rather for the piety which set her there with such care and thought to her glory than for her beauty. Signor Rooskin, it is true, saw her as a symbol of sadness, and some of the most exquisite sentences of "The Stones of Venice" belong to her; but had her robe been of less lovely hues it is possible that he might have written differently.

When the church was built, probably in the tenth century, the Virgin was its patron saint. S. Donato's body being brought hither by Doge Domenico Michiel (1118-1130), the church was known as Santa Maria, or San Donato; and to-day it is called S. Donato. And when the time comes for the old sacristan to die, I hope (no matter

what kind of a muddle his life has been) that S. Donato
will be at hand, near the gate, to pull him through, for
sheer faithfulness to his church.

The gondola returns by the same route, and as we pass
the Campo Santo the rays of the afternoon sun seem so to
saturate its russet walls that they give out light of their
own.   It is in order to pass slowly beneath these walls and
cypresses that I recommend the gondola as the medium
for a visit to Murano.   But the regular steamers go to a
pier close to S. Donato and are frequent.

Murano is within every visitor's range, no matter how
brief his stay, but Burano is another matter.   The steamer
which sails from the pier opposite Danieli's on all fine
afternoons except Sundays and holidays requires four hours;
but if the day be fine they are four hours not to be forgotten.   The way out is round the green island of S. Elena,
skirting the Arsenal, the vastness of which is apparent from
the water, and under the north wall of Murano, where its
pleasant gardens spread, once so gay with the Venetian
aristocracy but now the property of market gardeners and
lizards.   Then through the channels among the shallows,
north, towards the two tall minarets in the distance, the one
of Burano the other of Torcello.   Far away may be seen the
Tyrolean Alps, with, if it is spring, their snow-clad peaks
poised in the air; nearer, between us and the islands, is a
military or naval station, and here and there yellow and
red sail which we are to catch and pass.   Venice has nothing more beautiful than her coloured sails, both upon the
water and reflected in it.

The entrance to Burano is by a long winding canal,
which at the Campo Santo, with its battered campanile
and sentinel cypress at the corner, branches to left and
right—left to Torcello and right to Burano.   Here the

steamer is surrounded by boatmen calling seductively in their soft rich voices " Goon-dola ! Goon-dola ! " their aim being to take the visitor either to the cypress-covered island of S. Francesco in Deserto, where S. Francis is believed to have taken refuge, or to Torcello, to allow of a longer stay there than this steamer permits ; and unless one is enamoured of such foul canals and importunate children as Burano possesses it is well to listen to this lure. But Burano has charms, notwithstanding its dirt. Its squalid houses are painted every hue that the prism knows, and through the open doors are such arrays of copper and brass utensils as one associates with Holland. Every husband is a fisherman ; every wife a mother and a lace maker, as the doorways bear testimony, for both the pillow and the baby in arms are punctually there for the procession of visitors to witness. Whether they would be there did not the word go round that the steamer approached, I cannot say, but here and there the display seems a thought theatrical. Meanwhile in their boats in the canals, or on the pavement mending nets, are the Burano men.

Everybody is dirty. If Venice is the bride of the Adriatic, Burano is the kitchen slut.

Yet there is an oasis of smiling cleanliness, and that is the chief sight of the place—the Scuola Merletti, under the patronage of Royalty itself, the centre of the lace-making industry. This building, which is by the church, is, outside, merely one more decayed habitation. You pass within, past the little glass box of the custodian, whose small daughter is steering four inactive snails over the open page of a ledger, and ascend a flight of stairs, and behold you are in the midst of what seem to be thousands of girls in rows, each nursing her baby. On closer inspection the babies are revealed to be pillows held much as babies are held, and every hand is busy with a bobbin (or whatever it is), and every mouth seems to be munching. Passing on, you enter another room—if the first has not abashed you—and here are thousands more. Pretty girls too, some of them, with their black massed hair and olive skins, and all so neat and happy. Specimens of their work, some of it of miraculous delicacy, may be bought and kept as a souvenir of a most delightful experience.

For the rest, the interest of Burano is in Burano itself in the aggregate; for the church is a poor gaudy thing and there is no architecture of mark. And so, fighting one's way through small boys who turn indifferent somersaults, and little girls whose accomplishment is to rattle clogged feet and who equally were born with an extended hand, you rejoin the steamer.

Torcello is of a different quality. Burano is intensely and rather shockingly living; Torcello is nobly dead. It is in fact nothing but market gardens, a few houses where Venetian sportsmen stay when they shoot duck and are royally fed by kitcheners whose brass and copper make the mouth water, and a great forlorn solitary cathedral.

History tells us that in the sixth century, a hundred and more years after the flight of the mainlanders to Rialto and Malamocco, another exodus occurred, under fear of Alboin and the invading Lombards, this time to Torcello. The way was led by the clergy, and quickly a church was built to hearten the emigrants. Of this church there remain the deserted buildings before us, springing from the weeds, but on a scale which makes simple the realization of the populousness of the ancient colony.

The charming octagonal little building on the right

with its encircling arcade is the church of S. Fosca, now undergoing very thorough repair : in fact everything that a church can ask is being restored to it, save religion. No sea cave could be less human than these deserted temples, given over now to sightseers and to custodians who demand admittance money. The pit railed in on the left before the cathedral's west wall is the ancient baptistery, where complete immersion was practised. The cathedral within is remarkable chiefly for its marble throne high up in the apse, where the bishop sat with his clergy about him on semi-circular seats gained by steps. Above them are mosaics, the Virgin again, as at S. Donato, in the place of honour, but here she is given her Son and instantly becomes more tender. The twelve apostles attend. On the opposite wall is a quaint mosaic of the Last Judgment with the usual sharp division of parties. The floor is very beautiful in places, and I have a mental picture of an ancient and attractive carved marble pulpit.

The vigorous climb the campanile, from which, as Signor Rooskin says, may be seen Torcello and Venice—" Mother and Daughter . . . in their widowhood ". Looking down, it is strange indeed to think that here once were populous streets.

On the way to the campanile do not forget to notice the great stone shutters of the windows of the cathedral ; which suggest a security impossible to be conveyed by iron. No easy task setting these in their place and hinging them. What purpose the stone arm-chair in the grass between the baptistery and S. Fosca served is not known. One guide will have it the throne of Attila ; another, a seat of justice. Be that as it may, tired ladies can find it very consoling in this our twentieth century.

For antiquaries there is a museum of excavated relics of

Torcello; but with time so short it is better to wander a little, seeking for those wild flowers which in England are objects of solicitude to gardeners, or watching butterflies that are seen in our country only when pinned on cork.

The return voyage leaves S. Franceso in Deserto on the right, with the long low Lido straight ahead. Then we turn to the right and the Lido is on the left for most of the way to Venice. After a mile or so the mouth of the Adriatic is passed, where the Doge dropped his ring from the Bucintoro and thus renewed the espousals. On the day which I have in mind two airships were circling the city, and now and then the rays of the sun caught their envelopes and turned them to silver. Beneath, the lagoon was still as a pond; a few fishing boats with yellow sails lay at anchor near the Porto di Lido, like brimstone butterflies on a hot stone; and far away the snow of the Tyrolean alps still hung between heaven and earth.

VENUS, RULER OF THE WORLD
FROM THE PAINTING BY GIOVANNI BELLINI
In the Accademia

CHAPTER XV

LEAVING the Piazza at the corner diagonally opposite the Merceria clock, we come at once into
the busy Salizzada S. Moïse, where the shops for the more
wealthy tourists are to be found. A little way on the
right is the beginning of the Frezzeria, a Venetian shopping
centre second only to the Merceria. A little way on the
left is the Calle del Ridotto where, divided now into a
cinema theatre, auction rooms, a restaurant, and the Grand
Canal Hotel, is the once famous Ridotto of which Casanova
has much to tell. Here were held masquerades ; here were
gambling tables ; hither Venice resorted to forget that
she had ever been great and to make sure that she should
be great no longer. The Austrians suppressed it.

The church of S. Moïse, with its very florid façade of
statuary, has little of interest in it. Keeping with the
stream, we come in a few minutes to a bridge — the
Ponte delle Ostreghe (or Oysters)—over a rio at the end
of which, looking to the right, we see the great Venetian
theatre, the Fenice.

The Fenice is, I suppose, the most romantic theatre in
the world, for the simple reason that the audience, at any

rate those who occupy the boxes, all arrive in boats. Before it is a basin for the convenience of navigation, but even with that the confusion on a gala night must be excessive, and a vast space of time must divide the first comers from the last, if the last are to be punctual.   And when one translates our own difficulties over cars and cabs at the end of a performance into the terms of gondolas and canals, one can imagine how long it must be before the theatre is emptied.

The Fenice is also remarkable among the world's theatres for its size, holding, as it does, three thousand persons.   It is peculiar furthermore in being open only for a few weeks in the spring.

I have not been to the Fenice, but I once attended a performance of *Amleto* by " G. Shakespeare " in the Goldoni. It is the gayest of theatres, and the most intimate, for all save the floor and a trifling space under the flat ceiling is boxes : one hundred and twenty-three little ones and eight big ones, each packed with Venetians who really do enjoy a play while it is in progress, and really do enjoy every minute of the interval while it is not.   When the lights are up they eat and chatter and scrutinize the other boxes ; when the lights are down they follow the drama breathlessly and hiss if any one dares to whisper a word to a neighbour.

As for the melancholy Prince of Danimarca, he was not my conception of the part, but he was certainly the Venetians'.   Either from a national love of rhetoric, or a personal fancy of the chief actor for the centre of the stage, or from economical reasons, the version of " G. Shakespeare's " meritorious tragedy which was placed before us was almost wholly monologue.   Thinking about it now, I can scarcely recall any action on the part of the few other characters, whereas Amleto's millions of rapid words still rain uncomprehended on my ears, and I still see his myriad grimaces and gestures. It was like *Hamlet* very unintelligently arranged for a very noisy cinema, and watching it I was conscious of what a vast improvement might be effected in many plays if the cinema producer as well as the author attended the rehearsals. But to the Venetians this was as impressive and entertaining a Hamlet as could be wished, and four jolly Jack-tars from one of the men-of-war in the lagoon nearly fell out of their private box in their delight, and after each of the six atti Amleto was called several times through the little door in the curtain. Nor did he fail to respond.

About the staging of the play there was a right Shakespearian parsimony. If all the scenery and costumes cost twenty-five pounds, I am surprised. No attempt was made to invest "lo spettro del padre del Amleto" with supernatural graces. He merely walked on sideways, a burly, very living Italian, and with a nervous quick glance, to see if he was clearing the wing (which he sometimes did not), off again. So far as the Goldoni is concerned, Sir Henry Irving, Sir Herbert Beerbohm Tree, Sir Augustus Harris, and Herr Reinhardt all toiled in vain. Amleto's principle, "The play's the thing," was refined down to "Amleto's the thing". Yet no English theatre was ever in better spirits.

Continuing from the Bridge of the Oysters, we come shortly to S. Zobenigo, or S. Maria del Giglio (of the lily), of which the guide-books take very little account, but it is a friendly, cheerful church with a sweet little dark panelled chapel at the side, all black and gold with rich tints in its scriptural frieze. The church is not famous for any picture, but it has a quaint relief of S. Jerome in

11

his cell, with his lion and his books about him, in the entrance hall, and the first altar-piece on the left seemed to me a pleasant suave thing, and over the door are four female saints freely done. On the façade are stone maps of Zara, Candia, Padua, Rome, Corfu, and Spalata, which originally were probably coloured and must then have been very gay, and above are stone representations of five naval engagements.

All that remains of S. Zobenigo's campanile is the isolated structure in the Piazza. It did not fall but was taken down in time.

Still following the stream and maintaining as direct a line as the calli permit, we come, by way of two more bridges, a church (S. Maurizio), and another bridge, to the great Campo Morosoni where S. Stefano is situated.

For sheer comfort and pleasure I think that S. Stefano is the first church in Venice. It is spacious and cheerful, with a charming rosetted ceiling and carved and coloured beams across the nave, and a bland light illumines all. It is remarkable also as being one of the very few Venetian churches with cloisters. Here one may fancy oneself in Florence if one has the mind. The frescoes are by Pordenone, but they have almost perished. By some visitors to Venice, S. Stefano may be esteemed furthermore as offering a harbour of refuge from pictures, for it has nothing that need be too conscientiously scrutinized.

The fine floor tomb with brass ornaments is that of Francesco Morosoni, the heroic defender of Candia against the Turks until, in 1669, further resistance was found to be useless and he made an honourable retreat. Later he was commander of the forces in a new war against the Turks, and in 1686 he was present at the sack of Athens and did what he could (being a lover of the arts as well as a soldier) to check the destroying zeal of his army. It was there that he at last fulfilled his dreams of conquering the Morea. It was while he was conducting this campaign that the Doge Marcantonio Giustinian died, and Morosoni being elected in his place was crowned on his battleship at Porto Porro in Cephalonia. The carousals of the army and navy lasted for three days, at the new Doge's cost, the resources of the fleet having no difficulty in running to every kind of pageantry and pyrotechny. Returning to Venice, after the somewhat inglorious end of his campaign, Morosoni was again crowned.

Although a sick man when a year or so later a strong hand was again needed in the Morea, the Doge once more volunteered and sailed from the Lido with the fleet. But he was too old and too infirm, and he died in Nauplia in 1694. Venice was proud of him, and with reason ; for he won back territory for her (although she was not able to keep it), and he loved her with a pure flame. But he was behind his time : he was an iron ruler, and iron rule was out of date. The new way was compromise and pleasure.

The marble lions that now guard the gate of the Arsenal were saved and brought home by Morosoni, as his great fighting ducal predecessor Enrico Dandolo had in his day of triumph brought trophies from Constantinople. The careers of the two men are not dissimilar ; but Morosoni was a child beside Dandolo, for at his death he was but seventy-six.

The campo in front of S. Stefano bears Morosoni's name, but the statue in the midst is not that of General Booth, as the English visitor might think, but of Niccolò Tommaseo (1802-1874), patriot and author and the ally of Daniele Manin. This was once a popular arena for bull-fights, but there has not been one in Venice for more than a hundred years.

Morosoni's palace, once famous for its pictures, is the palace on the left (No. 2802) as we leave the church for the Accademia bridge. Opposite is another ancient palace, now a scholastic establishment with a fine Neptune knocker. Farther down on the left is a tiny campo, across which is the vast Palazzo Pisani, a very good example of the decay of Venice, for it is now a thousand offices and a conservatory of music.

Outside S. Vitale I met, in the space of one minute, two red-haired girls, after seeking the type in vain for days; and again I lost it. But certain artists, when painting in Venice, have never seen anything else.

And now, being close to the iron bridge which leads to the door of the Accademia, let us look at some pictures.

THE ASSUMPTION OF THE VIRGIN
FROM THE PAINTING BY TITIAN
In the Frari

CHAPTER XVI

THE ACCADEMIA. I: TITIAN, TINTORETTO, AND PAUL VERONESE

THE Accademia, which is to Venice what the National Gallery is to London, the Louvre to Paris, and the Uffizi to Florence, is, I may say, at once, as a whole a disappointment; and my advice to visitors is to disregard much of it absolutely. The reasons are two. One is that so wide a gulf is fixed between the best Venetian painters—Bellini, Titian, Carpaccio, Giorgione (but he is not represented here), Palma, Tintoretto, Veronese, and the next best; and the other, that Venetian painting of the second order is rarely interesting. In the Tuscan school an effort to do something authentic or arresting persists even to the fifth and sixth rank of painter; but not so here.

Were it not for the Accademia's Tintorettos, Carpaccios and Bellinis, our own Venetian collection in Trafalgar Square would be much more interesting; and even as it is we have in "The Origin of the Milky Way" a Tintoretto more fascinating than any here; in " Bacchus and Ariadne " a more brilliant Titian than any here; some Bellinis, such as "The Agony in the Garden," the portrait of Loredano, and "The Death of S. Peter Martyr," that challenge his best here; several pictures of Giorgione's school that can-not be matched here; some fine Cimas; the finest Catena that exists; a more charming Basaiti than any here; a better Antonello da Messina; and according to some judges, the best Paul Veronese in the world: "The House of Darius "; while when it comes to Carlo Crivelli, he does not exist here at all.

But it has to be remembered that one does not go to Venice to see pictures. One goes to see Venice : that is to say, an unbelievable and wonderful city of spires and palaces, whose streets are water and whose sunsets are liquid gold. Pictures, as we use the word, meaning paint-ings in frames on the wall, as in the National Gallery or the Louvre, are not among its first treasures. But in painting as decoration of churches and palaces Venice is rich indeed, and by anyone who would study the three great Venetian masters of that art—Tintoretto, Titian and Paul Veronese—it must not only be visited but haunted. Venice alone can prove to the world what giants these men —and especially Tintoretto—could be when given vast spaces to play with; and since they were Venetians it is well that we should be forced to their well-beloved and well-served city to learn it.

Owing to the fact that the Accademia is being re-arranged, I refer but seldom to the actual position of the pictures. The pictures, however, are there somewhere. If there is any confusion I hope that the index will help to remove it. The first room (with a fine ceiling which might be called the ceiling of the thousand wings, around which are portraits of painters ranged like the Doges in the great council halls) belongs to the very early men, of whom Jacobello del Fiore (1400-1439) is the most agreeable. It was he who painted one of the two lions that we saw in the museum of the Doges' Palace, the other and better being Carpaccio's. To him also is given, by some critics, the equestrian S. Chrysogonus, in S. Trovaso. His Accademia picture, on the end wall, is strictly local, representing Justice with her lion and S. Michael and S. Gabriel attending. It is a rich piece of decoration and you will notice that it grows richer on each visit. Two other pictures in this room that I like are a "Coronation of the Virgin," painted by Michele Giambono in 1440, making it a very complete ceremony, and a good church picture with an entertaining predella, by Michele di Matteo Lambertini (died 1469). The "Madonna and Child" by Bonconsiglio remains gaily in the memory too. No doubt about the Child being the Madonna's own !

Having finished with this room, we seek the Bellinis in a little room that leads out of it on the left, opposite the photograph stall, because Giovanni Bellini was the father of Venetian painting and the instructor of Titian and Giorgione. He was born in 1426, nearly a century after Giotto died. His father and teacher was Jacopo Bellini, who had a school of painting in Padua and was the rival in that city of Squarcione, a scientific instructor who depended largely on casts from the antique to point his lessons. Squarcione's most famous pupil was Andrea Mantegna, who subsequently married Giovanni Bellini's sister and alienated his master.

According to Vasari, oil-painting reached Venice through Antonello da Messina, who had learned the art

in the Netherlands. But that cannot be true. It came
to Venice from Verona or Padua long after Florence could
boast many fine masters, the delay being due to the circumstance that the Venetians thought more of architecture than the sister art. The first painters to make any
success in Venice were the Vivarini of Murano. The next
were Giovanni Bellini and Gentile his brother, who
arrived from Padua about 1460, the one to paint altar-
pieces in the Tuscan manner (for there is little doubt that
the sweet simplicity and gentle radiance of the Giotto
frescoes in the chapel of the Madonna dell' Arena, which
the Paduans had the privilege of seeing for two or three
generations before Squarcione was born, had greater influence than either Jacopo Bellini or Mantegna); and
the other to paint church pageants, such as we saw in an
earlier room.

Giovanni remained in Venice till his death, in 1516, at
the ripe age of ninety, and nearly to the end was he both
a busy painter and an interested and impressionable investigator of art, open to the influence of his own pupil
Giorgione, and, when eighty, being the only painter in
Venice to recognize the genius of Dürer, who was then
on a visit to the city. Dürer, writing home, says that
Bellini had implored him for a work and wanted to pay
for it. "Every one gives him such a good character that I
feel an affection for him. He is very old and is yet the
best in painting."

In his long life Bellini saw all the changes and helped
in their making. He is the most varied and flexible
painter of his time, both in manner and matter. None
could be more deeply religious than he, none more tender,
none more simple, none more happy. In manner he was
equally diverse, and could paint like a Paduan, a Tuscan,

a Fleming, a Venetian, and a modern Frenchman. I doubt if he ever was really great as we use the word of Leonardo, Titian, Tintoretto, Mantegna; but he was everything else. And he was Titian's master.

The National Gallery is rich indeed in Bellini's work. We have many pictures that are certainly his, and others that might be; and practically the whole range of his gifts is illustrated among them. There may not be anything as fine as the S. Zaccaria or Frari altar-pieces, or anything as exquisite as the Allegories in the Accademia and the Uffizi; but after that our collection is unexcelled in its examples.

In the Accademia are many also, each in its way a gem; enough to prove that variousness of which I spoke. The "Madonna degli Alberetti," for example, with its un-expected apple-green screen, almost Bouguereau carried out to the highest power, would, if hung in any exhibition to-day, be remarkable but not anachronistic. And then one thinks of the Gethsemane picture in our National Gallery, and of the Christ recently acquired by the Louvre, and marvels. For sheer delight of fancy, colour, and design the five scenes of Allegory are the flower of the room; and here again our thoughts leap forward as we look, for is not the second of the series, "Venus the Ruler of the World," sheer Burne-Jones? The pictures run thus: (1) "Bacchus tempting Endeavour," (2) either Venus, with the sporting babies, or as some think, Science (see the reproduction opposite page 158), (3) with its lovely river landscape, "Blind Chance," (4) the Naked Truth, and (5) Slander. Of the other pictures I like best is that reproduced opposite page 260, with the Leonardesque saint on the right; and the Madonna with the Child stretched across her knees, reproduced opposite page 144.

Giovanni Bellini did not often paint anything that can be described as essentially Venetian. He is called the father of Venetian painting, but his child only faintly resembles him, if at all. That curious change of which one is conscious at the National Gallery in passing from the schools of Tuscany and Umbria to that of Venice, is due less to the Bellinis in the Venetian room than to any painter there. The Bellinis could be hung in the Tuscan room without violence; the Giorgiones and Titians and Tintorettos would conflict. Bellini's simplicity allies him to Giotto traditions; but there was no simplicity about Giorgione, Titian, and Tintoretto. They were sophisticated, and the two last were also the painters of a wealthy and commanding Republic. One can believe that Bellini, wherever he was, even in the Doges' Palace, carried a little enclosed portion of the Kingdom of God within him: but one does not think of those others in that way. He makes his Madonnas so much more real and protective too. Note the strong large hands which hold the Child in his every picture.

Having seen the Bellinis we can now, after looking at the works of certain of his milder followers—such as Basaiti and Catena and Cima and Bissolo—and at some Tintoretto portraits, return to the first room and leave it by the far door which leads to the room where Titian's " Assumption " once used to hang, before it went to the Frari, and which is now made memorable by Tintoretto's " Miracle of S. Mark," which I reproduce opposite page 170.

This picture was painted between 1544 and 1548, before the artist was thirty. The story tells that a pious slave, forbidden by his master to visit and venerate the house of S. Mark, disobeyed the command and went. As a punishment his master ordered him to be blinded and maimed;

THE MIRACLE OF S. MARK
FROM THE PAINTING BY TINTORETTO
In the Accademia

but the hands of the executioners were miraculously stayed and their weapons refused to act. The master, looking on, was naturally at once converted.

Tintoretto painted his picture of this incident for the Scuola of S. Mark (now a hospital) ; but when it was delivered, the novelty of its dramatic vigour—a palpitating actuality almost of the cinema—was too much for the authorities. The coolness of their welcome infuriated the painter, conscious as he was that he had done a great thing, and he demanded the work back ; but fortunately there were a few good judges to see it first, and their enthusiasm carried the day. Very swiftly the picture became a wonder of the city. Thus has it always been with the great innovators in art, except that Tintoretto's triumph was more speedy : they have almost invariably been condemned first.

An interesting derivative detail of the work is the gateway at the back over which the sculptured figures recline, for these obviously were suggested by casts, which we know Tintoretto to have possessed, of Michael Angelo's tombs in S. Lorenzo's sacristy at Florence. Every individual in the picture is alive and breathing, but none more remarkably so than the woman on the left with a child in her arms and her knee momentarily resting on a slope of the pillar. No doubt some of the crowd are drawn, after the fashion of the time, from public men in Venice ; but I know not if they can now be identified.

Another legend of S. Mark which, by the way, should have its Venetian pictorial rendering, tells how a man who was working on the Campanile fell, and as he fell had the presence of mind to cry " S. Mark ! S. Mark ! " whereupon a branch instantly sprang forth from the masonry below and sustained him until help arrived.

Tintoretto, who has other miracles of S. Mark here and in the Brera at Milan, would have drawn that falling workman magnificently.

Other Tintorettos include the beautiful grave picture of the Madonna and Child giving a reception to Venetian Senators who were pleased to represent the Magi; the "Purification of the Virgin," a nice scene with one of his vividly natural children in it; a "Deposition" rich and glowing and very like Rubens; and the "Crucifixion," painted as an altar-piece for SS. Giovanni e Paolo before his sublime picture of the same subject—his masterpiece— was begun for the Scuola of S. Rocco. If one sees this, the earlier, version first, one is the more impressed; to come to it after that other is to be too conscious of a huddle. But it has most of the great painter's virtues, and the soldiers throwing dice are peculiarly his own.

In this room also is the last picture that Titian painted— a "Deposition". It was intended for the aged artist's tomb in the Frari, but that purpose was not fulfilled. Palma the younger finished it. With what feelings, one wonders, did Titian approach what he knew was his last work? He painted it in 1576, when he was either ninety-nine or eighty-nine; he died in the same year. To me it is one of his most beautiful things: not perhaps at first, but after one has returned to it again and again, and then for ever. It has a quality that his earlier works lack, both of simplicity and pathos. The very weakness of the picture engages and convinces. But now that the "Assumption" has gone, the most popular Titian is his charming conception of "The Presentation of the Virgin," which fills one wall of a room not far distant. I give a reproduction opposite page 36. The radiant figure of the thick-set little brave girl in blue, marching so steadily away from her

parents to the awe-inspiring but kindly priests at the head
of the steps, is unforgettable.   Notice the baby in the arms
of a woman among the crowd.   The picture as a whole is
disappointing in colour, and I cherish the belief that if
Tintoretto's beautiful variant at the Madonna dell' Orto
(see opposite page 282) could be cleaned and set up in
a good light it might conquer.

Before leaving this room one should give the ceiling a
little attention, for it is splendid in its lovely blue and gold,
and its coloured carvings are amusing.   The four Evangelists have each a medallion.   All are studious.   S. Matthew,
on the upper left as one stands with one's back to the
Titian, has an open-air study, and he makes notes as he
reads.   His eagle is in attendance.   S. Mark, with his lion
at ease under his chair, has also his open-air desk, and as he
reads he thinks.   S. John is indoors, reading intently, with
a box full of books to fall back on, and a little angel peeping at him from behind his chair.   Finally S. Luke, also
indoors, writing at a nice blue desk.   He holds his pen
very daintily and seems to be working against time, for
an hour-glass is before him.   His bull is also present.
Among the many good ceilings of Venice, this is at once
the most sumptuous and most charming.

High over the door by which we entered is a masterly
aristocratic allegory by Paul Veronese—Venice with
Hercules and Ceres—notable for the superb drawing and
vivacity of the cupid with the wheat sheaf.   I give a reproduction opposite page 102, but the Cupid unfortunately
is not distinct enough.

But Veronese's masterpiece at the Accademia is the vast
canvas representing "The Feast in the House of Levi," of
which I give a reproduction opposite page 176.   Veronese
is not a great favourite of mine ; but there is a blandness

and aristocratic ease and mastery here that are irresistible. As an illustration of scripture it is of course absurd ; but in Venice (whose Doges, as we have seen, had so little humour that they could commission pictures in which they were represented on intimate terms with the Holy Family) one is accustomed to that. As a fine massive arrangement of men, architecture, and colour, it is superb.

It was for painting this picture as a sacred subject—or rather for subordinating sacred history to splendid mundane effects—that the artist was summoned before the Holy Office in the chapel of S. Theodore on July 8, 1573. At the end of Ruskin's brief *Guide to the Principal Pictures in the Academy of Fine Arts at Venice*, a translation of the examination is given. Reading it, one feels that Veronese did not come out of it too well. Whistler would have done better. I quote a little.

Question. Do you know the reason why you have been summoned ?
Answer. No, my lord.
Q. Can you imagine it ?
A. I can imagine it.
Q. Tell us what you imagine.
A. For the reason which the Reverend Prior of SS. Giovanni and Paolo, whose name I know not, told me that he had been here, and that your illustrious lordships had given him orders that I should substitute the figure of the Magdalen for that of a dog ; and I replied that I would willingly have done this, or anything else for my own credit and the advantage of the picture, but that I did not think the figure of the Magdalen would be fitting or would look well, for many reasons, which I will always assign whenever the opportunity is given me.
Q. What picture is that which you have named ?
A. It is the picture representing the last supper that Jesus took with His disciples in the house of Simon.
Q. Where is this picture ?
A. In the refectory of the Friars of SS. Giovanni and Paolo.
Q. In this supper of Our Lord, have you painted any attendants ?
A. Yes, my lord.

Q.   Say how many attendants, and what each is doing.

A.   First, the master of the house, Simon; besides, I have placed below him a server, who I have supposed to have come for his own amusement to see the arrangement of the table.   There are besides several others, which, as there are many figures in the picture, I do not recollect.

Q.   What is the meaning of those men dressed in the German fashion each with a halberd in his hand ?

A.   It is now necessary that I should say a few words.

The Court.   Say on.

A.   We painters take the same license that is permitted to poets and jesters.   I have placed these two halberdiers—the one eating, the other drinking—by the staircase, to be supposed ready to perform any duty that may be required of them ; it appearing to me quite fitting that the master of such a house, who was rich and great (as I have been told), should have such attendants.

Q.   That fellow dressed like a buffoon, with the parrot on his wrist,— for what purpose is *he* introduced into the canvas ?

A.   For ornament, as is usually done.

Q.   At the table of the Lord whom have you placed ?

A.   The twelve Apostles.

Q.   What is St. Peter doing, who is the first ?

A.   He is cutting up a lamb, to send to the other end of the table.

Q.   What is he doing who is next to him ?

A.   He is holding a plate to receive what St. Peter will give him.

Q.   Tell us what he is doing who is next to this last ?

A.   He is using a fork as a tooth-pick.

Q.   Who do you really think were present at that supper ?

A.   I believe Christ and His Apostles were present ; but in the fore-ground of the picture I have placed figures for ornament, of my own invention.

Q.   Were you commissioned by any person to paint Germans and buffoons, and such-like things in this picture ?

A.   No, my lord; my commission was to ornament the picture as I judged best, which, being large, requires many figures, as it appears to me.

Q.   Are the ornaments that the painter is in the habit of introducing in his frescoes and pictures suited and fitting to the subject and to the principal persons represented, or does he really paint such as strike his own fancy without exercising his judgment or his discretion ?

A.   I design my pictures with all due consideration as to what is fitting, and to the best of my judgment.

Q.   Does it appear to you fitting that at our Lord's last supper you should paint buffoons, drunkards, Germans, dwarfs, and similar indecencies ?

A. No, my lord.

Q. Why, then, have you painted them ?

A. I have done it because I supposed that these were not in the place where the supper was served. . . .

Q. And have your predecessors, then, done such things ?

A. Michel-Angelo, in the Papal Chapel in Rome, has painted our Lord Jesus Christ, His mother, St. John and St. Peter, and all the Court of Heaven, from the Virgin Mary downwards, all naked, and in various attitudes, with little reverence.

Q. Do you not know that in a painting like the Last Judgment, where drapery is not supposed, dresses are not required, and that disembodied spirits only are represented ; but there are neither buffoons, nor dogs, nor armour, nor any other absurdity ? And does it not appear to you that neither by this nor any other example you have done right in painting the picture in this manner, and that it can be proved right and decent ?

A. Illustrious lord, I do not defend it; but I thought I was doing right. . . .

The result was that the painter was ordered to amend the picture, within the month, at his own expense ; but he does not seem to have done so. There are two dogs and no Magdalen. The dwarf and the parrot are there still. Under the table is a cat.

Other pictures to look for are Mantegna's "S. George," which I reproduce opposite page 190, a beautiful thing ; a fine Giorgionesque Palma Vecchio : a Holy Family, rich and strong and sweet; and Paris Bordone's representation of the famous story of the Fisherman and the Doge, full of gracious light and animation. It seems that on a night in 1340 so violent a storm broke that even the inner waters of the lagoon were perilously rough. A fisherman chanced to be anchoring his boat off the Riva when a man appeared and bade him row him to the island of S. Giorgio Maggiore. Very unwillingly he did so, and there they took on board another man who was in armour, and

THE FEAST IN THE HOUSE OF LEVI
FROM THE PAINTING BY VERONESE
In the Accademia

orders were given to proceed to S. Niccolò on the Lido. There a third man joined them, and the fisherman was told to put out to sea. They had not gone far when they met a ship laden with devils which was on her way to unload this cargo at Venice and overwhelm the city. But on the three men rising and making the sign of the cross, the vessel instantly vanished. The fisherman thus knew that his passengers were S. Mark, S. George, and S. Nicholas. S. Mark gave him a ring in token of their sanctity and the deliverance of Venice, and this, in the picture, he is handing to the Doge.

The visitor should also look for the Boccaccio Boccaccini, full of sweetness and pretty thoughts. The Madonna is surrounded by saints, the figure in the centre having the true Boccaccini face. The whole picture is a delight, whether as a group of nice holy people, a landscape, or a fantasy of embroidery. The condition of the picture is perfect too. The flight into Egypt, in two phases, goes on in the background. I reproduce it opposite page 266.

So much for the painters of the great period. The Accademia is also rich in the later Venetians : Tiepolo, Guardi, Canaletto, Longhi ; but for Tiepolo at his best the Labia Palace must be visited, and Longhi is more numerously represented at the Royal Palace than here. Both Canaletto and Guardi can be better studied in London, at the National Gallery and the Wallace Collection. There are indeed no works by either man to compare with the best of ours. No. 494 at Hertford House, a glittering view of the Dogana, is perhaps Guardi's masterpiece in England ; No. 135 in the National Gallery, Canaletto's.

Pietro Longhi was born in Venice in 1702, five years after Hogarth was born in London. He died in 1762, two

12

years before Hogarth in Chiswick. I mention the English painter because Longhi is often referred to as the Venetian Hogarth. We have a picture or two by him in the National Gallery. To see him once is to see all his pictures so far as technique goes, but a complete set would form an excellent microcosm of fashionable and frivolous Venice of his day. Hogarth, who no doubt approximates more to the Venetian style of painting than to any other, probably found that influence in the work of Sebastiano Ricci, a Venetian who taught in St. Martin's Lane.

The brave Tiepolo—Giovanni Battista or Giambattista, as the contraction has it—was born in Venice in 1696, the son of a wealthy merchant and shipowner. In 1721 he married a sister of Guardi, settled down in a house near the bridge of S. Francesco della Vigna, and had nine children. His chief artistic education came from the study of Titian and Paul Veronese, and he quickly became known as the most rapid and intrepid ceiling painter of the time. He worked with tremendous spirit, as one deduces from the examination of his many frescoes. Tiepolo drew with masterly precision and brio, and his colour can be very sprightly : but one always has the feeling that he had no right to be in a church at all, except possibly to confess.

At the National Gallery we have some small examples of Tiepolo's work, which, if greatly magnified, would convey an excellent impression of his mural manner. Tiepolo went to Spain in his old age to work for Charles III, and died there in 1770. His widow survived him by nine years, dying in 1779. She seems to have been a gambler, and there is a story of her staking all her losses one evening against her husband's sketches. Losing, she staked his villa, containing many of his frescoes, and lost again.

Antonio Canal, called Canaletto, was born in Venice in

1697, the son of a scene-painter. At first he too painted scenery, but visiting Rome he was fascinated by its architecture and made many studies of it. On returning to Venice he settled down as a topographical painter and practically reproduced his native city on canvas. He died in 1768. Venice possesses only inferior works from his hands; but No. 474 here—the view of the Scuola of S. Marco—is very fine.

Canaletto had a nephew named Bernardo Bellotto, who to much of his uncle's skill brought a mellow richness all his own, and since he also took the name of Canaletto, confusion has resulted. He is represented in the Accademia; but Vienna is richest in his work.

The great Canaletto has a special interest for us in that in later life he lived for a while in England and painted here. The National Gallery has views of Eton College and of Ranelagh seen through his Venetian eyes. In Venice Tiepolo often added the figures for him. In a recent volume of the *Walpole Society's Transactions* will be found much new material about Canaletto's English life.

Francesco Guardi was born in Venice in 1712 and died there in 1793, and all his life he was translating the sparkling charm of his watery city into paint. His master was Canaletto, whom he surpassed in charm but never equalled in foot-rule accuracy, or in that gravity which makes a really fine picture by the older man so distinguished a thing. Very little is known of Guardi's life. That he married is certain, and he had a daughter who eloped with an Irishman. We are told also that he was very indolent, and late in life came upon such evil days that he established himself at a corner of the Piazza, where Rosen's book-shop now is, and sold sketches to whomever would buy for whatever they would fetch; which is only one remove from a London screever. Guardi's picture of S. Giorgio Maggiore, in the Accademia, shows us that the earlier campanile, which fell in 1774, was higher and slenderer than the present one.

Finally let me say that the Accademia rejoices in the possession of some of the most beautiful drawings in the world, and is especially strong in Leonardo. These, however, are unhappily not on exhibition at the present time.

CHAPTER XVII

THE ACCADEMIA. II: THE SANTA CROCE MIRACLES AND CARPACCIO

The Holy Cross—Gentile Bellini's Venice—The empty windows— Carpaccio's Venice—The story of S. Ursula—Gay pageantry—A famous bedroom—Carpaccio's life—Ruskin's eulogy.

IN the larger room, once a chapel, are the famous pictures of the miracles of the Santa Croce—the Holy Cross which was brought by Filippo da Massaro and presented to the Scuola di S. Giovanni Evangelista. Every year it was carried in solemn procession through Venice and something remarkable was expected of it.

The great picture by Gentile Bellini, which shows the progress of the Holy Cross procession across the Piazza in 1496, is historically of much interest. One sees many changes and much that is still familiar. The only mosaic on the façade of S. Mark's which still remains is that in the arch over the left door; and that also is the only arch which has been left concave. The three flagstaffs are there, but they have wooden pediments and no lions on the top, as now. The Merceria clock tower is not yet, and the south arcade comes flush with the campanile's north wall; but I doubt if that was so. The miracle of that year was the healing of a youth who had been fatally injured in the head ; his father may be seen kneeling just behind the relic.

The next most noticeable picture, also Gentile Bellini's, records a miracle of 1500.   The procession was on its way to S. Lorenzo, near the Arsenal, from the Piazza, when the sacred emblem fell into the canal.   Straightway in jumped Andrea Vendramin, the chief of the Scuola, to save it, and was supernaturally buoyed up by his sanctified burden. The picture has a religious basis, but heaven is not likely, I think, to be seriously affronted if one smiles a little at these aquatic sports.   Legend has it that the little kneeling group on the right is Gentile's own family, and the kneeling lady on the left, with a nun behind her, is Caterina Cornaro, Queen of Cyprus.

Bellini has made the scene vivid, but it is odd that he should have put not a soul at a window.   When we turn to Carpaccio's " Miracle " of 1494, representing the healing of a man possessed of a devil, who may be seen in the loggia at the left, we find a slightly richer sense of history, for three or four women look from the windows ; but Mansueti, although a far inferior artist, is the only one to be really thorough and Venetian in this respect.

One very interesting detail of Carpaccio's "Miracle" picture is the Rialto bridge of his time.   It was of wood, on piles, and a portion in the centre could be drawn up either to let tall masts through or to stop the thoroughfare to pursuers.   It is valuable, too, for its costumes and architecture.   In a gondola is a dog, since one of those animals finds its way into most of his works.   This time it is S. Jerome's dog from the picture at S. Giorgio degli Schiavoni.   An English translation of the Santa Croce story might well be placed in this room.

It is the series of pictures depicting the life of S. Ursula

THE DEPARTURE OF THE BRIDEGROOM AND HIS MEETING WITH URSULA

FROM THE PAINTING BY CARPACCIO

In the Accademia

for which most visitors to Venice esteem the Accademia :
but to my mind the charm of Carpaccio is not displayed
here so fully as in his decorations at S. Giorgio. The
Ursula pictures are, however, of deep interest and are
unforgettable.

But first for the story. As *The Golden Legend* tells it,
it runs thus. Ursula was the daughter of a Christian king
in Britain named Notus or Maurus, and the fame of her
beauty and wisdom spread afar, so that the King of England, who was a heathen himself, heard of it and wished her
for his son's wife. His son, too, longed for the match, but
the paganism of his family was against it. Ursula therefore stipulated that before the marriage could be solemnized
the King of England should send to her ten virgins as
companions, and each of these virgins and herself, making
eleven, should have a retinue of a thousand other virgins,
making eleven thousand in all (or to be precise, eleven
thousand and eleven) for prayer and consecration ; and
that the prince moreover should be baptised ; and then at
the end of three years she would marry him. The conditions were agreed to, and the virgins collected, and
all, after some time spent in games and jousting, with
noblemen and bishops among the spectators, joined Ursula,
who converted them. Being converted, they set sail from
Britain for Rome. There they met the pope, who, having
a prevision of their subsequent martyrdom, resigned the
papacy, much against the will of the Church and for
reasons which are not too clear. In Rome they were seen
also by two fellow-princes named Maximus and Africanus,
who, disliking them for their Christianity, arranged with
one Julian, a prince of the Huns, that on their arrival at
Cologne, on their return journey, he should behead the whole
company, and thus prevent them from further mischief.

Meanwhile Ursula's betrothed went to Cologne to meet his bride. With the eleven thousand were many of the most eminent bishops and other men of mark, and directly they arrived at Cologne the Huns fell on them and killed every one except Ursula and another named Cordula. Julian offered to make Ursula his wife, but on her repudiation of the suggestion he shot her through the body with his bow and arrow. Cordula hid in a ship, but the next day suffered death by her own free will and earned a martyr's crown. All this happened in the year A.D. 238.

Carpaccio, it will be quickly seen, disregards certain details of this version. For example, he makes Ursula's father a King of the Moors, although there is nothing Moorish about either that monarch, his daughter, or his city. The first picture, which has the best light in it, shows the ambassadors from England craving the hand of the princess. At the back is one of those octagonal buildings so dear to this painter, also in the city. His affection for dogs, always noticeable, is to be seen here again, for he has placed three hounds on the quay. A clock somewhat like that of the Merceria is on the little tower. The English ship has a red flag. On the right is the King pondering with Ursula over his reply. In the next picture the ambassadors receive this reply. In the next the ambassadors depart, with the condition that a term of three years must first pass. They return to a strangely unfamiliar England : an England in which Carpaccio himself must have been living for some time in the rôle of architect. This is a delightful and richly mellow scene of activity, and not the least attractive feature of it is the little fiddling boy on the left. Carpaccio has so enjoyed the pageantry and detail, even to frescoes on the house, crowded bridges, and so forth, that his duty as a story-teller has suffered. In the next picture which is really two, divided by the flagstaff, we have on the left the departure of the English prince from an English seaport (of a kind which alas! has disappeared for ever) to join in his lady-love's pilgrimage to Rome. He bids his father farewell. Nothing could be more fascinating than the mountain town and its battlements, and every inch of the picture is amusing and alive. Crowds of gay people assemble and a ship has run on the rocks. On the right, the prince meets Ursula, who also has found a very delectable embarking place. Here are more gay crowds and sumptuous dresses, of which the King's flowered robe is not the least. Farther still to the right the young couple kneel before the monarch. I reproduce this.

The apotheosis of S. Ursula is here interposed, very inappropriately, for she is not yet dead or a saint, merely a pious princess.

The story is then resumed with a scene at Rome, as we know it to be by the castle of S. Angelo, in which Ursula and her prince are being blessed by the Pope Cyriacus, while an unending file of virgins extends into the distance.

In the next picture, reproduced opposite page 120, Ursula, in her nice great bed, in what is perhaps the best-known bedroom in the world, dreams of her martyrdom and sees an angel bringing her the rewards of fortitude. The picture has pretty thoughts but poor colour. Where the room is meant to be, I am not sure; but it is a very charming one. Note her little library of big books, her writing desk and hour-glass, her pen and ink. Carpaccio of course gives her a dog. Her slippers are beside the bed and her little feet make a tiny hillock in the bedclothes: Carpaccio was the man to think of that! The windows are open and she has no mosquito net. Her princess's crown is at the foot of the bed, or is it perchance her crown of glory?

We next see the shipload of bishops and virgins arriving at Cologne. There are fewer Carpaccio touches here, but he has characteristically put a mischievous youth at the end of a boom. There is also a dog on the landing-stage and a bird in the tree. A comely tower is behind with flags bearing three crowns. The next picture shows us, on the left, the horrid massacre of all these nice young women by a brutal German soldiery. Ursula herself is being shot by Julian, who is not more than six feet distant; but she meets her fate with a composure as perfect as if instead of the impending arrow it was a benediction. On the right is her bier, under a very pretty canopy. Wild flowers spring from the earth.

Now should come the apotheosis.

Carpaccio was not exactly a great painter, but he was human and ingratiating beyond any other that Venice can show, and his pictures here and at S. Giorgio degli Schiavoni make the city a sweeter and more lovable place. Vasari is very brief with Vittore Scarpaccia, as he calls him, and there are few known facts. Research has placed his birth at Capo d'Istria about 1450. His earliest picture is dated 1490: his last 1521 or 1522. Gentile Bellini was his master.

Ruskin found Carpaccio by far the most sympathetic Venetian painter. Everything that he painted, even, as I point out earlier, the Museo Civico picture of the two ladies, he exults in, here, there, and everywhere. In his little guide to the Accademia, published in 1877, he roundly calls Carpaccio's " Presentation of the Virgin " the " best picture" in the gallery. In one of the letters written from Venice in *Fors Clavigera*—and these were, I imagine, subjected to less critical examination by their author before they saw the light than any of his writings—is the following summary, which it may be interesting to read here. "This, then, is the truth which Carpaccio knows, and would teach : That the world is divided into two groups of men ; the first, those whose God is their God, and whose glory is their glory, who mind heavenly things; and the second, men whose God is their belly, and whose glory is in their shame, who mind earthly things. That is just as demonstrable a scientific fact as the separation of land from water. There may be any quantity of intermediate mind, in various conditions of bog ; some, wholesome Scotch peat, —some, Pontine marsh,—some, sulphurous slime, like what people call water in English manufacturing towns ; but the elements of Croyance and Mescroyance are always chemically separable out of the putrescent mess : by the faith that is in it, what life or good it can still keep, or do, is possible ; by the miscreance in it, what mischief it can do, or annihilation it can suffer, is appointed for its work and fate. All strong character curdles itself out of the scum into its own place and power, or impotence : and they that sow to the Flesh, do of the Flesh reap corruption ; and they that sow to the Spirit, do of the Spirit reap Life.

"I pause, without writing 'everlasting,' as perhaps you expected. Neither Carpaccio nor I know anything about duration of life, or what the word translated 'everlasting' means. Nay, the first sign of noble trust in God and man, is to be able to act without any such hope. All the heroic deeds, all the purely unselfish passions of our existence, depend on our being able to live, if need be, through the Shadow of Death and the daily heroism of simply honeymooners that this is done, since Venetians do not spend money to sit in stationary boats. These concerts are popular, but they are too self-conscious. Moreover, the songs are from all countries, even America; whereas purely Venetian, or at any rate Italian, operatic music should, I think, be given. The stray snatches of song which one hears at night from the hotel window; gondoliers trolling out folk choruses; the notes of a distant mandolin, brought down on the water—these make the true music of Venice.

But just as the motor-launch has invaded the lagoon, so has other machinery forced its way into this city—peculiarly the one place in the world which ought to have been meticulously safeguarded against every mechanical invention. When, in 1913, I was living near S. Sebastiano, on my way home at night the gondolier used to take me up the Grand Canal as far as the Foscari lantern and then to the left. In time we came to the campo of S. Pantaleone, where, outside a café, a little group was always seated, over its wine and beer, listening raptly to the music of—what? A gramophone. This means that while the motor is ousting the gondolier, the Venetian minstrel is also under death sentence.

It was the same if I chose to walk part of the way, for then I took the steamer to S. Toma and passed through the campo of S. Margherita, which does for the poor of its neighbourhood very much what the Piazza of S. Mark does for the centre of the city and the élite of the world. This campo is one of the largest in Venice, and at night it is very gay. There is a church at one end which, having lost its sanctity, is now a cinema theatre, with luridities pasted on the walls. There is another ancient building converted into a cinema at the opposite end. Between

S. GEORGE

FROM THE PAINTING BY MANTEGNA

In the Accademia

these alluring extremities are various cafés, each with its chairs and tables, and each with a gramophone that pours its notes into the night.

In summer there are occasional firework displays on the water between S. Giorgio and the Riva, supplied by the Municipality. The Riva is then crowded, while gondolas put out in great numbers, and myriad overloaded crafts full of poorer sightseers enter the lagoon by all the small canals. Having seen Venetian pyrotechny, one realizes that all fireworks should be ignited over water. It is the only way. A rocket can climb as fiercely and dazzlingly into any sky, no doubt, but over land the falling stars and sparks have but one existence; over water, like the swan " on St. Mary's lake," they have two. The displays last for nearly an hour, and consist almost entirely of rockets. Every kind of rocket is there : rockets which simply soar with a rush, burst into stars and fall; rockets which when they reach the highest point of their trajectory explode with a report that shakes the city and must make some of the campanili very nervous ; rockets which burst into a million sparks; rockets which burst into a thousand streamers; rockets whose stars change colour as they fall; rockets whose stars do not fall at once but hang and hover in the air. All Venice is watching, either from the land or the water, and the band plays to a deserted Piazza, but directly the display is over every one hastens back to hear its strains.

To get to the beautiful island of S. Giorgio it is almost necessary to take a gondola ; for although there is the Giudecca steamer every half hour, it is an erratic boat, and you may be left stranded too long waiting to return. The island is military, save for the church, and that is chiefly a show-place to-day. It is large and light, but it has no charm, for that was not Palladio's gift. That he was a great man, every visitor to Vicenza knows ; but it is both easy and permissible to dislike the architecture to which he gives his name. Not that any fault can be found with S. Giorgio Maggiore as a detail in the landscape : to me it will always be the perfect disposition of buildings in the perfect place ; but then, on the other hand, the campanile was not Palladio's, nor was the façade, while the principal attraction of his dome is its green copper. The church of the Redentore, on the Giudecca, is much more thoroughly Palladian.

Andrea Palladio was born in Vicenza in 1518. In Venice he built S. Giorgio Maggiore (all but the façade), the façade of S. Francesco della Vigna, the Redentore, Le Zitelle and S. Lucia. Such was Palladio's influence that for centuries he practically governed European architecture. Our own St. Paul's would be very different but for him. He died in 1580 and was buried at Vicenza. By the merest chance, but very fortunately, he was prevented from bedevilling the Ducal Palace after the fire in 1576. He had the plans all ready, but a wiser than he, one Da Ponte, undertook to make the structure good without rebuilding, and carried out his word. Terrible to think of what the Vicenza classicist would have done with that gentle, gay, and human façade !

The Tintorettos belong to his most spacious and dramatic style. One, "The Last Supper," is a busy scene of conviviality. The company is all at one side of the table and the two ends, except the wretched foredoomed Judas. There is plenty to eat. Attendants bustle about bringing more food. A girl, superbly drawn and painted, washes plates, with a cat beside her. A dog steals a bone. The disciples seem restless and the air is filled with angels.

MADONNA AND CHILD
FROM THE PAINTING BY GIOVANNI BELLINI
In the Accademia

Compared with the intensity and single-mindedness of Leonardo, this is a commonplace rendering; but as an illustration to the Venetian Bible, it is fine; and as a work of art by a mighty and original genius glorying in difficulties of light and shade, it is tremendous. Opposite is a quieter representation of the miracle of the manna, which has very charming details of a domestic character in it, the women who wash and sew and carry on other employments being done with splendid ease and naturalness. The manna lies about like little buttons; Moses discourses in the foreground; in the distance is the Israelite host. All that the picture lacks is light : a double portion : light to fall on it, and its own light to be allowed to shine through the grime of ages.

Tintoretto also has two altar-pieces here, one an " Entombment," in the Mortuary Chapel—very rich and grave and painful, in which Christ's mother is seen swooning in the background ; and the other a death of S. Stephen, a subject rare with the Old Masters, but one which, were there occasion to paint it, they must have enjoyed. Tintoretto has covered the ground with stones.

The choir is famous for its series of forty-six carved panels, representing scenes in the life of S. Benedict ; but some vandal having recently injured one or two, the visitor is no longer allowed to approach near enough to examine them with the thoroughness that they demand and deserve. They are the work of a carver named Albert de Brule, of whose life I have been able to discover nothing. Since before studying them it is well to know something of the Saint's career, I tell the story here, from *The Golden Legend*, but not all the incidents which the artist fixed upon are to be found in that biography.

Benedict as a child was sent to Rome to be educated,

13

mediately behind the long busy façade of the island are gardens, and then the shallow lagoon stretching for miles, where fishermen are mysteriously employed, day and night. The gardens are restful rather than beautiful—at least that one, open to visitors, on the Rio della Croce, may be thus described, for it is formal in its parallelograms divided by gritty paths, and its flowers are crudely coloured. But it has fine old twisted mulberry trees, and a long walk beside the water, where lizards dart among the stones on the land side and on the other crabs may be seen creeping.

On the way to this garden I stopped to watch a family of gossiping bead-workers. The old woman who sat in the door did not thread the beads as the girl does in one of Whistler's Venetian etchings, but stabbed a basketful with a wire, each time gathering a few more.

The great outstanding buildings of the Giudecca are Palladio's massive Redentore and S. Eufemia, and at the west end the modern Gothic polenta mill of Signor or Herr Stucky, beyond which is the lagoon once more. In Turner's picture in the National Gallery entitled "San Benedetto, looking towards Fusina" there is a ruined tower where Stucky's mill now stands.

The steps of the Redentore are noble, but within it is vast and cold and inhuman, and the statues in its niches are painted on the flat. Tintoretto's "Descent from the Cross" in the church proper is very vivid. In the sacristy, however, the chilled visitor will be restored to life by a truly delightful Madonna and Child, with two little celestial musicians playing a lullaby, said to be by Bellini, but more probably by Alvise Vivarini, and two companion pictures of much charm. Like the Salute, the Redentore was a votive offering to heaven for stopping a plague. Every year, on the third Sunday in July, a bridge of boats crosses the Grand Canal at the Campo S. Zobenigo, and then from the Zattere it crosses the Giudecca canal to this church. That day and night the island is *en fête.* Originally these bridges were constructed in order that the Doges might attend a solemn service ; but to-day the occasion is chiefly one of high spirits. In the gallery of the Palazzo Pesaro is a painting representing the event at a recent date ; in the Querini Stampalia gallery a more ancient procession may be seen.

There, too, are many views of regattas which of old were held on the Grand Canal but now belong to the canal of the Giudecca. The Venetians, who love these races, assemble in great numbers, both on the water, in every variety of craft, and on the quay. The winning-post is off the end of the island of S. Giorgio ; the races start from varying points towards the harbour. In April I saw races for six oars, four oars, two oars, and men-of-war's boats. The ordinary rowers were dull, but the powerful bending gondoliers urging their frail craft along with tremendous strokes in unison were a magnificent spectacle. The excitement was intense towards the end, but there was no close finish. Between the races the exchange of chaff among the spectators was continuous.

The question of where to live in Venice must, I think, be a difficult one to solve. I mean by live, to make one's home, as so many English and Americans have done. At the first blush, of course, one would say on the Grand Canal ; but there are objections to this. It is noisy with steamboat whistles and motor horns, and will become noisier every day and night, as the motor gains increasing popularity. On the other hand, one must not forget that so fine a Venetian taster as Mr. Howells wrote, "for myself I must count as half lost the year spent in Venice before I took a house upon the Grand Canal".

Personally, I think, I should seek my home else-where. There is a house on this Giudecca—a little way along from the S. Giorgio end—which should make a charming abode; for it has good windows over the water, immediately facing, first, the little forest of masts by the Custom House, and then the Molo and the Ducal Palace, and upon it in the evening would fall the sinking sun, while behind it is a pleasant garden. The drawbacks are the blasts of the big steamers entering and leaving the harbour, the contiguity of some rather noisy works, and the infrequency of steamboats to the mainland.

Ruskin was fond of this view. Writing to old Samuel Rogers, he said: "There was only one place in Venice which I never lost the feeling of joy in—at least the pleasure which is better than joy; and that was just half way between the end of the Giudecca and St. George of the Seaweed, at sunset. If you tie your boat to one of the posts there you can see the Euganeans where the sun goes down, and all the Alps and Venice behind you by the rosy sunlight: there is no other spot so beautiful. Near the Armenian convent is, however, very good too also; the city is handsomer, but the place is not so simple and lovely. I have got all the right feeling back now, how-ever and hope to write a word or two about Venice yet, when I have got the mouldings well out of my head—and the mud. For the fact is, with reverence be it spoken, that whereas Rogers says: 'There is a glorious city in the Sea,' a truthful person must say, 'There is a glorious city in the mud'. It is startling at first to say so, but it goes well enough with marble. 'Oh, Queen of Marble and of Mud.'"

TRAGHETTO OF S. ZOBENIGO, GRAND CANAL

Another delectable house is that one, on the island of
S. Giorgio Maggiore, which looks right up the Giudecca
canal and in the late afternoon flings back the sun's rays·
But that is the property of the army.   Another is at the
corner of the Rio di S. Trovaso and the Fondamenta delle
Zattere, with wistaria on it, looking over to the Redentore ;
but every one, I find, wants this.

when the Doge visited it in state every Easter. It is now chiefly famous for its very beautiful Bellini altar-piece, of which I give a reproduction on the opposite page. The picture in its grouping is typical of its painter, and nothing from his hand has a more pervading sweetness. The musical angel at the foot of the throne is among his best and the bland old men are more righteous than rectitude itself. To see this altar-piece aright one must go in the early morning: as I did on my first visit, only to find the central aisle given up to a funeral mass.

The coffin was in the midst, and about it, cn their knees, were the family, a typical gondolier all in black being the chief mourner. Such prayers as he might have been uttering were constantly broken into by the repeated calls of an attendant with a box for alms, and it was in- teresting to watch the struggle going on in the simple fellow's mind between native prudence and good form. How much he ought to give? Whether it was quite the thing to bring the box so often and at such a season? Whether shaking it so noisily was not peculiarly tact- less? What the spectators and church officials would think if he refused? Could he refuse? and, However much were these obsequies going to cost?—these questions one could discern revolving almost visibly beneath his short-haired scalp. At last the priests left the high altar and came down to the coffin, to sprinkle it and do whatever was now possible for its occupant; and in a few minutes the church was empty save for the undertaker's men, myself, and the Bellini. It is truly a lovely picture, although perhaps a thought too mild, and one should go often to see it.

The sculptor Alessandro Vittoria, who did so much to perpetuate the features of great Venetians and was the friend of so many artists, including Tintoretto and Paul

MADONNA AND CHILD WITH SAINTS
FROM THE PAINTING BY GIOVANNI BELLINI
In the Church of S. Zaccaria

Veronese, is buried here. The floor slabs of red stone with beautiful lettering should be noticed; but all over Venice such memorials have a noble dignity and simplicity.

It will be remembered that the site of this church was determined by the vision of Bishop Magnus, S. John appearing to him and commanding it to be built in honour of his father. The first structure probably dates from the seventh century; the present is fifteenth century, and beneath it is the ancient crypt adjoining the chapel of S. Tarasio, where in the twelfth century a hundred nuns seeking refuge from a fire were suffocated. In the chapel are ecclesiastical paintings, but no proper provision is made for seeing them. Eight Doges lie in S. Zaccaria.

Outside I found a great crowd to see the embarcation of the corpse for its last home, the Campo Santo. This, I may say, was rather a late funeral. Most of them are at eight or even earlier.

It is best now to return to the Riva by the calle which comes out beside Danieli's and then walk Lido-wards over two bridges and take the first calle after them. This brings us to S. Giovanni in Bragora, S. John's own church, built also according to his instructions to Bishop Magnus, and it used to have one of the keenest sacristans in Venice. From altar to altar he bustled, fixing you in the best positions for light. The great picture here is the Cima behind the high altar, of which I give a reproduction opposite page 136. A little perch has been made, the better to see it. It represents "The Baptism of Christ," and must in its heyday have been very beautiful. Christ stands at the edge of the water and the Baptist holds a little bowl— a very different scene from that mosaic version in S. Mark's where Christ is half submerged. It has a sky full of cherubs, delectable mountains and towns in the distance, and all Cima's sweetness; and when the picture-cleaning millionaire, of whom I speak elsewhere, has done his work it will be a joy. There is also a fine Bartolommeo Vivarini here, and the sacristan insists on your admiring a very ornate font which he says is by Sansovino.

As you leave, ask the way to S. Giorgio degli Schiavoni, which is close by, and prepare to be very happy.

I have said something about the most beautiful spacious places in Venice—S. Mark's, the Doges' Palace, the Scuola di S. Rocco, and so forth; we now come to what is, without question, the most fascinating small room in Venice. It is no bigger than a billiard-room and unhappily very dark, with a wooden ceiling done in brown, gold, and blue; an altar with a blue and gold canopy; rich panels on the walls; and as a frieze a number of paintings by Vittore Carpaccio, which, in my opinion, transcend in interest the S. Ursula series at the Accademia.

The story of the little precious room is this. In the multitude of seafaring men who in the course of their trade came to Venice with cargoes or for cargoes were a large number of Dalmatians, or Sclavonians, whose ships lay as a rule opposite that part of the city which is known as the Riva degli Schiavoni. Their lot being somewhat noticeably hard, a few wealthy Dalmatian merchants decided in 1451 to make a kind of Seamen's Institute (as we should now say), and a little building was the result of this effort, the patron saints of the altar in it being S. George and S. Tryphonius. Fifty years later the original "Institute" was rebuilt and Carpaccio was called in to decorate it.

The most famous of the pictures are those on the left wall as you enter—S. George attacking the dragon, S. George subduing the dragon, and (on the end wall) S. George baptizing the king and princess. These are not only lovely

autumnal schemes of colour, but they are perfect illustrations to a fairy tale, for no artist has ever equalled this
Venetian in the art of being entertaining.   Look at the
spirit of the first picture : the onset of both antagonists ;
and then examine the detail—the remains of the dragon's
victims, the half-consumed maidens ; the princess in despair ; the ships on the sea ; the adorable city mounting
up and up the hill, with spectators at every balcony.   (I
reproduce it opposite page 212)   And then in the next
how Carpaccio must have enjoyed his work on the costumes !
Look at the crowds, the band in full blast, the restless
horses which like dragons no more than they like bears.

The third, although the subject is less entertaining,
shows no decrease of liveliness.   Carpaccio's humour
underlies every touch of colour.   The dog's averted face
is one of the funniest things in art—a dog with sceptical
views as to baptism !—and the band is hard at it, even
though the ceremony, which, from the size of the vase,
promises to be very thorough, is beginning.

S. George is a link between Venice and England, for we
both honour him as a patron.   He is to be seen in pictures
again and again in Venetian churches, but these three scenes
by Carpaccio are the finest.   The Saint was a Cappadocian
gentleman and the dragon ranged and terrorized the
Libyan desert.   Every day the people of the city which
the dragon most affected bribed him away with two sheep.
When the sheep gave out a man was substituted.   Then
children and young people, to be selected by lot, and the
lot in time fell on the king's daughter.   The king in
despair offered his subjects gold and silver instead, but
they refused saying that it was his own law and must be
obeyed.   They gave her, however (this, though from the
lives of the saints, is sheer fairy tale, isn't it ?) eight days

grace, in which anything might happen; but nothing happened, and so she was led out to the dragon's lair.

As she stood there waiting to be devoured, S. George passed by. He asked her what she was doing, and she replied by imploring him to run or the dragon would eat him too. But S. George refused, and instead swore to rescue her and the city in the name (and here the fairy tale disappears) of Jesus Christ. The dragon then advancing, S. George spurred his horse, charged and wounded him grievously with his spear. (On English gold coins, as we all know to our shame, he is given nothing but a short dagger which could not reach the enemy at all; Carpaccio knew better.) Most of the painters make this stroke of the saint decisive; according to them, S. George thrust at the dragon and all was over. But the true story, as Caxton and Carpaccio knew, is, that having wounded the dragon, S. George took the maiden's girdle and tied it round the creature's neck, and it became "a meek beast and debonair," and she led it into the city. (Carpaccio makes the saint himself its leader.) The people were terrified and fled, but S. George reassured them, and promised that if they would be baptized and believe in Jesus Christ he would slay the dragon once and for all. They promised, and he smote off its head; and in the third picture we see him baptizing.

I have given the charming story as *The Golden Legend* tells it; but one may also hold the opinion, more acceptable to the orthodox hagiologist, that the dreadful monster was merely symbolical of sin.

As for S. George himself, the most picturesque and comely of all the saints and one whom all the nations reverence, he was born in Cappadocia, in the third century, of noble Christian parents. Becoming a soldier in Diocletian's army he was made a tribune or colonel. The Emperor showed him marks of especial favour, but when the imperial forces were turned against the Christians, George remonstrated and refused. He was therefore beheaded.

For broad comedy the picture of S. Jerome and the lion on the right wall is the best. The story tells us that S. Jerome was one day sitting with the brethren listening to a holy lesson when a lion came hobbling painfully into the monastery. The brethren fled, but S. Jerome, like Androcles, approached the beast, and finding that it had a sore foot, commanded the others to return and minister to it. This they did, and the lion was ever after attached to the monastery, one of its duties being to take care of an ass. Carpaccio has not spared the monks: he makes their terror utterly absurd in the presence of so puzzled and gentle a man-eater. In the next picture, the death of the saint, we see the lion again, asleep on the right, and the donkey quietly grazing at the back. As an impressive picture of the death of a good man it can hardly be called successful; but how could it be, coming immediately after the comic Jerome whom we have just seen? Carpaccio's mischief was a little too much for him—look at the pince-nez of the monk on the right reading the service.

Then we have S. Jerome many years younger, busy at his desk. He is just thinking of a word when the camera, I almost said—when Carpaccio caught him. His tiny dog gazes at him with fascination. Not bad surroundings for a saint, are they? A comfortable study, with a more private study leading from it; books; scientific instruments; music; works of art (note the little pagan bronze on the shelf); and an exceedingly amusing dog. I repro- duce the picture opposite page 82.

Two pictures with scriptural subjects represent Christ in the garden of Gethsemane, and Matthew (an Evangelist rarely painted in Venice, where his colleague Mark has all the attention) being called from the receipt of custom. And finally there is the delightful and vivid representation of S. Tryphonius and the basilisk. This picture, of which I give a reproduction opposite page 76, is both charming and funny. The basilisk is surely in the highest rank of the comic beasts of art. It seems to be singing, but that is improbable; what it is unmistakably not doing is basilisking. The little saint stands by in an attitude of prayer, and all about are comely courtiers of the king. In the distance are delightful palaces in the Carpaccio style of architecture, cool marble spaces, and crowded windows and stairs. The steps of the raised temple in which the saint and the basilisk perform have a beautiful intarsia of foliage similar to that on the Giants' Staircase at the Doges' Palace. So much for the ingredients of this bewitching picture ; but as to what it is all about I have no knowledge, for I have looked in vain among books for any information. I find a S. Tryphonius, but only as a grown man ; not a word of his tender years and his grotesque attendant. How amusing it would be to forget the halo and set the picture as a theme among a class of fanciful fantastic writers, to fit it with an appropriate fairy story ! For of course it is as absolute a fairy tale illustration as the dragon pictures on the other wall.

It is now well to ask the way to S. Francesco della Vigna, where we shall find S. Jerome and his lion again. This vast church, with its pretentious and very unwelcoming façade by Palladio covering the friendly red brick, is at the first sight unattractive, so huge and cold and deserted is it. But it has details. It has, for example, just inside

the door on the entrance wall, high up, a very beautiful
early Christian coloured relief of the Madonna and Child :
white on blue, but far earlier than the Della Robbias. The
Madonna is slender as a pole but memorably sweet. It has
also a curious great altar picture on wood by a strange
painter, Frater Antonius da Negropoñ, as he signs himself—
this in a little chapel in the right transept—with most
charming details of birds, and flowers, and scrolls, and
monochrome reliefs surrounding a Madonna and Child
who beam comfort and assurance of joy. The date is supposed to be about 1450 and the source of Brother Antonio's
inspiration must have been similar to that of the great
Mantegna's.

There are also the very delightful marble pictures in the
chapel of the Giustiniani family to the left of the choir,
the work of the Lombardi. About the walls are the
evangelists and prophets (S. John no more than a beautiful
and sensitive boy), while over the altar are scenes in the
life of S. Jerome, whom we again see with his lion. In
one relief he extracts the thorn from its foot; in another
the lion assists in holding up the theological work which
the saint is perusing, while in his other hand the saint
poises a model of the church and campanile of S. Zaccaria.
Below, on the altar cloth, is a Last Judgment, with the
prettiest little angel boys to sound the dreadful trumps.
To these must be added two pictures by Paul Veronese,
one with a kneeling woman in it who at once brings to
mind the S. Helena in our National Gallery.

Furthermore, in the little Cappella Santa is a rich and
lovely Giovanni Bellini, with sacred relics in jars above
and below it, and outside is the gay little cloistered garden
of the still existing monastery, with a figure of S. Francis
in the midst of its greenery.

14

The great church has also various tombs of Doges, the most splendid being that noble floor slab in front of the high altar, beneath which repose the bones of Marcantonio Trevisan (1553-1554). What Trevisan was like may be learned from the relief over the sacristy entrance, where he kneels to the crucifix. He made no mark on his times. Andrea Gritti (1523-1538), who also is buried here, was a more noticeable ruler, a born monarch who had a good diplomatic and fighting training abroad before he came to the throne. He was generous, long-memoried, astute, jovial, angry, healthy, voluptuous and an enthusiast for his country. He not only did all that he could for Venice (and one of his unfulfilled projects was to extend the Ducal Palace to absorb the prison) but he was quite capable of single-handed negotiations with foreign rulers.

Other Doges who lie here are the two Contarini, Francesco (1623-1624) and Alvise (1676-1684), but neither was of account; and here, too, in his own chapel lies Alvise's predecessor, Niccolò Sagredo (1674-1676) who had trouble in Candia for his constant companion. Of the Giustiniani only Marcantonio became a Doge and he succeeded Alvise Contarini not only to the throne but to the Candia difficulty, giving way after four years, in 1688, to the great soldier who solved it—Francesco Morosini.

CHAPTER XX

ON FOOT. III. THE MERCERIA AND THE RIALTO

Walking in Venice—The late Colonel Douglas—Shops—The Merceria clock — S. Zulian — S. Salvatore — Sansovino — Carlo Goldoni — the Campo Bartolommeo and Mr. Howells—S. Giovanni Crisostomo—Piombo and Giorgione—Marino Faliero's house—SS. Apostoli and Tiepolo—Venetian skittles — A broad walk — Filled-in canals — The Rialto Bridge—S. Giacomo di Rialto—The two Ghettos—The Rialto hunchback — Vegetables and fruits — The fish market — Symmetrical irony —S. Giovanni Elemosinario—A busy thoroughfare—Old books—The convivial gondoliers.

THE best of Venice—Venice itself, that is—can never find its way into a book ; and even if it did, no reader could extract it again. The best of Venice must be one's own discovery and one's own possession ; and one must seek it, as Browning loved to do, in the narrow calli, in the tiny canals, in the smaller campi, or seated idly on bridges, careless of time. Chiefly on foot does one realize the inner Venice.

I make no effort in this work to pass on any detailed account of my researches in this way. All I would say is that every calle leads to another ; there is hardly a dull inch in the whole city ; and for the weary some kind of resting-place—a church, a wine shop, a café, or a stone step—is always close by. If you are lost—and in Venice in the poorer populous districts a map is merely an aggravation of dismay, while there is no really good map of the city to be obtained—there is but one thing to do and that is to go on. Before very long you must of necessity come to a calle with more traffic than the others and then you need but flow with the stream to reach some recognizable centre; or merely say "San Marco" or "gondola" to the first boy and he will consider it a privilege to guide you. Do not, however, give up before you must, for it is a privilege to be lost in Venice.

For those who prefer exercise to sitting in a gondola there is the stimulating and instructive book by the late Col. Douglas, *Venice on Foot*, which is a mine of information and interest; but I must admit that the title is against it. Youthful travellers in particular will have none of it. If Venice is anything at all to them, it is a city of water, every footstep in which is an act of treachery to romance.

Even they, however, are pleased to jostle in the Merceria.

The shops of Venice, I may say at once, are not good. They satisfy the Venetians, no doubt, but the Venetians are not hard to please; there is no Bond Street or Rue de la Paix. But a busy shopping centre always being amusing, the Merceria and Frezzeria become attractive haunts of the stranger; the Merceria particularly so. To gain this happy hunting ground one must melt away with the crowd through the gateway under the famous blue clock, which is worth a visit on account of its two bronze giants: one punctual and one late, for that one on the left of the bell, as we face the tower from the Piazza, is always a minute or two after his brother in striking the hours. The right hand giant strikes first, swinging all his upper part as he does so; and then the other. From their altitude much of Venice is revealed, but only the thin can enjoy this view, such being the narrowness of the winding stairs and doorway by which

S. GEORGE AND THE DRAGON

FROM THE PAINTING BY CARPACCIO

At S. Giorgio degli Schiavoni

it is gained. On Ascension Day a procession of mechanical figures below the clock-face delights the spectators.

It was while Coryat was in Venice that one of these giants, I know not which, performed a deed of fatal savagery. The traveller thus describes it: "A certaine fellow that had the charge to looke to the clocke, was very busie about the bell, according to his usuall custome every day, to the end to amend something in it that was amisse. But in the meane time one of those wilde men that at the quarters of the howers doe use to strike the bell, strooke the man in the head with his brazen hammer, giving him such a violent blow, that therewith he fel down dead presently in his place, and never spake more."

At the third turning to the right out of the Merceria is the church of S. Giuliano, or S. Zulian, which the great Sansovino built. One evening, hearing singing as I passed, I entered, but found standing-room only, and that only with the greatest discomfort. Yet the congregation was so happy and the scene was so animated that I stayed on and on—long enough at any rate for the offertory box to reach me three separate times. Every one present was either poor or on the borders of poverty ; and the fervour was almost that of a salvation army meeting. And why not, since the religion both of the Pope and of General Booth was pre-eminently designed for the poor ? I came away with a tiny coloured picture of the Virgin and many fleas.

At the end of the Merceria is S. Salvatore, a big quiet church in the Renaissance style, containing the ashes of S. Theodore, the tombs of various Doges, and a good Bellini: a warm, rich, and very human scene of a wayside inn at Emmaus and Christ appearing there. An " An-nunciation " by Titian is in the church proper, painted

when he was getting very old, and framed by Sansovino;
a " Transfiguration " by Titian is in the pretty sacristy,
which, like many of the Venetian churches, is presided
over by a dwarf. A procession of Venetian sacristans
would, by the way, be a strange and grotesque spectacle.

The best of the S. Salvatore monuments is that by
Sansovino of Doge Francesco Venier (1554-1556), with
beautiful figures in the niches from the same hand—that
of Charity, on the left, being singularly sweet. When
Sansovino made these he was nearly eighty. Sansovino also
designed the fine doorway beneath the organ. The most
imposing monuments are those of Caterina Cornaro
(or Corner) the deposed queen of Cyprus, in the south
transept; of three Cardinals of the Corner family; and
of the Doges Lorenzo and Girolamo Priuli, each with his
patron saint above him. The oddity of its architecture,
together with its situation at a point where a little silence
is peculiarly grateful, makes this church a favourite of
mine, but there are many buildings in Venice which are
more beautiful.

Opposite, diagonally, is one of the depressing sights of
Venice, a church turned into a cinema.

Leaving S. Salvatore by the main door and turning to
the left, we soon come to the Goldoni Theatre. Leaving
San Salvatore by the same door and turning to the right,
we come to Goldoni himself, in an easy bright posture,
in bronze, in the midst of the Campo S. Bartolommeo:
the little brisk observant satirist upon whom Browning
wrote the admirable critical sonnet which I quote earlier
in this book.

The comedies of Carlo Goldoni (1707-1793) still hold
the Italian stage, but so far as translations can tell me
they are very far from justifying any comparison between

himself and Molière. Goldoni's *Autobiography* is not a very entertaining work, but it is told with the engaging minuteness which seems to have been a Venetian trait.

The church of S. Bartolommeo contains altar pieces by Giorgione's pupil, Sebastian del Piombo, but there is no light by which to see them.

It was in this campo that Mr. Howells had rooms before he married and blossomed out on the Grand Canal, and his description of the life here is still so good and so true, although many years have passed, that I make bold to quote it, not only to enrich my own pages, but in the hope that the tastes of the urbane American book which I give now and then may send readers to it. The campo has changed little except that the conquering Austrians have gone and Goldoni's statue is now here. Mr. Howells thus describes it : " Before the winter passed, I had changed my habitation from rooms near the Piazza to quarters on the Campo San Bartolommeo, through which the busiest street in Venice passes, from S. Mark's to the Rialto Bridge. It is one of the smallest squares of the city, and the very noisiest, and here the spring came with intolerable uproar. I had taken my rooms early in March, when the tumult under my windows amounted only to a cheerful stir, and made company for me ; but when the winter broke, and the windows were opened, I found that I had too much society.

" Each campo in Venice is a little city, self-contained and independent. Each has its church, of which it was in the earliest times the burial-ground ; and each within its limits compasses an apothecary's shop, a blacksmith's and shoemaker's shop, a café more or less brilliant, a green-grocer's and fruiterer's, a family grocery—nay, there is also a second-hand merchant's shop where you buy and sell every kind of worn out thing at the lowest rates. Of course there is a coppersmith's and a watchmaker's, and pretty certainly a wood carver's and gilder's, while without a barber's shop no campo could preserve its integrity or inform itself of the social and political news of the day. In addition to all these elements of bustle and disturbance, San Bartolommeo swarmed with the traffic and rang with the bargains of the Rialto market.

"Here the small dealer makes up in boastful clamour for the absence of quantity and assortment in his wares; and it often happens that an almost imperceptible boy, with a card of shirt buttons and a paper of hair pins, is much worse than the Anvil Chorus with real anvils. Fishermen, with baskets of fish upon their heads; peddlers, with trays of housewife wares; louts who dragged baskets of lemons and oranges back and forth by long cords; men who sold water by the glass; charlatans who advertised cement for mending broken dishes, and drops for the cure of toothache; jugglers who spread their carpets and arranged their temples of magic upon the ground; organists who ground their organs; and poets of the people who brought out new songs, and sang and sold them to the crowd—these were the children of confusion, whom the pleasant sun and friendly air woke to frantic and interminable uproar in San Bartolommeo.

"In San Bartolommeo, as in other squares, the buildings are palaces above and shops below. The ground floor is devoted to the small commerce of various kinds already mentioned; the first story above is occupied by tradesmen's families; and on the third or fourth is the appartamento signorile. From the balconies of these stories hung the cages of innumerable finches, canaries, blackbirds, and savage parrots, which sang and screamed with delight in the noise that rose from the crowd. All the human life, therefore, which the spring drew to the casements was perceptible only in dumb show. One of the palaces opposite was used as a hotel, and faces continually appeared at the windows. By all the odds the most interesting figure there was that of a stout peasant serving-girl, dressed in a white knitted jacket, a crimson neckerchief, and a bright coloured gown, and wearing long dangling earrings of yellowest gold. For hours this idle maiden balanced herself half over the balcony rail in perusal of the people under her, and I suspect made love at that distance, and in that constrained position, to some one in the crowd. On another balcony a lady sat; at the window of still another house, a damsel now looked out upon the square, and now gave a glance into the room, in the evident direction of a mirror. Venetian neighbours have the amiable custom of studying one another's features through opera-glasses; but I could not persuade myself to use this means of learning the mirror's response to the damsel's constant 'Fair or not?' being a believer in every woman's right to look well a little way off. I shunned whatever trifling temptation there was in the case, and turned again to the campo beneath—to the placid dandies about the door of the café; to the tide of passers-by from the Merceria; the smooth shaven Venetians of other days, and the bearded Venetians of these; the dark-eyed white-faced Venetians, hooped in cruel disproportion to the narrow streets, but richly clad, and moving with southern grace; the files of heavily burdened soldiers; the little policemen loitering lazily about with their swords at their sides, and in their spotless Austrian uniforms."

Having reached Goldoni's statue there are two courses open to us if we are in a mood for walking. One is to cross the Rialto bridge and join the stream which always fills the narrow busy calli that run parallel with the Grand Canal to the Frari.   The other is to leave this campo at the far end, at Goldoni's back, and join the stream which is always flowing backwards and forwards along the new Via Vittorio Emmanuele.

Let me describe both routes, beginning with the second. A few yards after leaving the campo we come on the right to the little church of S. Giovanni Crisostomo where there are two unusually delightful pictures: a Sebastiano del Piombo and a Bellini. The Bellini is his last signed work, and was painted when the old man was in his eighty-fifth year. The restorer has been at it, but not to its detriment. S. Christopher, S. Jerome, and S. Augustine are sweetly together in a delectable country ; S. Christopher (as the photograph on the opposite page shows) bearing perhaps the most charming Christ Child of all, with his thumb in his mouth. The Piombo—another company of saints—over the high altar, is a fine mellow thing with a very Giorgionesque figure of the Baptist dominating it, and a lovely Giorgionesque landscape spreading away. The picture (which I reproduce opposite page 116) is known to be the last which Sebastiano painted before he went to Rome and gave up Giorgione's influence for Michael Angelo's. It has been suggested that Giorgione merely supplied the design; but I think one might safely go further and affirm that the painting of the right side was his too, and the left, Piombo's. How far Piombo departed from Giorgione's spell and came under the other may be seen in our National Gallery by any visitor standing before No. 1—his " Raising of Lazarus." Very little of the divine chromatic melody of Castel Franco there !

THE GRAND CANAL, SHOWING S. MARIA DELLA SALUTE

S. Giovanni Crisostomo has also two fine reliefs, one by Tullio Lombardi with a sweet little Virgin (who, however, is no mother) in it, and the twelve Apostles gathered about.

Continuing on our way we come soon to a point where the Calle Dolfin meets a canal at right angles, with a large notice tablet like a gravestone to keep us from falling into the water. It bears an ancient, and I imagine, obsolete, injunction with regard to the sale of bread by unauthorized persons. Turning to the left we are beneath the arcade of the house of the ill-fated Marino Faliero, the Doge who was put to death for treason, as I have related elsewhere. It is now shops and tenements. Opposite is the church of SS. Apostoli, which is proud of possessing an altar-piece by Tiepolo which some think his finest work, and of which the late John Addington Symonds wrote in terms of excessive rapture. It represents the last communion of S. Lucy, whose eyes were put out. Her eyes are here, in fact, on a plate. No one can deny the masterly drawing and grouping of the picture.

I do not suggest the diversion at this moment; but from SS. Apostoli one easily gains the Fondamenta Nuova, on the way passing through a rather opener Venice where canals are completely forgotten. Hereabouts are two or three popular drinking places with gardens, and on one Sunday afternoon I sat for some time in the largest of them—the Trattoria alla Libra—watching several games of bowls—the giuoco di bocca—in full swing. The Venetian workman—and indeed the Italian workman generally—is never so happy as when playing this game, or perhaps he is happiest when—ball in hand—he discusses with his allies various lines of strategy. The Giudecca is another stronghold of the game, every little bar there having a stamped-down bowling alley at the back of it.

The longest direct broad walk in Venice—longer than the Riva—begins at SS. Apostoli and extends to the railway station. The name of the street is the Via Vittorio Emmanuele, and in order to obtain it many canals had to be filled-in. To the loss of canals the visitor is never reconciled. Wherever one sees the words Rio Terra before the name of a calle, one knows that it is a filled-in canal. For perhaps the best example of the picturesque loss which this filling-in entails one should seek the Rio Terra delle Colonne, which runs out of the Calle dei Fabri close to the Piazza of S. Mark. When this curved row of pillars was at the side of water it must have been impressive indeed.

And now we must return to the Goldoni statue to resume that other itinerary over the Rialto bridge, which is as much the centre of Venice by day as S. Mark's Square is by night. In another chapter I speak of the bridge as seen from the Grand Canal, which it so nobly leaps. More attractive is the Grand Canal as seen from it; and the visitor to Venice should spend much time leaning upon the parapet of one side and the other at the highest point. He will have it for the most part to himself, for the Venetians prefer the middle way between the shops. These shops are, however, very dull—principally cheap clothiers and inferior jewellers—and the two outer tracks are better. From here may best be seen the façade of the central Post Office, once the Fondaco dei Tedeschi splendid with the frescoes of Giorgione and Titian. The frescoes have gone and it is now re-faced with stucco. From here, too, the beautiful palace of the Camerlenghi at the edge of the Erberia is most easily studied.

The Rialto bridge itself exerts no spell. It is merely a steep hill from either side.

The busiest and noisiest part of Venice begins at the

S. CHRISTOPHER, S. JEROME AND S. AUGUSTINE
FROM THE PAINTING BY GIOVANNI BELLINI
In the Church of S. Giovanni Crisostomo

further foot of the bridge, for here are the markets, crowded by housewives with their bags or baskets, and a thousand busy wayfarers.

The little church of the market-place—the oldest in Venice—is S. Giacomo di Rialto, but I have never been able to find it open. Commerce now washes up to its walls and practically engulfs it. A garden is on its roof, and its clock has stopped permanently at four.

It was in this campo that the merchants anciently met: here, in the district of the Rialto, and not on the bridge itself, as many readers suppose, did Antonio transact his business with one Shylock a Jew. There are plenty of Jews left in Venice; in fact, I have been told that they are gradually getting possession of the city, and judging by their ability in that direction elsewhere, I can readily believe it; but I saw none in the least like the Shylock of the English stage, although I spent some time both in the New Ghetto and the Old by the Cannaregio. All unwilling I once had the company of a small Jewish boy in a gaberdine for the whole way from the New Ghetto to the steamboat station of S. Toma, his object in life being to acquire for nothing a coin similar to one which I had given to another boy who had been really useful. If he avowed once that he was a starving Jewish boy and I was a millionaire, he said it fifty times. Every now and then he paused for an anxious second to throw a somersault. But I was obdurate, and embarking on the steamer, left the two falsehoods to fight it out.

The two Ghettos, by the way, are not interesting; no traveller, missing them, need feel that he has been in Venice in vain.

At the other end of the Rialto campo, opposite the church, is the famous hunchback, the Gobbo of the Rialto, who supports a rostrum from which the laws of the Republic were read to the people, after they had been read, for a wider audience, from the porphyry block at the corner of S. Mark's.

Leaving the Gobbo on our left and passing from the campo at the right-hand corner, we come to the great arcaded markets for fruit and vegetables, and further to the wholesale and retail fish markets, all of which are amusing to loiter in, particularly in the early hours of the morning.   To the Erberia are all the fruit-laden barges bound, chiefly from Malamocco, the short cut from the lagoon being through the Rio del Palazzo beneath the Bridge of Sighs and into the Grand Canal, just opposite us, by the Post Office.   The fruit market is busy twice a day, in the early morning and in the late afternoon; the fish market in the morning only.

The vegetables and fruit differ according to the seasons; the fish are always the same.   In the autumn when the quay is piled high with golden melons and flaming tomatoes, the sight is perhaps the most splendid. The strangest of the fish to English eyes are the great cuttle-fish, which are sold in long slices.   It strikes one as a refinement of symmetrical irony that the ink which exudes from these fish and stains everything around should be used for indicating what their price is.

Here also are great joints of tunny, huge red scarpenna, sturgeon, mullet, live whole eels (to prove to me how living they were, a fishmonger one morning allowed one to bite him) and eels in writhing sections, aragosta, or langouste, and all the little Adriatic and lagoon fish— the scampi and shrimps and calimari—spread out in little wet heaps on the leaves of the plane-tree.   One sees them here lying dead; one can see them also, alive and swimming about, in the aquarium on the Lido, where the prettiest creatures are the little cavalli marini, or sea horses, roosting in the tiny submarine branches.

From all the restlessness and turmoil of these markets there is escape in the church of S. Giovanni Elemosinario, a few yards along the Ruga Vecchia di San Giovanni on the left. Here one may sit and rest and collect one's thoughts and then look at a fine rich altar-piece by Pordenone—S. Sebastian, S. Rocco, and S. Catherine. The lion of the church is a Titian, but it is not really visible.

As typical a walk as one can take in democratic Venice is that from this church to the Frari, along the Ruga Vecchia di San Giovanni, parallel with the Grand Canal. I have been here often both by day and by night, and it is equally characteristic at either time. Every kind of shop is here, including, in 1913, two old book-shops containing a surprising proportion of American minor verse. Another interesting shop here supplies Venetians with the small singing birds which they love so much, a cage by a window being the rule rather than the exception ; and it was hereabouts that an old humorous greengrocer once did his voluble best to make me buy a couple of grilli, or crickets, in a tiny barred prison, to make their shrill mysterious music for me. But I resisted.

At night, perhaps, is this walk best, for several very popular wine shops for gondoliers are hereabouts, one or two quite large, with rows of barrels along the walls ; and it is good to see every seat full, and an arm round many a waist, and everybody merry. Such a clatter of tongues as comes from these taverns is not to be beaten ; and now and then a tenor voice or a mandolin adds a grace.

CHAPTER XXI

S. ROCCO AND TINTORETTO

THERE are Tintorettos everywhere in Venice, in
addition to the immense canvases in the Doges'
Palace, but I imagine that were we able to ask the great
man the question, Where would he choose to be judged ? he
would reply, " At the Scuola di S. Rocco,"—with perhaps
a reservation in favour of "The Miracle of S. Mark " at
the Accademia, and possibly the " Presentation " (for I feel
he must have loved that work) at the Madonna dell' Orto,
and "The Marriage in Cana," that fascinating scene, in
the Salute.   In the superb building of the S. Rocco Scuola
he reigns alone, and there his " Crucifixion " is.

The Scuola and the church, in white stone, hide behind
the lofty red-brick apse of the Frari.   The Scuola's façade
has, in particular, the confidence of a successful people.
Within, it is magnificent, while to its architectural glories
it adds no fewer than six-and-fifty Tintorettos ; many of
which, however, can be only dimly seen, for the great

Bartolommeo Bon, who designed the Scuola, forgot that
pictures require light. Nor was he unique among Venice's
builders in this matter; they mostly either forgot it or
allowed their jealousy of a sister art to influence them.
"Light, more light," is as much the cry of the groping
enthusiast for painting in this fair city, as it was of the
dying Goethe.

The story of Tintoretto's connexion with the Scuola
illustrates his decision and swiftness. The Scuola having
been built, where, under the banner of S. Rocco, a philan-
thropical confraternity might meet to confer as to schemes
of social amelioration, it was, in 1560, decided to invite
the more prominent artists to make proposals as to its
decoration. Tintoretto, then forty-two, Paul Veronese
and Schiavone were among them. They were to meet in
the Refectory and display their sketches; and on a given
day all were there. Tintoretto stood aside while the others
unfolded their designs, which were examined and criticized.
Then came his turn, but instead of producing a roll he
twitched a covering, which none had noticed, and revealed in the middle of the ceiling the finished painting of
S. Rocco in glory. A scene of amazement and perplexity
ensued. The other artists, accepting defeat, retired from
the field; the authorities gazed in a fine state of confusion
over the unconventional foreshortening of the saint and
his angel. They also pointed out that Tintoretto had
broken the condition of the competition in providing a
painting when only sketches were required. "Very well,"
he said, "I make you a present of it." Since by the rules of
the confraternity all gifts offered to it had to be accepted,
he thus won his footing; and the rest was easy. Two or
three years later he was made a brother of the Order, at
fifty pounds a year, in return for which he was each year

15

to provide three paintings ; and this salary he drew for seventeen years, until the great work was complete.

The task comprises the scenes in the life of the Virgin, in the lower hall ; the scenes in the life of Christ, on the walls of the upper hall ; the scenes from the Old Testament, on the ceiling of the upper hall ; and the last scenes in the life of Christ, in the Refectory. In short, the Scuola di S. Rocco is Tintoretto's Sistine Chapel.

We enter to an " Annunciation " ; and if we had not perceived before, we at once perceive here, in this building, Tintoretto's innovating gift of realism. He brought dailiness into art. Tremendous as was his method, he never forgot the little things. His domestic details leaven the whole.

This " Annunciation " is the most dramatic version that exists. The Virgin has been sitting quietly sewing in her little room, poorly enough furnished, with a broken chair by the bed, when suddenly this celestial irruption—this urgent flying angel attended by a horde of cherubim or cupids and heralded by the Holy Spirit. At the first glance you think that the angel has burst through the wall, but that is not so. But as it is, even without that violence, how utterly different from the demure treatment of the Tuscans ! To think of Fra Angelico and Tintoretto together is like placing a violet beside a tiger lily.

A little touch in the picture should be noticed : a carpenter at work outside. Very characteristic of Tintoretto.

Next—but here let me remind or inform the reader that the Venetian Index at the end of the later editions of *The Stones of Venice* contains an analysis of these works, by Ruskin, which is as characteristic of that writer as the pictures are of their artist. In particular is Ruskin de-

lighted by "The Annunciation," by "The Murder of the
Innocents," and, upstairs, by the ceiling paintings and the
Refectory series.

Next is " The Adoration of the Magi," with all the ingredients that one can ask, except possibly any spiritual
rapture ; and then the flight into a country less like the
Egypt to which the little family were bound, or the Palestine
from which they were driven, than one can imagine, but a
dashing work. Then " The Slaughter of the Innocents," a
confused scene of fine and daring drawing, in which, owing
to gloom and grime, no innocents can be discerned. Then
a slender nocturnal pastoral which is even more difficult
to see, representing Mary Magdalen in a rocky landscape,
and opposite it a similar work representing S. Mary of
Egypt, which one knows to be austere and beautiful but
again cannot see.

Since the story of S. Mary of Egypt is little known, I
may perhaps be permitted to tell it here. This Mary, before
her conversion, lived in Alexandria at the end of the fourth
century and was famous for her licentiousness. Then one
day, by a caprice, joining a company of pilgrims to Jerusalem, she embraced Christianity, and in answer to her
prayers for peace of mind was bidden by a supernatural
voice to pass beyond Jordan, where rest and comfort were
to be found. There, in the desert, she roamed for forty-
seven years, when she was found, naked and grey, by a
holy man named Zosimus who was travelling in search of a
hermit more pious than himself with whom he might have
profitable converse. Zosimus, having given her his mantle
for covering, left her, but he returned in two years, bringing with him the Sacrament and some food.

When they caught sight of each other, Mary was on the
other side of the Jordan, but she at once walked to him

In the mass the picture is overpowering; in detail, to which one comes later, its interest is inexhaustible. As an example of the painter's minute thought, one writer has pointed out that the donkey in the background is eating withered palm leaves—a touch of ironical genius, if you like. Ruskin describes this work as the most exquisite instance of what he calls the "imagination penetrative." I reproduce a detail showing the soldiers with the ropes and the group of women at the foot of the cross.

The same room has Tintoretto's noble picture of Christ before Pilate and the fine tragic composition "The Road to Calvary," and on the ceiling is the S. Rocco of which I have already spoken—the germ from which sprang the whole wonderful series.

The story of this, the most Venetian of the Venetian painters and the truest to his native city (for all his life was spent here), may more fittingly be told in this place, near his masterpiece and his portrait (which is just by the door), than elsewhere. He was born in 1518, in the ninth year of our Henry VIII's reign, the son of a dyer, or tintore, named Battista Robusti, and since the young Jacopo Robusti helped his father in his trade he was called the little dyer, or il tintoretto. His father was well to do, and the boy had enough leisure to enable him to copy and to frequent the arcades of S. Mark's Square, under which such artists as were too poor to afford studios were allowed to work.

The greatest name in Venetian art at that time, and indeed still, was that of Titian, and Tintoretto was naturally anxious to become his pupil. Titian was by many years Tintoretto's senior when, at the age of seventeen, the little dyer obtained leave to study under him. The story has it that so masterly were Tintoretto's early drawings that Titian, fearing rivalry, refused to teach him any longer. Whether this be true or not, and one dislikes to think of Titian in this way, Tintoretto left the studio and was thrown upon his own resources and ambition. Fortunately he did not need money : he was able even to form a collection of casts from the antique and also from Michael Angelo, the boy's other idol, who when Tintoretto was seventeen was sixty-one. Thus supplied, Tintoretto practised drawing and painting, day and night, his motto being "Titian's colour and Michael Angelo's form"; and he expressed himself as willing to paint anything anywhere, inside a house or outside, and if necessary for nothing, rather than be idle. Practice was what he believed in : practice and study ; and he never tired. All painting worth anything, he held, must be based on sound drawing. "You can buy colours on the Rialto," he would remark, "but drawing can come only by labour." Some say that he was stung by a sarcasm of his Tuscan hero that the Venetians could not draw ; be that as it may, he made accurate drawing his corner-stone ; and so thorough was he in his study of chiaroscuro that he devised little toy houses in which to manufacture effects of light and shade. One of his first pictures to attract attention was a portrait of himself and his brother illuminated by a lamp.

So passed, in miscellaneous work, even to painting furniture, at least ten years, towards the close of which he painted for the Madonna dell' Orto his earliest important work, "The Last Judgment," which though derived from Michael Angelo yet indicates much personal force. It was in 1548, when he was thirty, that Tintoretto's real chance came, for he was then invited to contribute to the decoration of the Scuola of S. Marco, and for it he produced one of his greatest works, "The Miracle of S. Mark."

now in the Accademia. The novelty of its vivid force
and drama, together with its power and assurance, although, as I have said, at first disconcerting to the unpre-
pared critics, soon made an impression; spectators were
carried off their feet; and Tintoretto's fame was assured.
See opposite page 170.

I have not counted the Venetian churches with examples
of Tintoretto's genius in them (it would be simpler to
count those that have none); but they are many and his
industry was enormous. One likes to think of his studio
being visited continually by church patrons and prelates
anxious to see how their particular commission was getting
on.

Tintoretto married in 1558, two years after Shakespeare's birth, his wife being something of an heiress, and
in 1562 his eldest son, Domenico, who also became an
artist, was born. We have seen how in 1560 Tintoretto
competed for the S. Rocco decorations; in 1565 he
painted "The Crucifixion"; and he was working on the
walls of the Scuola until 1588. In the meantime he
worked also for the Doges' Palace, his first picture, that
of the Battle of Lepanto, being destroyed with many others
in the fire of 1576, but first obtaining him as a reward a
sinecure post in the Fondaco dei Tedeschi, that central
office of German merchants and brokers on the façade of
which Giorgione and Titian painted their famous (now
obliterated) frescoes. Small posts here with no obligations
were given to public servants, much as we give Civil List
pensions.

Tintoretto's life was very methodical, and was divided
strictly between painting and domestic affairs, with few
outside diversions. He had settled down in the house
which now bears his name and a tablet, close to the church

of the Madonna dell' Orto. His children were eight in number, among whom his favourite was Marietta, his eldest daughter. He and she were in fact inseparable, Marietta even donning boy's attire in order to be with him at his work on occasions when as a girl it would have been difficult. Perhaps it is she who so often appears in his pictures as a beautiful sympathetic human girl among so much that is somewhat frigidly Biblical and detached. Among his closer friends were some of the best Venetian intellects, and, among the artists, Andrea Schiavone, who hovers like a ghost about so many painters and their work, Paolo Caliari, known as Veronese, Jacopo da Ponte, or Bassano, and Alessandro Vittoria, the sculptor. He had musician friends, too; for Tintoretto, like Giorgione before him, was devoted to music, and himself played many instruments. He was a man of simple tastes and a quiet and somewhat dry humour; liked home best; chaffed his wife, who was a bit of a manager and had to check his indiscriminate generosity by limiting him to one coin a day; and, there is no doubt whatever, studied his Bible with minuteness. His collected works make the most copious illustrated edition of scripture that exists.

Certain of Tintoretto's sayings prove his humour to have had a caustic turn. Being once much harassed by a crowd of spectators, including men of civic eminence, he was asked why he painted so quickly when Bellini and Titian had been so deliberate. "They had not so many onlookers to drive them to distraction," he replied. Of Titian, in spite of his admiration for his colour, he was always a little jealous and could not bear to hear him much praised; and colour without drawing eternally vexed him. His own colour is always subservient.

hence the presence of a dog in all representations of the
saint. In the church of S. Rocco across the way Tintoretto has a picture of this scene in which we discern the
dog to have been a liver-and-white spaniel.

Golard, discovering the dog's fidelity to Rocco, himself
passed into the saint's service and was so thoroughly converted by him that he became a humble mendicant in the
Piacenza streets. Rocco meanwhile continued to heal,
although he could not heal himself, and he even cured the
wild animals of their complaints, as Tintoretto also shows
us. Being at last healed by heaven, he travelled to
Lombardy, where he was taken as a spy and imprisoned for
five years, and in prison he died, after being revealed as
a saint to his gaoler. His dying prayer was that all
Christians who prayed to him in the name of Jesus might
be delivered from pestilence. Shortly after Rocco's death
an angel descended to earth with a table written in letters
of gold stating that this wish had been granted. In the
carvings in the chancel, the bronzes on the gate and in
Tintoretto's pictures in the neighbouring church, much
of this story may be traced.

The most noteworthy carvings round the room represent types and attributes. Here is the musician, the con-
spirator (a very Guy Fawkes, with dark lantern and all),
the scholar, and so forth, all done with humorous detail
by one Pianta. When he came to the artist he had a little
quiet fun with the master himself, this figure being a cari-
cature of no less a performer than the great Tintoretto.

The little room leading from the upper hall is that
rare thing in Venice, a council chamber which presents a
tight fit for the council. Just inside is a wax model of
the head of one of the four Doges named Alvise Mocenigo,
I know not which. Upstairs is a Treasury filled with

THE CRUCIFIXION (CENTRAL DETAIL)
FROM THE PAINTING BY TINTORETTO
In the Scuola di S. Rocco

valuable ecclesiastical vessels, missals and vestments, and two fine religious pictures from the masterly worldly hand of Tiepolo. Among the sacred objects enshrined in gold and silver reliquaries are a piece of the jawbone of S. Barbara, a piece of the cranium of S. Martin, a tiny portion of the veil of the Madonna, and a tooth of S. Apollonia held in triumph in a pair of forceps by a little golden cherub. And now, descending again, let us look once more at the great picture of Him whose Life and Crucifixion put into motion all this curious ecclesiastical machinery— so strangely far from the original idea.

The church of S. Rocco is opposite, and one must enter it for Tintoretto's scenes in the life of the saint, and for a possible Giorgione over the altar to the right of the choir in a beautiful old frame. The subject is Christ carrying the cross, with a few urging Him on. The theory that Giorgione painted this picture is gaining ground, and we know that only about a century after Giorgione's death Van Dyck, when sketching in Venice, made some notes of the work under the impression that it was by the divine Castel Francan. The light is poor and the picture is in a bad state, but one is conscious of being in the presence of a work of very delicate beauty and a profound soft richness. The picture, Vasari says, once worked miracles, and years ago it brought in, in votive money, great sums. One grateful admirer has set up a version of it in marble, on the left wall of the choir. Standing before this Giorgione, as before the Tintorettos here and over the way, one again wishes, as so often in Venice, that some American millionaire, in love with this lovely city and in doubt as to how to apply his superfluity of cash, would offer to clean the pictures in the churches. What glorious hues would then come to light !

CHAPTER XXII

THE FRARI AND TITIAN

A noble church—The tomb of Titian—A painter-prince—A lost garden—Pomp and colour—A ceaseless learner—Canova—Titian's Assumption—The Pesaro Madonna—The Frari cat—Bellini's altar-piece—Tombs vulgar and otherwise—Francesco Foscari—Niccolò Tron's beard.

FROM S. Rocco to the Frari is but a step, and plenty of assistance in taking that step will be offered you by small boys.

Outside, the Frari—whose full title is Santa Maria Gloriosa dei Frari—is worth more attention than it wins. At the first glance it is a barn built of millions of bricks; but if you give it time it grows into a most beautiful Gothic church with lovely details, such as the corbelling under the eaves, the borders of the circular windows, and still more delightful borders of the long windows, and so forth; while its campanile is magnificent. In size alone the Frari is worthy of all respect, and its age is above five centuries. It shares with SS. Giovanni e Paolo the duty of providing Venice with a Westminster Abbey, for between them they preserve most of the illustrious dead.

Within, it is a gay light church with fine sombre choir stalls. Next to S. Stefano, it is the most cheerful church in Venice, and one should often be there. Nothing is easier than to frequent it, for it is close to the S. Toma steamboat station, and every visit will discover a new charm.

S. MARIA GLORIOSA DEI FRARI

The most cherished possession of the Frari is, I suppose, now, after its return from long exile in the Accademia, Titian's "Assumption"; but formerly it was the painter's tomb to which the sacristan first led you. It is not a very fine monument, dating from as late as 1852, but it marks reverently the resting-place of the great man. He sits there, the old painter, with a laurel crown. Behind him is a relief of his "Assumption," now behind the high altar; above is the lion of Venice. Titian's work is to be seen throughout Venice, either in fact or in influence, and all the great cities of the world have some superb creation from his hand, London being peculiarly fortunate in the possession of his "Bacchus and Ariadne". Standing before the tomb of this tireless maker of beauty, let us recall the story of his life. Titian, as we call him—Tiziano Vecellio, or Vecelli, or Tiziano da Cadore, as he was called by his contemporaries—was born in Cadore, a Venetian province. The year of his birth varies according to the biographer. Some say 1477, some 1480, some 1487 or even 1489 and 1490. Be that as it may, he was born in Cadore, the son of a soldier and councillor, Gregorio Vecelli. As a child he was sent to Venice and placed under art teachers, one of whom was Gentile Bellini, and one Giovanni Bellini, in whose studio he found Giorgione. And it is here that his age becomes important, because if he was born in 1477 he was Giorgione's contemporary as a scholar; if ten years later he was much his junior. In either case there is no doubt that Giorgione's influence was very powerful. On Titian's death in 1576 he was thought to be ninety-nine.

One of Titian's earliest known works is the visitation of S. Mary and S. Elizabeth, in the Accademia; his last work also hangs there. In 1507 he helped Giorgione with the Fondaco dei Tedeschi frescoes. In 1511 he went to Padua.

In 1512 he obtained a sinecure in the Fondaco dei Tedeschi and was appointed a State artist, his first task being the completion of certain pictures left unfinished by his predecessor Giovanni Bellini, and in 1516 he was put in possession of a patent granting him a painting monopoly, with a salary of 120 crowns and 80 crowns in addition for the portrait of each successive Doge. Thereafter his career was one long triumph and his brush was sought by foreign kings and princes as well as the aristocracy of Venice. Honours were showered upon him at home and abroad, and Charles V made him a Count and ennobled his progeny. He married and had many children, his favourite being, as with Tintoretto, a daughter, whose early death left him, again as with Tintoretto, inconsolable. He made large sums and spent large sums, and his house was the scene of splendid entertainments. It still stands, not far from the Jesuits' church, but it is now the centre of a slum, and his large garden, which extended to the lagoon where the Fondamenta Nuovo now is, has been built over.

Titian's place in art is high and unassailable. What it would have been in colour without Giorgione we cannot say; but Giorgione could not affect his draughtsmanship. As it is, the word Titianesque means everything that is rich and glorious in paint. The Venetians, with their ostentation, love of pageantry, and intense pride in their city and themselves, could not have had a painter more to their taste. Had Giorgione lived he would have disappointed them by his preoccupation with romantic dreams; Bellini no doubt did disappoint them by a certain simplicity and divinity; Tintoretto was stern and sparing of gorgeous hues. But Titian was all for sumptuousness.

Not much is known of his inner life. He seems to have been over-quick to suspect a successful rival, and his treatment of the young Tintoretto, if the story is true, is not admirable. He was more friendly with Aretino than one would expect an adorner of altars to be. His love of money grew steadily stronger. As an artist he was a pattern, for he was never satisfied with his work but continually experimented and sought for new secrets, and although quite old when he met Michael Angelo in Rome he returned with renewed ambitions. Among his last words, on his death-bed, was the remark that he was at last almost ready to begin painting.

It is the pyramidal tomb opposite Titian's that was really intended to hold his remains. But it became the tomb of Canova. Why it was not put to its designer's purpose, I do not know, but to my mind it is a far finer thing than the Titian monument and worthier of Titian than of Canova, as indeed Canova would have been the first to admit. But there was some hitch, and the design was laid in a drawer and not taken out again until Canova died ; and certain of his pupils then completed it—for himself. Canova was not a Venetian by birth. He was born at Passagno, near Asolo, in 1757, and was taught the elements of art by his grandfather and afterwards by a sculptor named Torretto, who recommended him to the Falier family as a "phenomenon". The Faliers made him their protégé, continued his education in Venice, and when the time was ripe sent him to Rome, the sculptors' Mecca. In Rome he remained practically to the end of his life, returning to Venice to die in 1822. It is possible not too highly to esteem Canova's works, but the man's career was marked by splendid qualities of industry and purpose and he won every worldly honour. In private life he practised unremittingly that benevolence and philanthropy which many Italians have brought to a fine art.

Titian's "Assumption" was more easily seen at the
Accademia than in its position over the high altar, with
light behind it, but none the less one likes it to be where it
was intended to be.   It is massive and wonderful : perhaps
indeed too massive in the conception of the Madonna, for
the suggestion of flight is lacking ; but it has an earthiness,
even a theatricalness, which one cannot forget, superb
though that earthiness may be.   The cherubs, however,
copies of which are always being made by diligent commercial artists, are a joy.   The Titians that hang in the
gallery of my mind are other than this.   A Madonna and
Child and a rollicking baby at Vienna ; our own " Bacchus
and Ariadne " ; the " Amoretti " at Madrid ; the Louvre
" Man with a Glove " ; these are among them, but the
" Assumption " is not there.

Another great Frari picture—simpler than this but
not as attractive—is the famous Titian altar-piece, the
" Pesaro Madonna ".   This is an altar-piece indeed, and in
it unite with peculiar success the world and the spirit.
The picture was painted for Jacopo Pesaro, a member of
a family closely associated with this church, as the tombs
will show us.   Jacopo, known as " Baffo," is the kneeling
figure, and, as his tonsure indicates, a man of God.   He
was in fact Bishop of Paphos in Cyprus, and being of the
church militant he had in 1501 commanded the Papal
fleet against the Turks.   The expedition was triumphant
enough to lead the Bishop to commission Titian to paint
two pictures commemorating it.   In the first the Pope,
Alexander Borgia, in full canonicals, standing, introduces
Baffo, kneeling, to S. Peter, on the eve of starting with
the ships to chastise the Infidel.   S. Peter blesses him and
the Papal standard which he grasps.   In the second, the
picture at which we are now looking (see the repro-

THE MADONNA OF THE PESARO FAMILY
FROM THE PAINTING BY TITIAN
In the Church of the Frari

duction opposite page 242), Baffo again kneels to S. Peter, while behind him a soldier in armour (who might be S. George and might merely be a Venetian warrior and a portrait) exhibits a captured Turk. Above S. Peter is the Madonna, with one of Titian's most adorable and vigorous Babes. Beside her are S. Francis and S. Anthony of Padua, S. Francis being the speaking brother who seems to be saying much good of the intrepid but by no means over-modest Baffo. The other kneeling figures are various Pesari. Everything about the picture is masterly and aristocratic, and S. Peter yields to no other old man in Venetian art, which so valued and respected age, in dignity and grandeur. In the clouds above all are two outrageously plump cherubs—fat as butter, as we say—sporting (it is the only word) with the cross.

As I sat one day looking at this picture, a small grey and white cat sprang on my knee from nowhere and immediately sank into a profound slumber from which I hesitated to wake it. Such ingratiating acts are not common in Venice, where animals are scarce and all dogs must be muzzled. Whether or not the spirit of Titian had instructed the little creature to keep me there, I cannot say, but the result was that I sat for a quarter of an hour before the altar without a movement, so that every particular of the painting is photographed on my retina. Six months later the same cat led me to a courtyard opposite the Sacristy door and proudly exhibited three kittens.

The Frari is famous also for Bellini's altar-piece in the Sacristy. This work represents the Madonna enthroned, about her being saints and the little angelic musicians of whom Bellini was so fond. In this work these musicians are younger than usual; one pipes while the other plays a mandolin. Above them is the Madonna, grave and sweet, with a resolute little Son standing on her knee. The venerable holy men on either side have all Bellini's suave benignancy and incapacity for sin : celestial grandfathers The whole is set in a very splendid frame. I give a reproduction opposite page 252, but the colour cannot be suggested.

Jacopo Pesaro's tomb is near the Baptistery. The enormous and repellent tomb on the same wall as the Titian altar-piece is that of a later Pesaro, Giovanni, an unimportant Doge of Venice for less than a year, 1658-1659. It has grotesque details, including a camel, giant negroes and skeletons, and it was designed by the architect of S Maria della Salute, who ought to have known better.

As a gentle contrast look at the wall tomb of a bishop on the right of the Pesaro picture. The old priest lies on his bier resting his head on his hand and gazing for ever at the choir screen and stalls. Behind him are coloured stones beautifully set. It is one of the simplest and most satisfactory tombs in this church.

But it is in the right transept, about the Sacristy door, that the best tombs cluster, and here also, in the end chapel, is another picture, by an early Muranese painter of whom we have seen far too little, Bartolommeo Vivarini, who is credited with having produced the first oil picture ever seen in Venice. His Frari altar-piece undoubtedly had influence on the Bellini in the Sacristy, but it is less beautiful, although possibly a deeper sincerity informs it. Other musicianly angels are here, and this time they make their melody to S. Mark. In the next chapel are some pretty cool grey and blue tombs.

Chief of the tombs in this corner is the fine monument to Jacopo Marcello, the admiral. This lovely thing is one of the most Florentine sculptures in Venice ; above is a delicate fresco record of the hero's triumphs. Near by is the monument of Pacifico Bon, the architect of the Frari, with a Florentine relief of the Baptism of Christ in terra-cotta, a little too high to be seen well. The wooden equestrian figure of Paolo Savello, an early work, is very attractive. In his red cap he rides with a fine assurance and is the best horseman in Venice after the great Colleoni.

In the choir are two more dead Doges. One is Francesco Foscari, who reigned from 1423-1457, and is one of the two Foscari (his son being the other) of Byron's drama. Francesco Foscari, whom we know so well by reason of his position in the relief on the Piazzetta façade of the Doges' Palace, and again on the Porta della Carta, was unique among the Doges both in the beginning and end of his reign. He was the first to be introduced to the populace in the new phrase "This is your Doge," instead of "This is your Doge, an it please you," and the first to quit the ducal throne not by death but deposition. But in many of the intervening thirty-four years he reigned with brilliance and liberality and encouraged the arts. His fall was due to the political folly of his son Jacopo and the unpopularity of a struggle with Milan. He died in the famous Foscari palace on the Grand Canal and, in spite of his recent degradation, was given a Doge's funeral.

The other Doge here, who has the more ambitious tomb, is Niccolò Tron (1471-1473), who was before all a successful merchant. Foscari, it will be noticed, is clean shaven; Tron bearded; and to this beard belongs a story, for on losing a dearly loved son he refused ever after to have it cut and carried it to the grave as a sign of his grief.

agreed that this is the finest horse and horseman ever cast in bronze; and it is a surprise to me that South Kensington has no reproduction of it, as the Trocadero in Paris has. Warrior and steed equally are splendid: they are magnificent and they are war. The only really competitive statue is that of Gattamelata (who was Colleoni's commander) by Donatello at Padua; but personally I think this the finer.

Bartolommeo Colleoni was born in 1400, at Bergamo, of fighting stock, and his early years were stained with blood. The boy was still very young when he saw his father's castle besieged by Filippo Maria Visconti, Duke of Milan, and his father killed. On becoming himself a condottiere, he joined the Venetians, who were then busy in the field, and against the Milanese naturally fought with peculiar ardour. But on the declaration of peace in 1441 he forgot his ancient hostility, and in the desire for more battle assisted the Milanese in their campaigns. Fighting was meat and drink to him. Seven years later he returned to the Venetians, expecting to be appointed Captain-General of the Republic's forces, but failing in this wish he put his arm again at the service of the Milanese. A little later, however, Venice afforded him the coveted honour, and for the rest of his life he was true to her, although when she was miserably at peace he did not refrain from a little strife on his own account, to keep his hand in. Venice gave him not only honours and money but much land, and he divided his old age between agriculture and—thus becoming still more the darling of the populace—almsgiving.

Colleoni died in 1475 and left a large part of his fortune to the Republic to be spent in the war with the Turks, and a little for a statue in the Piazza of S. Mark. But

THE COLLEONI STATUE AND S. S. GIOVENNI E PAOLO

the rules against statues being erected there being adamant, the site was changed to the campo of SS. Giovanni e Paolo, and Andrea Verrocchio was brought from Florence to prepare the group. He began it in 1479 and died while still working on it, leaving word that his pupil, Lorenzo di Credi, should complete it. Di Credi, however, was discouraged by the authorities, and the task was given to Alessandro Leopardi (who made the sockets for the three flagstaffs opposite S. Mark's), and it is his name which is inscribed on the statue. But to Verrocchio the real honour.

Among the Colleoni statue's great admirers was Robert Browning, who never tired of telling the story of the hero to those unacquainted with it.

The vast church of SS. Giovanni e Paolo does for the Dominicans what the Frari does for the Franciscans ; the two churches being the Venetian equivalents of Florence's S. Maria Novella and Santa Croce. Like too many of the church façades of Venice, this one is unfinished and probably ever will be, and for several years the church has been under repair within. Unlike the Frari, to which it has a general resemblance, the church of John and Paul is domed ; or rather it possesses a dome, with golden balls upon its cupola like those of S. Mark. Within, it is light and immense. It may contain no Titian's ashes, but both Giovanni and Gentile Bellini lie here ; and its forty-six Doges give it a cachet. We come at once to two of them, for on the outside wall are the tombs of Doge Jacopo Tiepolo, who gave the land for the church, and his son, Doge Lorenzo Tiepolo.

Just within we find Alvise Mocenigo (1570-1577) who was on the throne when Venice was swept by the plague in which Titian died, and who offered the church of the

Redentore on the Giudecca as a bribe to Heaven to stop the pestilence. Close by lie his predecessors and ancestors, Pietro Mocenigo, the admiral, and Giovanni Mocenigo, his brother, whose reign (1478-1485) was peculiarly belligerent and witnessed the great fire which destroyed so many treasures in the Ducal Palace. What he was like you may see in the picture numbered 750 in our National Gallery, once given to Carpaccio, then to Lorenzo Bastiani, and now to the school of Gentile Bellini. In this work the Doge kneels to the Virgin and implores intercession for the plague-stricken city. Pietro's monument is the most splendid, with a number of statues by Pietro Lombardi, architect of the Ducal Palace after the same fire. S. Christopher is among these figures, with a nice little Christ holding on to his ear.

In the right aisle we find the monument of Bragadino, a Venetian commander who, on the fall of Cyprus, which he had been defending against the Turks, was flayed alive. But this was not all the punishment put upon him by the Turks for daring to hold out so long. First his nose and ears were cut off; then for some days he was made to work like the lowest labourer. Then came the flaying, after which his skin was stuffed with straw and fastened as a figure-head to the Turkish admiral's prow on his triumphant return to Constantinople. For years the trophy was kept in the arsenal of that city, but it was removed by some means or other, purchase or theft, and now reposes in the tomb at which we are looking. This monument greatly affected old Coryat. "Truly," he says, "I could not read it with dry eyes."

Farther on is the pretentious Valier monument, a triumph of bad taste. Here we see Doge Bertucci Valier (1656-1658) with his courtly abundant dame, and Doge

Silvestro Valier (1694-1700), all proud and foolish in death, as I feel sure they must have been in life to have commissioned such a memorial. In the choir are more Doges, some of sterner stuff: Michele Morosini (1382), who after only a few months was killed by a visitation of the plague, which carried off also twenty thousand more ordinary Venetians, but who has a tomb of great distinction worthy of commemorating a full and sagacious reign; Leonardo Loredan (1501-1521) whose features we know so well by reason of Bellini's portrait in the National Gallery, the Doge on the throne when the League of Cambray was formed by the Powers to crush the Republic; and Andrea Vendramini (1476-1478) who has the most beautiful monument of all, the work of Tullio and Antonio Lombardi. Vendramini, who came between Pietro and Giovanni Mocenigo, had a brief and bellicose reign. Lastly here lies Doge Marco Corner (1365-1368), who made little history, but was a fine character.

In the left transept we find warlike metal, for here is the modern statue of the great Sebastian Venier whom we have already seen in the Ducal Palace as the hero of the battle of Lepanto in 1571, and it is peculiarly fitting that he should be honoured in the same church as the luckless Bragadino, for it was at Lepanto that the Turks who had triumphed at Cyprus and behaved so vilely were for the moment utterly defeated. On the death of Alvise Mocenigo, Venier was made Doge, at the age of eighty, but he occupied the throne only for a year, and his end was hastened by grief at another of those disastrous fires, in 1576, which destroyed some of the finest pictures that the world then contained. This statue is vigorous, and one feels that it is true to life, but for the old admiral at his finest and most vivid you must go to Vienna, where Tintoretto's superb and magnificent portrait of him is preserved. There he stands, the old sea dog, in his armour, but bare-headed, and through a window you see the Venetian fleet riding on a blue sea. It is one of the greatest portraits in the world and it ought to be in Venice.

The chapel of the Rosary, which is entered just by the statue of Venier, was built in honour of his Lepanto victory. It was largely destroyed by fire in 1867. Such wood carving as was saved is in the church proper, in the left aisle. Not to be rescued were Titian's great "Death of S. Peter, Martyr," a copy of which, presented by King Victor Emmanuel, is in the church, and a priceless altar-piece by Giovanni Bellini. The beautiful stone reliefs by Sansovino are in their original places, and remain to-day as they were mutilated by the flames. Their unharmed portions prove their exquisite workmanship, and fortunately photography has preserved for us their unimpaired form. An American gentleman who followed me into the church, after having considered for some time as to whether or not he (who had "seen ten thousand churches") would risk the necessary entrance fee, expressed himself, before these Sansovino masterpieces, as glad he came. "These reliefs," he said to me, "seem to be of a high order of merit."

Returning to the church proper, we find more Doges. An earlier Venier Doge, Antonio (1382-1400), is here. In the left aisle is another fine Ducal monument, that of Pasquale Malipiero (1457-1462), who succeeded Foscari on his deposal and was the first Doge to be present at the funeral of another, for Foscari died only ten days after his fall. Here also lie Doge Michele Steno (1400-1413) who succeeded Antonio Venier, and who as a young man is credited with the insult which may be said to have led to

THE MADONNA TRIPTYCH
BY GIOVANNI BELLINI
In the Church of the Frari

all Marino Faliero's troubles.   For Steno having annoyed
the Doge by falling in love with a maid of honour, Faliero
forbade him the palace, and in retaliation Steno scribbled
on the throne itself a scurrilous commentary on the Doge's
wife.   Faliero's inability to induce the judges to punish
Steno sufficiently was the beginning of that rage against
the State which led to his ruin.   It was during Steno's
reign that Carlo Zeno was so foolishly arrested and imprisoned, to the loss of the Republic of one of its finest
patriots.

The next Ducal tomb is the imposing one of the illustrious Tommaso Mocenigo (1413-1423) who succeeded Steno
and brought really great qualities to his office.   Had his
counsels been followed the whole history of Venice might
have changed, for he was firm against the Republic's land
campaigns, holding that she had territory enough and
should concentrate on sea power : a sound and sagacious
policy which found its principal opponent in Francesco
Foscari, Mocenigo's successor, and its justification years
later in the calamitous League of Cambray, to which I have
referred elsewhere.   Mocenigo was not only wise for Venice
abroad, but at home too.   A fine of a thousand ducats had
been fixed as the punishment of anyone who, in those days
of expenses connected with so many campaigns, chiefly
against the Genoese, dared to mention the rebuilding or
beautifying of the Ducal Palace.   But Mocenigo was not
to be deterred, and rising in his place with his thousand
ducat penalty in his hand, he urged with such force
upon the Council the necessity of rebuilding that he
carried his point, and the lovely building much as we
now know it was begun.   That was in 1422.   In 1423
Mocenigo died, his last words being a warning against
the election of Foscari as his successor.   But Foscari

Mr. Howells speaks in his *Venetian Life* of the Giardini Pubblici as being an inevitable resort in the sixties; but they must, I think, have lost their vogue. The Venetians who want to walk now do so with more comfort and entertainment in S. Mark's Square.

At the Via Garibaldi entrance is a monument to the fine old Liberator, who stands, wearing the famous cap and cloak, sword in hand, on the summit of a rock. Below him on one side is a lion, but a lion without wings, and on the other one of his watchful Italian soldiers. There is a rugged simplicity about it that is very pleasing. Among other statues in the gardens is one to perpetuate the memory of Querini, the Arctic explorer, with Esquimaux dogs at his side; Wagner also is here.

In the public gardens are the buildings in which international art exhibitions are held every other year. These exhibitions are not very remarkable, but it is extremely entertaining to be in Venice on the opening day, for all the State barges and private gondolas turn out in their richest colours, some with as many as eighteen rowers all bending to the oar at the same moment, and in a splendid procession they convey important gentlemen in tall hats to the scene of the ceremony, while overhead dirigible airships solemnly swim like distended whales.

Pavilions have been dedicated to the principal European nations, so that in a short walk you may learn how and what the English paint, the Germans, the Dutch, the Spanish, the Belgians, the Hungarians, the French, and the Italians. The difference is becoming more noticeable in subject than in manner. Since the Exhibition is on Italian soil, the Italians take the lion's share, their gallery being immense and varied. Much vigour and vivacity go to modern Italian art, but one finds few pictures or statues

BARTOLOMMEO COLLEONI
FROM THE STATUE BY ANDREA VERROCCHIO

to-day that are likely to be attracting our posterity to
Venice in the twenty-third century as the artists of the
fifteenth or sixteenth century are now attracting us.

Beyond the gardens, and connected with them by a bridge,
is the island of S. Elena, where the foundry was built in
which were recast the campanile bells after the fall of 1902.
This is a waste space of grass and a few trees, and here the
children play, and here, a few years ago, a football ground
—or campo di giuoco—was laid out, with a galvanized-
iron and pitch-pine shed called splendidly the Tribuna.
One afternoon I watched a match there between those
ancient enemies Venice and Genoa: ancient, that is, on the
sea, as Chioggia can tell. Owing to the heat the match
was not to begin until half-past four; but even then the
sun blazed. No sooner was I on the ground than I found
that some of the Genoese team were old friends, for in the
morning I had seen them in the water and on the sand at
the Lido, and wondered who so solid a band of brothers could
be. Then they had played a thousand pranks on each
other, the prime butt being the dark young Hercules
with a little gold charm on his mighty chest, which he
wore then and was wearing now, who guarded the Genoese
goal and whose name was Frederici.

It was soon apparent that Venice was outplayed in every
department, but they tried gallantly. The Genoese, I
imagine, had adopted the game much earlier; but an even
more cogent reason for their superiority was apparent
when I read through the list of players, for whereas
the Venetians were strictly Italian, I found in the Genoese
eleven several names from the conquering Land of
Cakes.

This island of S. Elena has more interest to the
English than meets the eye. It is not merely that it

17

than in the city itself. I say fewer mosquitoes with great emphasis, because there are a few, although every hotel manager will affirm that there are none. If by any chance he should say " practically none " you should insist at once on a net, because nights are never such agonies as when there are practically no mosquitoes. Even a single spy can completely rout sleep.

But in Venice, of course, a net is a necessity, particularly as the bite of a Venetian mosquito can be really a danger.

From July to the middle of September the sands of the Lido, on the Adriatic side, are covered with bathers and baskers. There is nowhere more buoyant or exhilarating water, nowhere out of the tropics a hotter sun. If I could order my life as I wished I should stay on the Lido every August. There one eats the lotus indeed.

The Venetians use the sands also as a Rotten Row, and a a job-master close to the landing station does a thriving trade not only by supplying horses but by teaching riding. His little grounds, with their jumps and gallops, are just beside the road for all to see, and the spectacle of Venetians learning to stick on is not the least of the Lido's Sunday amusements.

MADONNA WITH THE MAGDALEN AND S. CATHERINE

FROM THE PAINTING BY GIOVANNI BELLINI

In the Accademia

CHAPTER XXV

ON FOOT. IV: FROM THE DOGANA TO S. SEBASTIANO

The Dogana—A scene of shipping—The Giudecca Canal—On the Zattere—The debt of Venice to Ruskin—An artists' bridge—The painters of Venice—Turner and Whistler—A removal—S. Trovaso—Browning on the Zattere—S. Sebastiano—The life of Paul Veronese—S. Maria del Carmine—A Tuscan relief—A crowded calle—The grief of the bereaved.

FOR a cool day, after too much idling in gondolas, there is a good walk, tempered by an occasional picture, from the Custom House to S. Sebastiano and back to S. Mark's. The first thing is to cross the Grand Canal, either by ferry or a steamer to the Salute, and then all is easy.

The Dogana, as seen from Venice and from the water, is as familiar a sight almost as S. Mark's or the Doges' Palace, with its white stone columns, and the two giants supporting the globe, and the beautiful thistledown figure holding out his cloak to catch the wind. Everyone who has been to Venice can recall this scene and the decisive way in which the Dogana thrusts into the lagoon like the prow of a ship of which the Salute's domes form the canvas. But to see Venice from the Dogana is a rarer experience.

No sooner does one round the point—the Punta della Salute—and come to the Giudecca canal than everything changes. Palaces disappear and shipping asserts itself. One has promise of the ocean. Here there is always a huddle of masts, both of barges moored close together, mostly called after either saints or Garibaldi, with crude pictures of their namesakes painted on the gunwale, and of bigger vessels and perhaps a few pleasure yachts ; and as likely as not a big steamer is entering or leaving the harbour proper, which is at the far end of this Giudecca canal. And ever the water dances and there are hints of the great sea, of which the Grand Canal, on the other side of the Dogana, is ignorant.

The pavement of the Zattere, though not so broad as the Riva, is still wide, and, like the Riva, is broken by the only hills which the Venetian walker knows—the bridges. The first building of interest to which we come is the house, now a hotel, opposite a little alfresco restaurant above the water, which bears a tablet stating that it was Ruskin's Venetian home. That was in his later days, when he was writing *Fors Clavigera ;* earlier, while at work on *The Stones of Venice,* he had lived, as we have seen, near S. Zobenigo. Ruskin could be very rude to the Venetians : somewhere in *Fors* he refers to the " dirty population of Venice which is now neither fish nor flesh, neither noble nor fisherman," and he was furious alike with its tobacco and its steamboats ; yet for all that, if ever a distinguished man deserved honour at the hands of a city Ruskin deserves it from Venice. *The Stones of Venice* is such a book of praise as no other city ever had. In it we see a man of genius with a passion for the best and most sincere work devoting every gift of appraisement, exposition, and eulogy, fortified by the most loving thoroughness and patience, to the glory of the city's architecture, character, and art.

The first church is that of the Gesuati, but it is uninteresting. Passing on, we come shortly to a very attractive house with an overhanging first floor, most delectable

FROM THE DOGANA AT NIGHT

windows and a wistaria, beside a bridge; and looking up
the canal, the Rio di S. Trovaso, we see one of the
favourite subjects of artists in Venice—the huddled wooden
sheds of a squero, or boat-building yard; and as likely
as not some workmen will be firing the bottom of an old
gondola preliminary to painting her afresh. Venice can
show you artists at work by the score, on every fine day,
but there is no spot more certain in which to find one
than this bridge. It was here that I once overheard two
of these searchers for beauty comparing notes on the day's
fortune. "The bore is," said one, " that everything is so
good that one can never begin."

Of the myriad artists who have painted Venice, Turner
is the most wonderful. Her influence on him cannot be
stated in words : after his first residence in Venice, in the
early eighteen-thirties, when he was nearing sixty, his
whole genius became etherealized and a golden mist seems
to have swum for ever before his eyes. For many years
after that, whenever he took up his brush, his first thought
was to record yet another Venetian memory. In the Tate
Gallery and the National Gallery are many of the canvases to which this worshipper of light endeavoured with
such persistence and zeal to transfer some of the actual
glory of the universe : each one the arena of the unequal
struggle between pigment and atmosphere. But if
Turner failed, as every artist must fail, to recapture all,
his failures are always magnificent.

There are, of course, also numbers of his Venetian
water-colours.

Where Turner lived when in Venice, I have not been
able to discover ; but I feel sure it was not at Danieli's,
where Bonington was lodging on his memorable sojourn
there about 1825. Turner was too frugal for that. The

one of his letters he thus describes the view from his room : "Every morning at six, I see the sun rise ; far more wonderfully, to my mind, than his famous setting, which everybody glorifies. My bed-room window commands a perfect view—the still grey lagune, the few sea-gulls flying, the islet of S. Giorgio in deep shadow, and the clouds in a long purple rack, behind which a sort of spirit of rose burns up till presently all the ruins are on fire with gold, and last of all the orb sends before it a long column of its own essence apparently : so my day begins."

Still keeping beside the shipping, we proceed to the little Albergo of the Winds where the fondamenta ends. Here we turn to the right, cross a campo with a school beside it, and a hundred boys either playing on the stones or audible at their lessons within walls, and before us, on the other side of the canal, is the church of S. Sebastiano, where the superb Veronese painted and all that was mortal of him was laid to rest in 1588. Let us enter.

For Paolo Veronese at his best, in Venice, you must go to the Doges' Palace and the Accademia. Nearer home he is to be found in the Salon Carré in the Louvre, where his great banqueting scene hangs, and in our own National Gallery, notably in the beautiful S. Helena, more beautiful, to my mind, than anything of his in Venice, and not only more beautiful but more simple and sincere, and also in the magnificent " House of Darius ".

Not much is known of the life of Paolo Caliari of Verona. The son of a stone-cutter, he was born in 1528, and thus was younger than Titian and Tintoretto, with whom he was eternally to rank, who were born respectively in 1477 or 1487 and 1518. At the age of twenty-seven, Veronese went to Venice, and there he remained, with brief absences, for the rest of his life, full of work and

MADONNA AND SAINTS

FROM THE PAINTING BY BOCCACCINI

In the Accademia

honour. His first success came when he competed for the decoration of the ceiling of S. Mark's library and won. In 1560 he visited Rome in the Ambassador's service; in 1565 he married a Veronese woman. He died in 1588, leaving two painter sons. Vasari, who preferred Tuscans, merely mentions him.

More than any other painter, except possibly Velasquez, Veronese strikes the observer as an aristocrat. Everything that he did had a certain aloofness and distinction. In drawing, no Venetian was his superior, not even Tintoretto; and his colour, peculiarly his own, is characterized by a certain aureous splendour, as though he mixed gold with all his paints. Tintoretto and he, though latterly, in Titian's very old age, rivals, were close friends.

Veronese is the glory of this church, for it possesses not only his ashes but some fine works. It is a pity that the light is not good. The choir altar-piece is his and his also are the pictures of the martyrdom of S. Sebastian, S. Mark, and S. Marcellinus. They are vigorous and typical, but tell their stories none too well. Veronese painted also the ceiling, the organ, and other altar-pieces, and a bust of him is here to show what manner of man he was.

Close to the door, on the left as you leave, is a little Titian which might be very fine after cleaning.

There are two ways of returning from S. Sebastiano to, say, the iron bridge of the Accademia. One is direct, the other indirect. Let us take the indirect one first.

Leaving the church, you cross the bridge opposite its door and turn to the left beside the canal. At the far corner you turn into the fondamenta of the Rio di S. Margherita, which is a beautiful canal with a solitary cypress that few artists who come to Venice can resist. Keeping on the right side of the Rio di S. Margherita we come quickly to the campo of the Carmine, where another church awaits us.

S. Maria del Carmine is not beautiful, and such pictures as it possesses are only dimly visible—a " Circumcision " by Tintoretto, a Cima which looks as though it might be rather good, and four Giorgionesque scenes by Schiavone. But it has, what is rare in Venice, a bronze bas-relief from Tuscany, probably by Verrocchio and possibly by Leonardo himself. It is just inside the side door, on the right as you enter, and might easily be overlooked. Over the dead Christ bend women in grief; a younger woman stands by the cross, in agony; and in a corner are kneeling, very smug, the two donors, Federigo da Montefeltro and Battista Sforza.

Across the road is a Scuola with ceilings by the dashing Tiepolo—very free and luminous, with a glow that brought to my mind certain little pastorals by Karel du Jardin, of all people !

It is now necessary to get to the Campo di S. Barnaba, where under an arch a constant stream of people will be seen, making for the iron bridge of the Accademia, and into this stream you will naturally be absorbed ; and to find this campo you turn at once into the great campo of S. Margherita, leaving on your left an ancient building that is now a cinema and bearing to the right until you reach a canal. Cross the canal, turn to the left, and the Campo di S. Barnaba, with its archway under the houses, is before you.

The direct way from S. Sebastiano to this same point and the iron bridge is by the long Calle Avogadro and Calle Lunga running straight from the bridge before the church. There is no turning.

The Calle Lunga is the chief shopping centre of this

neighbourhood—its Merceria—and all the needs of poorer Venetian life are supplied there. But what most interested me was the death-notices in the shop windows. Every day there was a new one; sometimes two. These intimations of mortality are printed in a copper-plate type on large sheets of paper, usually with black edges and often with a portrait. They begin with records as to death, disease, and age, and pass on to eulogise the departed. It is the encomiastic mood that makes them so charming. If they mourn a man, he was the most generous, most punctilious, and most respected of Venetian citizens. His word was inviolable; as a husband and father he was something a little more than perfection, and his sorrowing and desolate widow and his eight children, two of them the merest bambini, will have the greatest difficulty in dragging through the tedious hours that must intervene before they are reunited to him in the paradise which his presence is now adorning. If they mourn a woman, she was a miracle of fortitude and piety, and nothing can ever efface her memory and no one take her place. "Ohè!" if only she had been spared, but death comes to all.

The composition is florid and emotional, with frequent exclamations of grief, and the intimations of mortality are so thorough and convincing that one has a feeling that many a death-bed would be alleviated if the dying man could hear what was to be printed about him.

After reading several one comes to the conclusion that a single author is responsible for many; and it may be a Venetian profession to write them. A good profession too, for they carry much comfort on their wings. Every one stops to read them, and I saw no cynical smile on any face.

CHAPTER XXVI

CHURCHES HERE AND THERE

S. Maria dei Miracoli—An exquisite casket—S. Maria Formosa—Pictures of old Venice—The Misericordia—Tintoretto's house—The Madonna dell' Orto—Tintoretto's " Presentation "—" The Last Judgment "—A Bellini—Titian's " Tobias "—S. Giobbe—Il Moro—Venetian by-ways—A few minor beauties.

AMONG the smaller beauties of Venice—its cabinet architectural gems, so to speak—S. Maria dei Miracoli comes first. This little church, so small as to be almost a casket, is tucked away among old houses on a canal off the Rio di S. Marina, and it might be visited after SS. Giovanni e Paolo as a contrast to the vastness of that "Panthéon de Venise," as the sacristan likes to call it. S. Maria dei Miracoli, so named from a picture of the Madonna over the altar which has performed many miracles, is a monument to the genius of the Lombardo family : Pietro and his sons having made it, in the fifteenth century, for the Amadi. To call the little church perfect is a natural impulse, although no doubt fault could be found with it : Ruskin, for example, finds some, but try as he will to be cross he cannot avoid conveying an impression of pleasure in it. For you and me, however, it is a joy unalloyed : a jewel of Byzantine Renaissance architecture, made more beautiful by gay and thoughtful detail. It is all of marble, white and coloured, with a massive wooden ceiling enriched and lightened by paint. Venice has nothing else at all like it. Fancy, in this city of aisles and columns and side chapels and wall tombs, a church with no interruptions or impediments whatever. The floor has its chairs (such poor cane-bottomed things too, just waiting for a rich patron to put in something good of rare wood, well carved and possibly a little gilded), and nothing else. The walls are unvexed. At the end is a flight of steps leading to the altar, and that is all, except that there is not an inch of the church which does not bear traces of a loving care. Every piece of the marble carving is worth study—the flowers and foliations, the birds and cupids and dolphins, and not least the saint with a book on the left ambone.

S. Maria Formosa, one of the churches mentioned in the beautiful legend of Bishop Magnus—to be built, you remember, where he saw a white cloud rest—which still has a blue door-curtain, is chiefly famous for a picture by a great Venetian painter who is too little represented in the city—Palma the elder. Palma loved beautiful, opulent women and rich colours, and even when he painted a saint, as he does here—S. Barbara (whose jawbone we saw in the S. Rocco treasury)—he could not much reduce his fine free fancy and therefore he made her more of a commanding queen than a Christian martyr. This church used to be visited every year by the Doge for a service in commemoration of the capture of the brides, of which we heard at S. Pietro in Castello. The campo, once a favourite centre for bull-fights and alfresco plays, has some fine palaces, notably those at No. 5250, the Malipiero, and No. 6125, the red Donà.

At the south of the campo is the Campiello Querini where we find the Palazzo Querini Stampalia, a seventeenth-century mansion, now the property of the city, which contains a library and a picture gallery. Among the older pictures which I recall are a Holy Family by Lorenzo di Credi in Room III and a Martyrdom of San Sebastian by Annibale Caracci in Room IV. A Judith boldly labelled Giorgione is not good. But although no very wonderful work of art is here, the house should be visited for its scenes of Venetian life, which bring the Venice of the past very vividly before one. Here you may see the famous struggles between the two factions of gondoliers, the Castellani and the Nicolotti, actually in progress on one of the bridges; the departure of the Bucintoro with the Doge on board to wed the Adriatic; the wedding ceremony off S. Niccolò; the marriage of a noble lady at the Salute; a bull-fight on the steps of the Rialto bridge; another in the courtyard of the Ducal Palace; a third in the Piazza of S. Mark in 1741; the game of pallone (now played in Venice no more) in the open space before the Gesuiti; fairs in the Piazzetta; church festivals and regattas. The paintings being contemporary, these records are of great value in ascertaining costumes, architecture, and so forth.

I speak elsewhere of the Palazzo Giovanelli as being an excellent destination to give one's gondolier when in doubt. After leaving it, with Giorgione's landscape still glowing in the memory, there are worse courses to take than to tell the poppé to row on up the Rio di Noale to the Misericordia, in which Tintoretto painted his "Paradiso". This great church, once the chief funeral church of Venice, is now a warehouse, lumber rooms, workshops. Beside it is the head-quarters of the *pompes funèbres*, wherein a jovial fellow in blue linen was singing as I passed.

At the back of the Misericordia is an ancient abbey now also secularized, with a very charming doorway surmounted by a pretty relief of cherubs. Farther north is the Sacco of the Misericordia opening into the lagoon. Here are stored the great rafts of timber that come down the rivers from the distant hill-country, and now and then you may see one of the huts in which the lumber-men live on the voyage.

From the Misericordia it is a short distance to the Fondamenta dei Mori, at No. 3399 of which is the Casa di Tintoretto, with a relief of the great painter's head upon it. Here he lived and died. The curious carved figures on this and the neighbouring house are thought to represent Morean merchants who once congregated here. Turning up the Campo dei Mori we come to the great chu. h of the Madonna dell' Orto, where Tintoretto was buried. It should be visited in the late afternoon, because the principal reason for seeing it is Tintoretto's "Pre sentation," and this lovely picture hangs in a dark chapel which obtains no light until the sinking sun penetrates its window and falls on the canvas. To my mind it is one of the most beautiful pictures that Tintoretto painted —a picture in which all his strength has turned to sweetness. We have studied Titian's version in the Accademia, where it has a room practically to itself (see opposite page 36); Tintoretto's is hung badly and has suffered seriously from age and conditions. Titian's was painted in 1540; this afterwards, and the painter cheerfully accepted the standard set by the earlier work. In both pictures there is a pyramidal spire the significance of which is unknown to me.

The Madonna dell' Orto is not a church much resorted to by visitors, as it lies far from the beaten track, but one can always find some one to open it, and as likely as not the sacristan will be seated by the rampino at the landing steps, awaiting custom.

18

The church was built in the fourteenth century as a shrine for a figure of the Madonna, which was dug up in a garden that spread hereabout and at once performed a number of miracles. On the façade is a noble slab of porphyry, and here is S. Christopher with his precious burden. The campanile has a round top and flowers sprout from the masonry. Within, the chief glory is Tintoretto. His tomb is in the chapel to the right of the chancel, where hang, on the left, his scene of "The Worship of the Golden Calf," and opposite it his "Last Judgment".

The "Last Judgment" is one of his Michael-Angelesque works and also one of his earliest, before he was strong enough or successful enough (often synonymous states) to be wholly himself. But it was a great effort, and the rushing cataract is a fine and terrifying idea. "The Worship of the Golden Calf" is a work interesting not only as a dramatic scriptural scene full of thoughtful detail, but as containing a portrait of the painter and his wife. Tintoretto is the most prominent of the calf's bearers; his Faustina is the woman in blue.

Two very different painters—the placid Cima and the serene Bellini—are to be seen here too, each happily represented. Cima has a sweet and gentle altar-piece depicting the Baptist and two saints, and Bellini's "Madonna and Child" is rich and warm and human.

The neighbouring church of S. Marziale is a gay little place famous for a "Tobias and the Angel" by Titian. This is a cheerful work. Tobias is a typical and very real Venetian boy, and his dog, a white and brown mongrel, also peculiarly credible. The chancel interrupts an "Annunciation," by Tintoretto's son, the angel being on one side and the Virgin on the other.

And now for the most north-westerly point of the city that I have reached—the church of S. Giobbe, off the squalid Cannaregio which leads to Mestre and Treviso. This church, which has, I suppose, the poorest congregation of all, is dedicated to one whom I had never before thought of either as Giobbe or as a saint, although his merits are unmistakable—Job. Its special distinction is the beautiful chapel of the high altar designed by the Lombardi (who made S. Maria dei Miracoli) for Doge Cristoforo Moro to the glory of S. Bernardino of Siena. S. Bernardino is represented, with S. Anthony of Padua and S. Lawrence. At each corner is an exquisite little figure holding a relief.

On the floor is the noble tombstone of the Doge himself (1462-1471) by Pietro Lombardi. Moro had a distinguished reign, which saw triumphs abroad and the introduction of printing into the city; but to the English he has yet another claim to distinction, and that is that most probably he was the Moro of Venice whom Shakespeare when writing *Othello* assumed to be a Moor.

The church also has a chapel with a Della Robbia ceiling and sculpture by Antonio Rossellino. The best picture is by Paris Bordone, a mellow and rich group of saints.

This book has been so much occupied with the high-ways of Venice—and far too superficially, I fear—that the by-ways have escaped attention; and yet the by-ways are the best. The by-ways, however, are for each of us separately, whereas the high-ways are common property : let that —and conditions of space—be my excuse. The by-ways must be sought individually, either straying where one's feet will or on some such thorough plan as that laid down in Col. Douglas's most admirable book, *Venice on Foot.* Some of my own unaided discoveries I may mention just as examples, but there is no real need : as good a harvest is for every quiet eye.

There used to be the tiniest medieval cobbler's shop you ever saw under a staircase in a courtyard reached by the

Sotto-portico Secondo Lucatello, not far from S. Zulian, with a medieval cobbler cobbling in it day and night. There is a relief of graceful boys on the Rio del Palazzo side of the Doges' Palace; there is a S. George and Dragon on a building on the Rio S. Salvatore just behind the Bank of Italy; there is a doorway at 3462 Rio di S. Margherita; there is the Campo S. Maria Mater Domini with a house on the north side into whose courtyard much ancient sculpture has been built. There is a yellow palace on the Rio di S. Marina whose reflection in the water is most beautiful. There is the overhanging street leading to the Ponte del Paradiso. There is the Campo of S. Giacomo dall' Orio, which is gained purely by accident, with its church in the midst and a vast trattoria close by, and beautiful vistas beneath this sottoportico and that. There are the two ancient chimneys seen from the lagoon on a house behind Danieli's. There is the lovely Gothic palace with a doorway and garden seen from the Ponte dell' Erbe—the Palazzo Van Axel. There is the red palace seen from the Fondamenta dell' Osmarin next the Ponte del Diavolo. There is in the little calle leading from the Campo Daniele Manin to the lovely piece of architecture known as the staircase dal Bovolo—a bovolo being a snail—from its convolutions. This staircase, which is a remnant of the Contarini palace and might be a distant relative of the tower of Pisa, is a shining reproach to the adjacent architecture, some of which is quite new. It is a miracle of delicacy and charm, and should certainly be sought for.

And above all there is the dancing reflection of the rippling water in the sun on the under sides of bridges seen from the gondola; and of all the bridges that give one this effect of gentle restless radiancy none is better than the Ponte S. Polo.

CHAPTER XXVII

GIORGIONE

IT will happen now and then that you will be in your gondola, with the afternoon before you, and will not have made up your mind where to go. It is then that I would have you remember the Palazzo Giovanelli. "The Palazzo Giovanelli, Rio di Noale," say to your gondolier; because this palace is not only open to the public but it contains the most sensuously beautiful picture in Venice— Giorgione's "Tempest". Giorgione, as I have said, is the one transcendentally great Venetian painter whom it is impossible, for certain, to find in any public gallery or church in the city of his adoption. There is a romantic scene at the Seminario next the Salute, an altar-piece in S. Rocco, another altar-piece in S. Giovanni Crisostomo, in each of which he may have had a hand. But none of these is Giorgione essential. For the one true work of this wistful beauty-adoring master we must seek the Palazzo Giovanelli.

You can enter the palace either from the water, or on foot at the Salizzada Santa Fosca, No. 2292. A massive custodian greets you and points to a winding stair. This you ascend and are met by a typical Venetian man-servant. Of the palace itself, which has been recently modernized, I have nothing to say. There are both magnificent and pretty rooms in it, and a little boudoir has a quite charming floor, and furniture covered in ivory silk. But everything is in my mind subordinated to the Giorgione : so much so that I have difficulty in writing that word Giovanelli at all. The pen will trace only the letters of the painter's name : it is to me the Palazzo Giorgione.

The picture, which I reproduce on the opposite page, is on an easel just inside a door and you come upon it suddenly. Not that any one could ever be completely ready for it; but you pass from one room to the next, and there it is—all green and blue and glory. Remember that Giorgione was not only a Venetian painter but in some ways the most remarkable and powerful of them all ; remember that his fellow-pupil Titian himself worshipped his genius and profited by it, and that he even influenced his master Bellini; and then remember that all the time you have been in Venice you have seen nothing that was unquestionably authentic and at the most only three pictures that might be his. It is as though Florence had but one Botticelli, or London but one Turner, or Madrid but one Velasquez. And then you turn the corner and find this !

The Venetian art that we have hitherto seen has been almost exclusively the handmaid of religion or the State. At the Ducal Palace we found the great painters exalting the Doges and the Republic; even the other picture in Venice which I associate with this for its pure beauty— Tintoretto's " Bacchus and Ariadne"—was probably an allegory of Venetian success. In the churches and at the Accademia we have seen the masters illustrating the

THE TEMPEST
FROM THE PAINTING BY GIORGIONE
In the Giovanelli Palace

Testaments Old and New. All their work has been for altars or church walls or large public places. We have seen nothing for a domestic wall but little mannered Longhis, without any imagination, or topographical Canalettos and Guardis. And then we turn a corner and are confronted by this!—not only a beautiful picture and a non-religious picture, but a picture painted to hang on a wall.

That was one of Giorgione's innovations : to paint pictures for private gentlemen. Another, was to paint pictures of sheer loveliness with no concern either with Scripture or history ; and this is one of his loveliest. It has all kinds of faults—and it is perfect. The drawing is not too good ; the painting is not too good ; that broken pillar is both commonplace and foolish ; and yet the work is perfect because a perfect artist made it. It is beautiful and mysterious and a little sad, all at once, just as an evening landscape can be, and it is unmistakably the work of one who felt beauty so deeply that his joyousness left him and the melancholy that comes of the knowledge of transitoriness took its place. Hence there is only one word that can adequately describe it and that is Giorgionesque.

The picture is known variously as " The Tempest," for a thunder-storm is working up ; as " The Soldier and the Gipsy," as " Adrastus and Hypsipyle," and as " Giorgione's Family ". In the last case the soldier watching the woman would be the painter himself (who never married) and the woman the mother of his child. Whatever we call it, the picture remains the same : profoundly beautiful, profoundly melancholy. A sense of impending calamity informs it. A lady observing it remarked to me, " Each is thinking thoughts unknown to the other " ; and they are thoughts of unhappy morrows.

This, the Giovanelli Giorgione, which in 1817 was in the Manfrini palace and was known as the "Famiglia di Giorgione," was the picture in all Venice—indeed the picture in all the world—which most delighted Byron. "To me," he wrote, "there are none like the Venetian— above all, Giorgione." *Beppo* has some stanzas on it. Thus :—

> They've pretty faces yet, those same Venetians,
>   Black eyes, arched brows, and sweet expressions still ;
> Such as of old were copied from the Grecians,
>   In ancient arts by moderns mimicked ill ;
> And like so many Venuses of Titian's
>   (The best's at Florence—see it, if ye will),
> They look when leaning over the balcony,
> Or stepped from out a picture by Giorgione,
>
> Whose tints are Truth and Beauty at their best;
>   And when you to Manfrini's palace go,
> That picture (howsoever fine the rest)
>   Is loveliest to my mind of all the show ;
> It may perhaps be also to *your* zest
>   And that's the cause I rhyme upon it so ;
> 'Tis but a portrait of his Son and Wife,
> And self, but *such* a Woman ! Love in life ;
>
> Love in full life and length, not love ideal,
>   No, nor ideal beauty, that fine name,
> But something better still, so very real,
>   That the sweet Model must have been the same ;
> A thing that you would purchase, beg, or steal,
>   Wer't not impossible, besides a shame ;
> The face recalls some face, as 'twere with pain,
> You once have seen, but ne'er will see again ;
>
> One of those forms which flit by us, when we
>   Are young, and fix our eyes on every face ;
> And, oh ! the Loveliness at times we see
>   In momentary gliding, the soft grace,

The Youth, the Bloom, the Beauty which agree,
In many a nameless being we retrace,
Whose course and home we knew not nor shall know,
Like the lost Pleiad seen no more below.

The Giovanelli picture is one of the paintings which all the critics agree to give to Giorgione, from Sir Sidney Colvin in the *Encyclopædia Britannica* to the very latest monographer, Signor Lionello Venturi, whose work, *Giorgione e Giorgionismo*, is a monument to the diversity of expert opinion. Giorgione, short as was his life, lived at any rate for thirty years and was known near and far as a great painter, and it is to be presumed that the work that he produced is still somewhere. But Signor Lionello Venturi reduces his output to the most meagre dimensions; the conclusion being that wherever his work may be, it is anywhere but in the pictures that bear his name. The result of this critic's heavy labours is to reduce the certain Giorgiones to thirteen, among which is the S. Rocco altarpiece. With great daring he goes on to say who painted all the others: Sebastian del Piombo this, Andrea Schiavone that, Romanino another, Titian another, and so forth. It may be so, but if one reads also the other experts—Sir Sidney Colvin, Morelli, Justi, the older Venturi, Mr. Berenson, Mr. Charles Ricketts, Mr. Herbert Cook—one is simply in a whirl. For all differ. Mr. Cook, for example, is lyrically rapturous about the two Padua panels, of which more anon, and their authenticity; Mr. Ricketts gives the Pitti "Concert" and the Caterina Cornaro to Titian without a tremor. Our own National Gallery "S. Liberale" is not mentioned by some at all; the Paris "Concert Champêtre," in which most of the judges believe so absolutely, Signor Lionello Venturi gives to Piombo. The Giovanelli picture and the Castel

Franco altar-piece alone remain above suspicion in every book.

Having visited the Giovanelli Palace, I found myself restless for this rare spirit, and therefore arranged a little diversion to Castel Franco, where he was born and where his great altar-piece is preserved.

But first let us look at Giorgione's career. Giorgio Barbarelli was born at Castel Franco in 1477 or 1478. The name by which we know him signifies the great Giorgio and was the reward of his personal charm and unusual genius. Very little is known of his life, Vasari being none too copious when it comes to the Venetians. What we do know, however, is that he was very popular, not only with other artists but with the fair, and in addition to being a great painter was an accomplished musician. His master was Giovanni Bellini, who in 1494, when we may assume that Giorgione, being sixteen, was beginning to paint, was approaching seventy.

Giorgione, says Vasari in an exultant passage, was "so enamoured of beauty in nature that he cared only to draw from life and to represent all that was fairest in the world around him". He had seen, says the same authority, "certain works from the hand of Leonardo which were painted with extraordinary softness, and thrown into powerful relief, as is said, by extreme darkness of the shadows, a manner which pleased him so much that he ever after continued to imitate it, and in oil painting approached very closely to the excellence of his model. A zealous admirer of the good in art, Giorgione always selected for representation the most beautiful objects that he could find, and these he treated in the most varied manner: he was endowed by nature with highly felicitous qualities, and gave to all that he painted, whether in oil

THE PRESENTATION
FROM THE PAINTING BY TINTORETTO
In the Church of the Madonna dell' Orto

or fresco, a degree of life, softness, and harmony (being more particularly successful in the shadows) which caused all the more eminent artists to confess that he was born to infuse spirit into the forms of painting, and they admitted that he copied the freshness of the living form more exactly than any other painter, not of Venice only, but of all other places."

Leonardo, who was born in 1452, was Giorgione's senior by a quarter of a century and one of the greatest names— if not quite the greatest name—in art when Giorgione was beginning to paint. A story says that they met when Leonardo was in Venice in 1500. One cannot exactly derive any of Giorgione's genius from Leonardo, but the fame of the great Lombardy painter was in the air, and we must remember that his master Verrocchio, after working in Venice on the Colleoni statue, had died there in 1488, and that Andrea da Solario, Leonardo's pupil and imitator, was long in Venice too. Leonardo and Giorgione share a profound interest in the dangerous and subtly alluring; but the difference is this, that we feel Leonardo to have been the master of his romantic emotions, while Giorgione suggests that for himself they could be too much.

It is not, however, influence upon Giorgione that is most interesting, but Giorgione's influence upon others. One of his great achievements was the invention of the *genre* picture. He was the first lyrical painter : the first to make a canvas represent a single mood, much as a sonnet does. He was the first to combine colour and pattern to no other end but sheer beauty. The picture had a subject, of course, but the subject no longer mattered. Il fuoco Giorgionesco—the Giorgionesque fire—was the phrase invented to describe the new wonder he brought into painting. A comparison of Venetian art before Giorgione and after shows instantly how this flame kindled. Not only did Giorgione give artists a liberty they had never enjoyed before, but he enriched their palettes. His colours burned and glowed. Much of the gorgeousness which we call Titianesque was born in the brain of Giorgione, Titian's fellow-worker, and (for Titian's birth date is uncertain : either 1477 or 1487) probably his senior. You may see the influence at work in our National Gallery : Nos. 41, 270, 35, and 635 by Titian would probably have been far different but for Giorgione. So stimulating was Giorgione's genius to Titian, who was his companion in Bellini's studio, that there are certain pictures which the critics divide impartially between the two, chief among them the "Concert" at the Pitti ; while together they decorated the Fondaco dei Tedeschi on the Grand Canal. It is assumed that Titian finished certain of Giorgione's works when he died in 1510. The plague which killed Giorgione killed also 20,000 other Venetians, and sixty-six years later, in another visitation of the scourge, Titian also died of it.

Castel Franco is five-and-twenty miles from Venice, but there are so few trains that it is practically a day's excursion there and back. I sat in the train with four commercial travellers and watched the water give way to maize, until chancing to look up for a wider view there were the blue mountains ahead of us, with clouds over them and here and there a patch of snow. Castel Franco is one of the last cities of the plain ; Browning's Asolo is on the slope above it, only four or five miles away.

The station being reached at last—for even in Italy journeys end—I rejected the offers of two cabmen, one cabwoman, and one bus driver, and walked. There was no doubt as to the direction, with the campanile of the duomo as a beacon. For a quarter of a mile the road is straight and narrow; then it broadens into an open space and Castel Franco appears. It is a castle indeed. All the old town is within vast crumbling red walls built on a mound with a moat around them. Civic zeal has trimmed the mound into public "grounds," and the moat is lively with ornamental ducks; while a hundred yards farther rises the white statue of Castel Franco's greatest son, no other than Giorgione himself, a dashing cavalier-like gentleman with a brush instead of a rapier. If he were like this, one can believe the story of his early death— little more than thirty—which came about through excessive love of a lady, she having taken the plague and he continuing to visit her.

Having examined the statue I penetrated the ramparts to the little town, in the midst of which is the church. It was however locked, as a band of children hastened to tell me: intimating also that if anyone on earth knew how to effect an entrance they were the little devils in question. So I was led to a side door, the residence of a fireman, and we pulled a bell, and in an instant out came the fireman to extinguish whatever was burning; but on learning my business he instantly became transformed into the gentlest of sacristans, returned for his key, and led me, followed by the whole pack of children, by this time greatly augmented, to a door up some steps on the farther side of the church. The pack was for coming in too, but a few brief yet sufficient threats from the sacristan acted so thoroughly that not only did they melt away then but were not there when I came out—this being, in Italy, unique as a merciful disappearance. More than merciful, miraculous, leading one to believe that Giorgione's picture really has supernatural powers.

The picture is on a wall behind the high altar, curtained. The fireman-sacristan pulled away the curtain, handed me a pair of opera glasses and sat down to watch me, a task in which he was joined by another man and a boy who had been cleaning the church. There they sat, the three of them, all huddled together, saying nothing, but staring hard at me (as I could feel) with gimlet eyes ; while a few feet distant I sat too, peering through the glasses at Giorgione's masterpiece, of which I give a reproduction on the opposite page.

It is very beautiful ; it grows more beautiful ; but it does not give me such pleasure as the Giovanelli pastoral. I doubt if Giorgione had the altar-piece temperament. He was not for churches ; and indeed there were so many brushes for churches, that his need never have been called upon. He was wholly individual, wistful, pleasure-seeking and pleasure-missing, conscious of the brevity of life and the elusiveness of joy ; of the earth earthy ; a kind of Keats in colour, with, as one critic—I think Mr. Ricketts —has pointed out, something of Rossetti too. Left to himself he would have painted only such idylls as the Giovanelli picture.

Yet this altar-piece is very beautiful, and, as I say, it grows more beautiful as you look at it, even under such conditions as I endured, and even after much restoration. The lines and pattern are Giorgione's, howsoever the re-painter may have toiled. The two saints are so kind and reasonable (and never let it be forgotten that we *may* have, in our National Gallery, one of the studies for S. Liberale), and so simple and natural in their movements and position ; the Madonna is at once so sweet and so little of a mother ; the landscape on the right is so very Giorgionesque, with all the right ingredients—the sea, the glade, the lovers, and

ALTAR-PIECE
BY GIORGIONE
At Castel Franco

the glow.   If anything disappoints it is the general colour
scheme, and in a Giorgione for that to disappoint is amazing.
Let us then blame the re-painter.   The influence of Giovanni Bellini in the arrangement is undoubtable; but
the painting was Giorgione's own and his the extra touch
of humanity.

Another day I went as far afield as Padua, also with
Giorgione in mind, for Baedeker, I noticed, gave one of
his pictures there a star.   Of Padua I want to write
much, but here, at this moment, Giotto being forgotten,
it is merely as a casket containing two (or more) Giorgiones that the city exists.   From Venice it is distant half
an hour by fast trains, or by way of Fusina, two hours.
I went on the occasion of this Giorgione pilgrimage by
fast train, and returned in the little tram to Fusina and
so, across the lagoon, into Venice, with the sun behind me,
and the red bricks of Venice flinging it back.

The picture gallery at Padua is crowded with pictures
of saints and the Madonna, few of them very good.   But
that is of no moment, since it has also three isolated
screens, upon each of which is inscribed the magic name.
The three screens carry four pictures—two long and
narrow, evidently panels from a cassone ; the others quite
small.   The best is No. 50, one of the two long narrow
panels which together purport to represent the story of
Adonis and Erys but do not take the duty of historian
very seriously.   Both are lovely, with a mellow sunset
lighting the scene.   Here and there in the glorious landscape occurs a nymph whose naked flesh burns with the
reflected fire ; here and there are lovers, and among
the darkling trees lurk beholders of the old romance.
The pictures remain in the vision much as rich autumnal
prospects can.

The other screen is more popular because the lower picture on it yet again shows us Leda and her uncomfortable amours—that favourite mythological legend. The little pictures are not equal to the larger ones, and No. 50 is by far the best, but all are beautiful, and all are exotics here. Do you suppose, however, that Signor Lionello Venturi will allow Giorgione to have painted a stroke to them? Not a bit of it. They come under the head of Giorgionismo. The little ones, according to him, are the work of that diligent and many-sided craftsman, "Anonimo"; the larger ones were painted by Romanino. But whether or not Giorgione painted any or all, the irrefutable fact remains that but for his genius and influence they would never have existed. He showed the way. The eyes of that beautiful sad pagan shine wistfully through.

According to Vasari, Giorgione, like his master Bellini, painted the Doge Leonardo Loredan ; but the picture, where is it? And where are others mentioned by Vasari and Ridolfi? So fervid a lover of nature and his art must have painted much ; yet there is but little left now. Can there be discoveries of Giorgiones still to be made? One wonders that it is possible for any of the glowing things from that hand to lie hidden : their colours should burn through any accumulation of rubbish, and now and then their pulses be heard.

THE ARMENIAN MONASTERY AND THE LAGOON

CHAPTER XXVIII AND LAST

ISLAND AFTERNOON'S ENTERTAINMENTS.
II: S. LAZZARO AND CHIOGGIA

An Armenian monastery—The black beards—An attractive cicerone—The refectory—Byron's Armenian studies—A little museum—A pleasant library—Tireless enthusiasm—The garden—Old age—The two campanili —Armenian proverbs—Chioggia—An amphibious town—The repulsiveness of roads—The return voyage—Porto Secco—Malamocco—An evening scene—The end.

A S one approaches the Lido from Venice one passes on the right two islands. The first is a grim enough colony, for thither are the male lunatics of Venice deported; but the second, with a graceful eastern campanile or minaret, a cool garden and warm red buildings, is alluring and serene, being no other than the island of S. Lazzaro, on which is situated the monastery of the Armenian Mechitarists, a little company of scholarly monks who collect old MSS., translate, edit and print their learned lucubrations, and instruct the young in religion and theology. Furthermore, the island is famous in our literature for having afforded Lord Byron a refuge, when, after too deep a draught of worldly beguilements, he decided to become a serious recluse; and for a brief while buried himself here, studied Armenian, and made a few translations: enough at any rate to provide himself with a cloistral interlude on which he might ever after reflect with pride and the wistful backward look of a born scholiast to whom the fates had been unkind.

According to a little history of the island which one of the brothers has written, S. Lazzaro was once a leper settlement. Then it fell into disuse, and in 1717 an Armenian monk of substance, one Mekhitar of Sebaste, was permitted to purchase it and here surround himself with companions. Since then the life of the little community has been easy and tranquil.

The extremely welcome visitor is received at the island stairs by a porter in uniform and led by him along the sunny cloisters and their very green garden to a waiting-room hung thickly with modern paintings: indifferent Madonnas and views of the city and the lagoon. By and by in comes a black-bearded father, in a cassock. All the Mechitarists, it seems, have black beards and cassocks and wide-brimmed beavers; and the young seminarists, whom one meets now and then in little bunches in Venice, are broad-brimmed, black-coated, and give promise of being hairy too. The father, who is genial and smiling, asks if we understand French, and deploring the difficulty of the English language, which has so many ways of pronouncing a single termination, whereas the Armenian never exceeds one, leads the way.

The first thing to admire is the garden once more, with its verdant cedars of Lebanon and a Judas-tree bent beneath its blood. On a seat in the midst another bearded father beneath a wide hat is reading a proof. And through the leaves the sunlight is splashing on the cloisters, pillars, and white walls.

The refectory is a long and rather sombre room. Here, says the little guide-book to the island, prepared by one of the fathers who had overcome most of the difficulties of our tongue, "before sitting down to dine grace is said in common; the president recites some prayer, two of the

scholars recite a psalm, the Lord's prayer is repeated and
the meal is despatched in silence. In the meantime one of
the novices appears in the pulpit and reads first a lesson
from the Bible, and then another from some other book.
The meal finished, the president rings a bell, the reader
retires to dine, the Community rises, they give thanks and
retire to the garden."

Next upstairs. We are taken first to the room which was
Byron's, where the visitors' book is kept. I looked from
the window to see upon what prospect those sated eyes
could fall, and found that immediately opposite is now
the huge Excelsior Hotel of the Lido. In Byron's day the
Lido was a waste, for bathing had hardly been invented.
The reverence in which the name and memory of his lordship
are still held suggests that he took in the simple brothers
very thoroughly. Not only have they his portrait and the
very table at which he sat, but his pens, inkstand, and
knife. His own letters on his refuge are interesting.
Writing to Moore in 1816 he says : " By way of divertise-
ment, I am studying daily, at an Armenian monastery, the
Armenian language. I found that my mind wanted something craggy to break upon ; and this—as the most difficult thing I could discover here for an amusement—I have
chosen, to torture me into attention. It is a rich language,
however, and would amply repay any one the trouble of
learning it. I try, and shall go on ; but I answer for
nothing, least of all for my intentions or my success." He
made a few metrical translations into Armenian, but his
principal task was to help with an English and Armenian
grammar, for which, when it was ready, he wrote a preface.
Byron usually came to the monastery only for the day,
but there was a bedroom for him which he occasionally
occupied. The superior, he says, had a "beard like a

meteor ". A brother who was there at the time and survived till the seventies told a visitor that his " Lordship was as handsome as a saint ".

In the lobby adjoining Byron's room are cases of autographs and photographs of distinguished visitors, such as Mr. Howells, Longfellow, Ruskin, Gladstone, King Edward VII when Prince of Wales, and so forth. Also a holograph sonnet on the monastery by Bryant. Elsewhere are various curiosities—dolls dressed in national costumes, medals, Egyptian relics, and so forth. In one case is some manna which actually fell from the skies in Armenia during a famine in 1833.

The chief room of the library contains not only its priceless MSS., but a famous mummy which the experts put at anything from 2200 to 3500 years old. Another precious possession is a Buddhist ritual on papyrus, which an Armenian wandering in Madras discovered and secured. The earliest manuscript dates from the twelfth century. In a central case are illuminated books and some beautiful bindings ; and I must put on record that if ever there was a cicerone who displayed no weariness and disdained merely mechanical interest in exhibiting for the thousandth time his treasures, it is Father Vardan Hatzouni. But the room is so pleasant that, were it not that one enjoys such enthusiasm and likes to stimulate it by questions, it would be good merely to be in it without too curiously examining its possessions.

Downstairs is a rather frigid little church, where an embroidered cloth is shown, presented by Queen Margherita. The S. Lazzaro Armenians, I may say, seem always to have attracted gifts, one of their great benefactors being Napoleon III. They are so simple and earnest and unobtrusive — and, I am sure, grateful —

that perhaps it is natural to feel generous towards them.

Finally we were shown to the printing-room, on our way to which, along the cloisters from the church, we passed through a group of elderly monks, cheerfully smoking and gossiping, who rose and made the most courtly salutation. Here we saw the printing-presses, some of English make, and then the books that these presses turn out. Two of these I bought—the little pamphlet from which I have already quoted and a collection of Armenian proverbs translated into English.

The garden is spreading and very inviting, and no sooner were we outside the door than Father Hatzouni returned to some horticultural pursuit. The walks are long and shady and the lagoon is lovely from every point ; and Venice is at once within a few minutes and as remote as a star.

In the garden is an enclosure for cows and poultry, and the little burial-ground where the good Mechitarists are laid to rest when their placid life is done. Among them is the famous poet of the community, the Reverend Father Gonidas Pakraduni, who translated into Armenian both the *Iliad* and *Paradise Lost*, as well as writing epics of his own. The *Paradise Lost* is dedicated to Queen Victoria. Some of the brothers have lived to a very great age, and Mr. Howells in his delightful account of a visit to this island tells of one, George Karabagiak, who survived until he was 108 and died in September, 1863. Life, it seems, can be too long; for having an illness in the preceding August, from which he recovered, the centenarian remarked sadly to one of his friends, " l fear that God has abandoned me and I shall live ". Being asked how he was, when his end was really imminent, he replied " Well," and died.

As we came away we saw over the wall of the playground the heads of a few black-haired boys, embryo priests; but they wore an air of gravity beyond their years. The future perhaps bears on them not lightly. They were not romping or shouting, nor were any in the water; and just below, at the edge of the sea, well within view and stone range, I noticed an empty bottle on its end, glistening in the sun. Think of so alluring a target disregarded and unbroken by an English school!

The returning gondola passes under the walls of the male mad-house. Just before reaching this melancholy island there is a spot at which it is possible still to realize what Venice was like when S. Mark's campanile fell, for one has the S. Giorgio campanile and this other so completely in line that S. Giorgio's alone is visible.

Some of the Armenian proverbs are very shrewd and all have a flavour of their own. Here are a few :—

" What can the rose do in the sea, and the violet before the fire ? "

"The mother who has a daughter always has a hand in her purse."

" Every one places wood under his own pot."

"The day can dawn without the cock's crowing."

" If you cannot become rich, become the neighbour of a rich man."

"Our dog is so good that the fox has pupped in our poultry house."

" One day the ass began to bray. They said to him : ' What a beautiful voice ! ' Since then he always brays."

" Whether I eat or not I shall have the fever, so better eat and have the fever."

"The sermon of a poor priest is not heard."

" When he rides a horse, he forgets God ; when he comes down from the horse, he forgets the horse."

" Dine with thy friend, but do no business with him."

" To a bald head a golden comb."

"Choose your consort with the eyes of an old man, and choose your horse with the eyes of a young man."

" A good girl is worth more than seven boys."

" When you are in town, if you observe that people wear the hat on one side, wear yours likewise."

" The fox's last hole is the furrier's shop."

" The Kurd asked the barber : ' Is my hair white or black ?' The other answered him : ' I will put it before you, and you will see '."

" He who mounts an ass, has one shame ; he who falls from it, has two."

" Be learned, but be taken for a fool."

Of a grumbler : " Every one's grain grows straight ; mine grows crooked ".

Of an impatient man : " He feeds the hen with one hand and with the other he looks for her eggs ".

I have not printed these exactly as they appear in the little pamphlet, because one has only to turn one page to realize that what the S. Lazzaro press most needs is a proof-reader.

I said at the beginning of this book that the perfect way to approach Venice for the first time is from Chioggia. But that is not too easy. What, however, is quite easy is to visit Chioggia from Venice and then, re-turning, catch some of the beauty—without, however, all the surprise and wonder—of that approach.

Steamers leave the Riva, opposite Danieli's, several times a day. They take their easy way up the lagoon towards the Lido for a little while, and then turn off to the right, always keeping in the enclosed channel, for eighteen miles. I took the two o'clock boat on a hot day and am not ashamed to confess that upon the outward voyage I converted it (as indeed did almost everybody else) into a dormitory. But Chioggia awakened me, and upon the voyage back I missed, I think, nothing.

Chioggia is amphibious. Parallel with its broad main street, with an arcade and cafés under awnings on one side, and in the roadway such weird and unfamiliar objects as vehicles drawn by horses, and even motor-cars noisy and fussy, is a long canal packed with orange-sailed fishing boats and crossed by many little bridges and one superb broad white one. All the men fish; all the women and children sit in the little side streets, making lace, knitting, and stringing beads. Beside this canal the dirt is abnormal, but it carries with it the usual alleviation of extreme picturesqueness, so that Chioggia is always artist-ridden.

The steamer gives you an hour in which to drift about in the sunshine and meditate upon the inferiority of any material other than water for the macadamizing of roads. There are sights too: Carpaccio's very last picture, painted in 1520, in S. Domenico; a Corso Vittorio Emmanuele; a cathedral; a Giardino Pubblico; and an attractive stone parapet with a famous Madonna on it revered by fishermen and sailors. The town is historically important, for was not the decisive battle of Chioggia fought here in 1379 between the Venetians and their ancient enemies the Genoese?

But I cannot pretend that Chioggia is to my taste. To come to it on the journey to Venice, knowing what is in store, might put one in a mood to forgive its earthy situation and earthy ways; but when, all in love with water, one visits it from Venice, one resents the sound and sight of traffic, the absence of gondolas, and the presence of heat unalleviated.

At five o'clock, punctually to the minute, the steamer leaves the quay and breaks the stillness of the placid lagoon. A few fishing boats are dotted about, one of them with sails of yellow and blue, as lovely as a Chinese rug; others the deep red that Clara Montalba has reproduced so charmingly; and a few with crosses or other religious symbols. The boat quickly passes the mouth of the Chioggia harbour, the third spot at which the long thread of land which divides the lagoon from the Adriatic is pierced, and then makes for Palestrina, surely the narrowest town on earth, with a narrower walled cemetery just outside, old boats decaying on the shore, and the skin of naked boys who frolic at the water's edge glowing in the declining sun. Never were such sun-traps as these strips of towns along this island bank, only a few inches above sea level and swept by every wind that blows.

Hugging the coast, which is fringed with tamarisk and an occasional sumach, we come next to Porto Secco, another tiny settlement among vegetable gardens. Its gay church, yellow washed, with a green door and three saints on the roof, we can see inverted in the water, so still is it, until our gentle wash blurs all. Porto Secco's front is all pinks and yellows, reds, ochres, and white; and the sun is now so low that the steamer's shadow creeps along these façades, keeping step with the boat. More market gardens, and then the next mouth of the harbour (known as Malamocco, although Malamocco town is still distant), with a coastguard station, a fort, acres of coal and other signs of militancy on the farther side. It is here that the Lido proper begins and the island broadens out into meadows.

At the fort pier we are kept waiting for ten minutes while a live duck submits to be weighed for fiscal purposes, and the delay gives an old man with razor-fish a chance to sell several pennyworths. By this time the sun is very near the horizon, setting in a roseate sky over a lagoon of jade. There is not a ripple. The tide is very low. Sea-birds fleck with white the vast fields of mud. The peacefulness of it all under such unearthly beauty is almost disquieting.

Next comes Malamocco itself, of which not much is seen but a little campo—almost an English village green —by the pier, and children playing on it. Yet three thousand people live here, chiefly growers of melons, tomatoes, and all the picturesque vegetables which are heaped up on the bank of the Grand Canal in the Rialto market and are carried to Venice in boats day after day for ever.

Malamocco was a seat of ducal government when Venice was only a village, and not until the seventh century did the honours pass to Venice : hence a certain alleged sense of superiority on the part of the Malamoccans, although not only has the original Malamocco but the island on which it was built disappeared beneath the tide. Popilia too, a city once also of some importance, is now the almost deserted island of Poveglia which we pass just after leaving Malamocco, as we steam along that splendid wide high-way direct to Venice—between the mud-flats and the sea-mews and those countless groups of piles marking the channel, which always resemble bunches of giant asparagus and sometimes seem to be little companies of drowning people who have sworn to die together.

Here we overtake boats on the way to the Rialto market, some are hastening with oars, others allowing their yellow sails to do the work, heaped high with vegetables and fruit. Just off the mud the sardine catchers are at work, waist high in the water.

The sun has now gone, the sky is burning brighter and brighter, and Venice is to be seen : either between her islands or peeping over them. S. Spirito, now a powder magazine, we pass, and S. Clemente, with its barrack-like red buildings, once a convent and now a refuge for poor mad women, and then La Grazia, where the consumptives are sent, and so we enter the narrow way between the Giudecca and S. Giorgio Maggiore, on the other side of which Venice awaits us in all her twilight loveliness. And disembarking we are glad to be at home again. For even an afternoon's absence is like an act of treachery.

And here, re-entering Venice in the way in which, in the first chapter, I advised all travellers to get their first sight of her, I come to an end, only too conscious of how ridiculous is the attempt to write a single book on this city. Where many books could not exhaust the theme, what chance has only one ? At most it can say and say again (like all of the singing) how it was good !

Venice needs a whole library to describe her : a book on her churches and a book on her palaces ; a book on her painters and a book on her sculptors ; a book on her old families and a book on her new ; a book on her builders and a book on her bridges ; a book—but why go on ? The fact is self-evident.

Yet there is something that a single book can do : it can testify to delight received and endeavour to kindle an enthusiasm in others ; and that I may perhaps have done.

INDEX

PRINTED IN GREAT BRITAIN AT THE UNIVERSITY PRESS, ABERDEEN

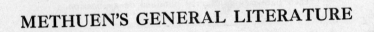

METHUEN'S GENERAL LITERATURE

A SELECTION OF

MESSRS. METHUEN'S
PUBLICATIONS

This Catalogue contains only a selection of the more important books published by Messrs. Methuen. A complete catalogue of their publications may be obtained on application.

PART I. GENERAL LITERATURE

Allen (R. Wilberforce)
METHODISM AND MODERN WORLD PROBLEMS. *Crown 8vo.* 7s. 6d. net.

Bain (F. W.)
A DIGIT OF THE MOON. THE DESCENT OF THE SUN. A HEIFER OF THE DAWN. IN THE GREAT GOD'S HAIR. A DRAUGHT OF THE BLUE. AN ESSENCE OF THE DUSK. AN INCARNATION OF THE SNOW. A MINE OF FAULTS. THE ASHES OF A GOD. BUBBLES OF THE FOAM. A SYRUP OF THE BEES. THE LIVERY OF EVE. THE SUBSTANCE OF A DREAM. *All Fcap. 8vo.* 5s. net. AN ECHO OF THE SPHERES. *Wide Demy 8vo.* 10s. 6d. net.

Balfour (Sir Graham)
THE LIFE OF ROBERT LOUIS STEVENSON. *Twentieth Edition. In one Volume. Cr. 8vo. Buckram,* 7s. 6d. net.

Barker (Ernest)
NATIONAL CHARACTER. *Demy 8vo.* 12s. 6d. net.

Belfield (Reginald)
FROM LANDSCAPE TO STUDIO. Illustrated. *Fcap. 4to.* 12s. 6d. net.

Belloc (Hilaire)
PARIS. THE PYRENEES. *Each 8s. 6d. net.* ON NOTHING. HILLS AND THE SEA. ON SOMETHING. FIRST AND LAST. THIS AND THAT AND THE OTHER. ON. ON EVERYTHING. ON ANYTHING. EMMANUEL BURDEN. *Each 3s. 6d. net.* MARIE ANTOINETTE. 18s. net. A HISTORY OF ENGLAND. In 4 vols. Vols. I and II. 15s. net each.

Birmingham (George A.)
A WAYFARER IN HUNGARY. Illustrated. 8s. 6d. net. A WAYFARER IN IRELAND. Illustrated. 7s. 6d. net. SPILLIKINS: a Book of Essays. 5s. net. SHIPS AND SEALING WAX: a Book of Essays. 5s. net.

Bowles (George F. S.)
THE STRENGTH OF ENGLAND. *Demy 8vo.* 8s. 6d. net.

Bryden (H. A.)
HORN AND HOUND: Memories of Hunting. Illustrated. *Demy 8vo.* 15s. net.

Bulley (M. H.)
ART AND COUNTERFEIT. Illustrated. 15s. net. ANCIENT AND MEDIEVAL ART : A SHORT HISTORY. Second Edition, Revised. Crown 8vo. 10s. 6d. net.

Burns (Robert)
THE POEMS AND SONGS. Edited by ANDREW LANG. Fourth Edition. Wide Demy 8vo. 10s. 6d. net.

Chandler (Arthur), D.D.
ARA CŒLI. 5s. net. FAITH AND EXPERI-ENCE. 5s. net. THE CULT OF THE PASS-ING MOMENT. 6s. net. THE ENGLISH CHURCH AND REUNION. 5s. net. SCALA MUNDI. 4s. 6d. net.

Chesterton (G. K.)
THE BALLAD OF THE WHITE HORSE. ALL THINGS CONSIDERED. TREMEN-DOUS TRIFLES. FANCIES VERSUS FADS. CHARLES DICKENS. Each Fcap. 8vo. 3s. 6d. net. ALARMS AND DISCURSIONS. A MISCELLANY OF MEN. THE USES OF DIVERSITY. THE OUTLINE OF SANITY. Each Fcap. 8vo. 6s. net. A GLEAMING COHORT. Fcap. 8vo. 2s. 6d. net. WINE, WATER, AND SONG. Fcap. 8vo. 1s. 6d. net.

Clutton-Brock (A.)
WHAT IS THE KINGDOM OF HEAVEN ? ESSAYS ON ART. SHAKESPEARE'S HAM-LET. Each 5s. net. ESSAYS ON BOOKS. MORE ESSAYS ON BOOKS. ESSAYS ON LIFE. ESSAYS ON RELIGION. ESSAYS ON LITERATURE AND LIFE. Each 6s. net. SHELLEY, THE MAN AND THE POET. 7s. 6d. net.

Cowling (George H.)
A PREFACE TO SHAKESPEARE. Illustrated. 5s. net. CHAUCER. Illustrated. 6s. net.

Crawley (Ernest)
THE MYSTIC ROSE. Revised and En-larged by THEODORE BESTERMAN. Two Vols. Demy 8vo. £1 10s. net.

Cromer (Countess of)
LAMURIAC and other Sketches. Small Demy 8vo. 6s. net.

Dolls' House (The Queen's)
THE BOOK OF THE QUEEN'S DOLLS' HOUSE. Vol. I. THE HOUSE, Edited by A. C. BENSON, C.V.O., and Sir LAWRENCE WEAVER, K.B.E. Vol. II. THE LIBRARY, Edited by E. V. LUCAS. Profusely Illustrated. A Limited Edi-tion. Crown 4to. £6 6s. net. EVERYBODY'S BOOK OF THE QUEEN'S DOLLS' HOUSE. An abridged edition of the above. Illustrated. Crown 4to. 5s. net.

Edwardes (Tickner)
THE LORE OF THE HONEYBEE. Thir-teenth Edition. 7s. 6d. net. BEEKEEPING FOR ALL. 3s. 6d. net. THE BEE-MASTER OF WARRILOW. Third Edition. 7s. 6d. net. All Illustrated. BEE-KEEPING DO's AND DON'TS. 2s. 6d. net.

Einstein (Albert)
RELATIVITY : THE SPECIAL AND GEN-ERAL THEORY. 5s. net. SIDELIGHTS ON RELATIVITY. 3s. 6d. net. THE MEANING OF RELATIVITY. 5s. net. THE BROWNIAN MOVEMENT. 5s. net. Other books on the Einstein Theory. AN INTRODUCTION TO THE THEORY OF RELATIVITY. By LYNDON BOLTON. 5s. net.
THE PRINCIPLE OF RELATIVITY. By A. EINSTEIN, H. A. LORENTZ, H. MINKOWSKI and H. WEYL. With Notes by A. SOMMERFELD. 12s. 6d. net.
Write for Complete List

Erman (Adolph)
THE LITERATURE OF THE ANCIENT EGYPTIANS. Translated by Dr. A. M. BLACKMAN. Demy 8vo. £1 1s. net.

Fouquet (Jean)
THE LIFE OF CHRIST AND HIS MOTHER. From Fouquet's "Book of Hours." Edited by FLORENCE HEYWOOD, B.A. With 24 Plates in Colours. Wide Royal 8vo. £3 3s net.

Fyleman (Rose)
FAIRIES AND CHIMNEYS. THE FAIRY GREEN. THE FAIRY FLUTE. THE RAINBOW CAT. EIGHT LITTLE PLAYS FOR CHILDREN. FORTY GOOD-NIGHT TALES. FAIRIES AND FRIENDS. THE ADVENTURE CLUB. FORTY GOOD-MOR-NING TALES. Each 3s. 6d. net. A SMALL CRUSE, 4s. 6d. net. THE ROSE FYLEMAN FAIRY BOOK. Illustrated. 10s. 6d. net. LETTY. Illustrated. 6s. net. A LITTLE CHRISTMAS BOOK. Illustrated. 2s. net.

Gibbon (Edward)
THE DECLINE AND FALL OF THE ROMAN EMPIRE. With Notes, Appendixes, and Maps, by J. B. BURY. Illustrated. Seven volumes. Demy 8vo. 15s. net each volume. Also, unillustrated. Crown 8vo. 7s. 6d. net each volume.

Glover (T. R.)
THE CONFLICT OF RELIGIONS IN THE EARLY ROMAN EMPIRE. POETS AND PURITANS. VIRGIL. Each 10s. 6d. net. FROM PERICLES TO PHILIP. 12s. 6d. net.

4   MESSRS. METHUEN'S PUBLICATIONS

Graham (Harry)

THE WORLD WE LAUGH IN: More Deportmental Ditties. Illustrated by "FISH." *Sixth Edition. Fcap. 8vo.* 5s. net. STRAINED RELATIONS. Illustrated by H. STUART MENZIES and HENDY. *Royal 16mo.* 6s. net.

Grahame (Kenneth)

THE WIND IN THE WILLOWS. *Nineteenth Edition. Crown 8vo.* 7s. 6d. net. Also, Illustrated by NANCY BARNHART. *Small, 4to.* 10s. 6d. net. Also unillustrated. *Fcap. 8vo.* 3s. 6d. net.

Hadfield (J. A.)

PSYCHOLOGY AND MORALS. *Sixth Edition. Crown 8vo.* 6s. net.

Hall (H. R.)

THE ANCIENT HISTORY OF THE NEAR EAST. *Sixth Edition, Revised. Demy 8vo.* £1 1s. net. THE CIVILIZATION OF GREECE IN THE BRONZE AGE. Illustrated. *Wide Royal 8vo.* £1 10s. net.

Hamer (Sir W. H.), and Hutt (C. W.)

A MANUAL OF HYGIENE. Illustrated. *Demy 8vo.* £1 10s. net.

Hewlett (Maurice)

THE LETTERS OF MAURICE HEWLETT. Edited by LAURENCE BINYON. Illustrated. *Demy 8vo.* 18s. net.

Hind (A. M.)

A CATALOGUE OF REMBRANDT'S ETCHINGS. Two Vols. Profusely Illustrated. *Wide Royal 8vo.* £1 15s. net.

Holdsworth (W. S.)

A HISTORY OF ENGLISH LAW. Nine Volumes. *Demy 8vo.* £1 5s. net each.

Hudson (W. H.)

A SHEPHERD'S LIFE. Illustrated. *Demy 8vo.* 10s. 6d. net. Also, unillustrated. *Fcap. 8vo.* 3s. 6d. net.

Hutton (Edward)

CITIES OF SICILY. Illustrated. 10s. 6d. net. MILAN AND LOMBARDY. THE CITIES OF ROMAGNA AND THE MARCHES. SIENA AND SOUTHERN TUSCANY. VENICE AND VENETIA. THE CITIES OF SPAIN. NAPLES AND SOUTHERN ITALY. Illustrated. *Each,* 8s. 6d. net. A WAYFARER IN UNKNOWN TUSCANY. THE CITIES OF UMBRIA. COUNTRY WALKS ABOUT FLORENCE. ROME. FLORENCE AND NORTHERN TUSCANY. Illustrated. *Each,* 7s. 6d. net.

Imms (A. D.)

A GENERAL TEXTBOOK OF ENTOMOLOGY. Illustrated. *Royal 8vo.* £1 16s. net.

Inge (W. R.), D.D., Dean of St. Paul's

CHRISTIAN MYSTICISM. (The Bampton Lectures of 1899.) *Sixth Edition. Crown 8vo.* 7s. 6d. net.

Jackson (H. C.)

OSMAN DIGNA. *Demy 8vo.* 12s. 6d. net.

Kipling (Rudyard)

BARRACK-ROOM BALLADS. 241st Thousand.

THE SEVEN SEAS. 180th Thousand.

THE FIVE NATIONS. 139th Thousand.

DEPARTMENTAL DITTIES. 111th Thousand.

THE YEARS BETWEEN. 95th Thousand. Four Editions of these famous volumes of poems are now published, viz. :— *Crown 8vo. Buckram,* 7s. 6d. net. *Fcap. 8vo. Cloth,* 6s. net. *Leather,* 7s. 6d. net. Service Edition. Two volumes each book. *Square Fcap. 8vo.* 3s. net each volume.

A KIPLING ANTHOLOGY—Verse. *Fcap. 8vo. Cloth,* 6s. net. *Leather,* 7s. 6d. net.

TWENTY POEMS FROM RUDYARD KIPLING. 447th Thousand. *Fcap. 8vo.* 1s. net.

A CHOICE OF SONGS. *Second Edition. Fcap. 8vo.* 2s. net.

Lamb (Charles and Mary)

THE COMPLETE WORKS. Edited by E. V. LUCAS. A New and Revised Edition in Six Volumes. With Frontispieces. *Fcap. 8vo.* 6s. net each. The volumes are : I. MISCELLANEOUS PROSE. II. ELIA AND THE LAST ESSAYS OF ELIA. III. BOOKS FOR CHILDREN. IV. PLAYS AND POEMS. V. and VI. LETTERS.

SELECTED LETTERS. Chosen and Edited by G. T. CLAPTON. *Fcap. 8vo.* 3s. 6d. net.

THE CHARLES LAMB DAY BOOK. Compiled by E. V. LUCAS. *Fcap. 8vo.* 6s. net.

Lankester (Sir Ray)

SCIENCE FROM AN EASY CHAIR. SCIENCE FROM AN EASY CHAIR : Second Series. DIVERSIONS OF A NATURALIST. GREAT AND SMALL THINGS. Illustrated. *Crown 8vo.* 7s. 6d. net. SECRETS OF EARTH AND SEA. Illustrated. *Crown 8vo.* 8s. 6d. net.

Lodge (Sir Oliver)

MAN AND THE UNIVERSE (*Twentieth Edition*). THE SURVIVAL OF MAN (*Seventh Edition*). *Each Crown 8vo. 7s. 6d. net.* RAYMOND (*Thirteenth Edition*). *Demy 8vo. 10s. 6d. net.* RAYMOND REVISED. *Crown 8vo. 6s. net.* RELATIVITY (*Fourth Edition*). *Fcap.8vo. 1s.net.*

Lucas (E. V.)

THE LIFE OF CHARLES LAMB. 2 Vols. £1 1s. net. EDWIN AUSTIN ABBEY, R.A. 2 Vols. £6 6s. net. VERMEER OF DELFT. 10s. 6d. net. A WANDERER IN ROME. A WANDERER IN HOLLAND. A WANDERER IN LONDON. LONDON REVISITED (Revised). A WANDERER IN PARIS. A WANDERER IN FLORENCE. A WANDERER IN VENICE. *Each 10s. 6d. net.* A WANDERER AMONG PICTURES. 8s. 6d. net. E. V. LUCAS'S LONDON. £1 net. INTRODUCING LONDON. 2s. 6d. net. THE OPEN ROAD. 6s. net. Also, illustrated. 10s. 6d. net. Also, India Paper. *Leather, 7s. 6d. net.* THE FRIENDLY TOWN. FIRESIDE AND SUNSHINE. CHARACTER AND COMEDY. *Each 6s. net.* THE GENTLEST ART. 6s. 6d. net. AND THE SECOND POST. 6s. net. Also, together in one volume 7s. 6d. net. HER INFINITE VARIETY. GOOD COMPANY. ONE DAY AND ANOTHER. OLD LAMPS FOR NEW. LOITERER'S HARVEST. CLOUD AND SILVER. A BOSWELL OF BAGHDAD. 'TWIXT EAGLE AND DOVE. THE PHANTOM JOURNAL. GIVING AND RECEIVING. LUCK OF THE YEAR. ENCOUNTERS AND DIVERSIONS. ZIGZAGS IN FRANCE. EVENTS AND EMBROIDERIES. 365 DAYS (AND ONE MORE). *Each 6s. net.* SPECIALLY SELECTED. 5s. net. URBANITIES, 7s. 6d. net. *Each illustrated by* G. L. STAMPA. YOU KNOW WHAT PEOPLE ARE. *Illustrated by* GEORGE MORROW. 5s. net. THE SAME STAR: A Comedy in Three Acts. 3s. 6d. net. THE BRITISH SCHOOL. 6s. net. LITTLE BOOKS ON GREAT MASTERS. *Each 5s. net.* ROVING EAST AND ROVING WEST. 5s. net. PLAYTIME AND COMPANY. 7s. 6d. net. See also **Dolls' House (The Queen's)** and **Lamb (Charles)**

Lynd (Robert)

THE MONEY BOX. THE ORANGE TREE. THE LITTLE ANGEL. *Each Fcap. 8vo. 6s. net.* THE BLUE LION. THE PEAL OF BELLS. *Each Fcap. 8vo. 3s. 6d. net.*

Marie Louise (H.H. Princess)

A CHOICE OF CAROLS. *Fcap. 4to. 2s. 6d. net.* LETTERS FROM THE GOLD COAST. *Illustrated. Demy 8vo. 16s. net.*

McDougall (William)

AN INTRODUCTION TO SOCIAL PSYCHOLOGY (*Twentieth Edition, Revised*). 10s. 6d. net. NATIONAL WELFARE AND NATIONAL DECAY. 6s. net. AN OUTLINE OF PSYCHOLOGY *Third Edition*). 12s. net. AN OUTLINE OF ABNORMAL PSYCHOLOGY. 15s. net. BODY AND MIND (*Fifth Edition*). THE CONDUCT OF LIFE. *Each 12s. 6d. net.* ETHICS AND SOME MODERN WORLD PROBLEMS (*Second Edition*). 7s. 6d. net.

Mackenzie-Rogan (Lt.-Col. J.)

FIFTY YEARS OF ARMY MUSIC. *Illustrated. Demy 8vo. 15s. net.*

Maeterlinck (Maurice)

THE BLUE BIRD. 6s. net. Also, illustrated by F. CAYLEY ROBINSON. 10s. 6d. net. MARY MAGDALENE. 2s. net. DEATH. 3s. 6d. net. OUR ETERNITY. 6s. net. THE UNKNOWN GUEST. 6s. net. POEMS. 5s. net. THE WRACK OF THE STORM. 6s. net. THE MIRACLE OF ST. ANTHONY. 3s. 6d. net. THE BURGOMASTER OF STILEMONDE. 5s. net. THE BETROTHAL. 6s. net. MOUNTAIN PATHS. 6s. net. THE STORY OF TYLTYL. £1 1s. net. THE GREAT SECRET. 7s. 6d. net. THE CLOUD THAT LIFTED and THE POWER OF THE DEAD. 7s. 6d. net.

Masefield (John)

ON THE SPANISH MAIN. 8s. 6d. net. A SAILOR'S GARLAND. 6s. net. and 3s. 6d. net. SEA LIFE IN NELSON'S TIME. 5s. net.

Methuen (Sir A.)

AN ANTHOLOGY OF MODERN VERSE. 122nd Thousand. SHAKESPEARE TO HARDY: An Anthology of English Lyrics. 19th Thousand. *Each Fcap. 8vo. Cloth, 6s. net. Leather, 7s. 6d. net.*

Milne (A. A.)

NOT THAT IT MATTERS. IF I MAY. THE SUNNY SIDE. THE RED HOUSE MYSTERY. ONCE A WEEK. THE HOLIDAY ROUND. THE DAY'S PLAY. *Each 3s. 6d. net.* WHEN WE WERE VERY YOUNG. *Fourteenth Edition.* 139th Thousand. WINNIE-THE-POOH. *Fourth Edition.* 70th Thousand. *Each Illustrated by* E. H. SHEPARD. 7s. 6d. net. Leather, 10s. 6d. net. FOR THE LUNCHEON INTERVAL. 1s. 6d. net.

Milne (A. A.) and Fraser-Simson (H.)
FOURTEEN SONGS FROM "WHEN WE WERE VERY YOUNG." (*Tenth Edition.* 7s. 6d. net.) TEDDY BEAR AND OTHER SONGS FROM "WHEN WE WERE VERY YOUNG." (7s. 6d. net.) THE KING'S BREAKFAST. (*Second Edition.* 3s. 6d.net.) Words by A. A. Milne. Music by H. Fraser-Simson.

Montague (C. E.)
DRAMATIC VALUES. *Cr. 8vo.* 7s. 6d. net.

Morton (H. V.)
THE HEART OF LONDON. 3s. 6d. net. (Also illustrated, 7s. 6d. net.) THE SPELL OF LONDON. THE NIGHTS OF LONDON. *Each* 3s. 6d. net. THE LONDON YEAR. IN SEARCH OF ENGLAND. Each Illustrated. 7s. 6d. net.

Newman (Tom)
HOW TO PLAY BILLIARDS. *Second Edition.* Illustrated. *Cr. 8vo.* 8s. 6d. net. BILLIARD DO'S AND DON'TS. 2s. 6d. net.

Oman (Sir Charles)
A HISTORY OF THE ART OF WAR IN THE MIDDLE AGES, A.D. 378–1485. *Second Edition,* Revised and Enlarged. 2 Vols. Illustrated. *Demy 8vo.* £1 16s. net.

Oxenham (John)
BEES IN AMBER. *Small Pott 8vo.* 2s. net. ALL'S WELL. THE KING'S HIGH-WAY. THE VISION SPLENDID. THE FIERY CROSS. HIGH ALTARS. HEARTS COURAGEOUS. ALL CLEAR! *Each Small Pott 8vo. Paper,* 1s. 3d. net. *Cloth,* 2s. net. WINDS OF THE DAWN. 2s. net.

Perry (W. J.)
THE ORIGIN OF MAGIC AND RELIGION. THE GROWTH OF CIVILIZATION (*Second Edition*). *Each* 6s. net. THE CHILDREN OF THE SUN. 18s. net.

Petrie (Sir Flinders)
A HISTORY OF EGYPT. In 6 Volumes.
Vol. I. FROM THE 1ST TO THE XVITH DYNASTY. *Eleventh Edition, Revised.* 12s. net.
Vol. II. THE XVIITH AND XVIIITH DYNASTIES. *Seventh Edition, Revised.* 9s. net.
Vol. III. XIXTH TO XXXTH DYNAS-TIES. *Third Edition.* 12s. net.
Vol. IV. PTOLEMAIC EGYPT. By EDWYN BEVAN. 10s. 6d. net.
Vol. V. EGYPT UNDER ROMAN RULE. By J. G. MILNE. *Third Edition, Revised.* 12s. net.
Vol. VI. EGYPT IN THE MIDDLE AGES. By STANLEY LANE POOLE. *Fourth Edition.* 10s. net.

Raleigh (Sir Walter)
THE LETTERS OF SIR WALTER RALEIGH. Edited by LADY RALEIGH. Two Vols. Illustrated. *Second Edition Demy 8vo.* £1 10s. net.

Ridge (W. Pett) and Hoppé (E. O.)
LONDON TYPES : TAKEN FROM LIFE. The text by W. PETT RIDGE and the 25 Pictures by E. O. HOPPÉ. *Large Crown 8vo.* 10s. 6d. net.

Smith (Adam)
THE WEALTH OF NATIONS. Edited by EDWIN CANNAN. 2 Vols. *Demy 8vo.* £1 5s. net.

Smith (C. Fox)
SAILOR TOWN DAYS. SEA SONGS AND BALLADS. A BOOK OF FAMOUS SHIPS. SHIP ALLEY. *Each,* illustrated, 6s. net. FULL SAIL. Illustrated. 5s. net. TALES OF THE CLIPPER SHIPS. 5s. net. THE RETURN OF THE "CUTTY SARK." Illustrated. 3s. 6d. net. A BOOK OF SHANTIES. 6s. net.

Sommerfeld (Arnold)
ATOMIC STRUCTURE AND SPECTRAL LINES. £1 12s. net. THREE LECTURES ON ATOMIC PHYSICS. 2s. 6d. net.

Stevenson (R. L.)
THE LETTERS. Edited by Sir SIDNEY COLVIN. 4 Vols. *Fcap. 8vo. Each* 6s. net.

Surtees (R. S.)
HANDLEY CROSS. MR. SPONGE'S SPORTING TOUR. ASK MAMMA. MR. FACEY ROMFORD'S HOUNDS. PLAIN OR RINGLETS ? HILLINGDON HALL. *Each* illustrated, 7s. 6d. net. JORROCKS'S JAUNTS AND JOLLITIES. HAWBUCK GRANGE. *Each,* illustrated, 6s. net.

Taylor (A. E.)
PLATO : THE MAN AND HIS WORK. *Demy 8vo.* £1 1s. net.

Tilden (W. T.)
THE ART OF LAWN TENNIS. SINGLES AND DOUBLES. *Each,* illustrated, 6s. net. THE COMMON SENSE OF LAWN TENNIS. Illustrated. 5s. net.

Tileston (Mary W.)
DAILY STRENGTH FOR DAILY NEEDS. *32nd Edition.* 3s. 6d. net. *India Paper, Leather,* 6s. net.

Underhill (Evelyn)
MYSTICISM (*Eleventh Edition*). 15s. net. THE LIFE OF THE SPIRIT AND THE LIFE OF TO-DAY (*Sixth Edition*). 7s. 6d. net. CONCERNING THE INNER LIFE (*Fourth Edition*). 2s. net.

Vardon (Harry)
HOW TO PLAY GOLF. Illustrated. 19th Edition. Crown 8vo. 5s. net.

Waterhouse (Elizabeth)
A LITTLE BOOK OF LIFE AND DEATH. 22nd Edition. Small Pott 8vo. 2s. 6d. net.

Wilde (Oscar).
THE WORKS. In 16 Vols. Each 6s. 6d. net.

I. LORD ARTHUR SAVILE'S CRIME AND THE PORTRAIT OF MR. W. H. II. THE DUCHESS OF PADUA. III. POEMS. IV. LADY WINDERMERE'S FAN. V. A WOMAN OF NO IMPORTANCE. VI. AN IDEAL HUSBAND. VII. THE IMPOR- TANCE OF BEING EARNEST. VIII. A HOUSE OF POMEGRANATES. IX. IN- TENTIONS. X. DE PROFUNDIS AND PRISON LETTERS. XI. ESSAYS. XII. SALOME, A FLORENTINE TRAGEDY, and LA SAINTE COURTISANE. XIII. A CRITIC IN PALL MALL. XIV. SELECTED PROSE OF OSCAR WILDE. XV. ART AND DECORATION. XVI. FOR LOVE OF THE KING. (5s. net.)

William II. (Ex-German Emperor)
MY EARLY LIFE. Illustrated. Demy 8vo. £1 10s. net.

Williamson (G. C.)
THE BOOK OF FAMILLE ROSE. Richly Illustrated. Demy 4to. £8 8s. net.

PART II. A SELECTION OF SERIES

The Antiquary's Books
Each, illustrated, Demy 8vo. 10s. 6d. net. A series of volumes dealing with various branches of English Antiquities, com- prehensive and popular, as well as accurate and scholarly.

The Arden Shakespeare
Edited by W. J. CRAIG and R. H. CASE. Each, wide Demy 8vo. 6s. net. The Ideal Library Edition, in single plays, each edited with a full Introduc- tion, Textual Notes and a Commentary at the foot of the page. Now complete in 39 Vols.

Classics of Art
Edited by J. H. W. LAING. Each, pro- fusely illustrated, wide Royal 8vo. 15s. net to £3 3s. net. A Library of Art dealing with Great Artists and with branches of Art.

The " Complete " Series
Demy 8vo. Fully illustrated. 5s. net to 18s. net each. A series of books on various sports and pastimes, all written by acknowledged authorities.

The Connoisseur's Library
With numerous Illustrations. Wide Royal 8vo. £1 11s. 6d. net each vol. EUROPEAN ENAMELS. FINE BOOKS. GLASS. GOLDSMITHS' AND SILVER- SMITHS' WORK. IVORIES. JEWELLERY. MEZZOTINTS. PORCELAIN. SEALS.

The Do's and Dont's Series
Fcap. 8vo. 2s. 6d. net each. This series, although only in its in- fancy, is already famous. In due course it will comprise clear, crisp, informative volumes on all the activities of life. Write for full list

The Faiths : VARIETIES OF CHRISTIAN EXPRESSION. Edited by L. P. JACKS, M.A., D.D., LL.D. Crown 8vo. 5s. net each volume. The first volumes are : THE ANGLO-CATHOLIC FAITH (Rev. Canon T. A. LACEY) ; MODERNISM IN THE ENGLISH CHURCH (Prof. P. GARD- NER) ; THE FAITH AND PRACTICE OF THE QUAKERS (Prof. R. M. JONES) ; CONGREGATIONALISM (Rev. Princ. W. B. SELBIE) ; THE FAITH OF THE ROMAN CHURCH(Father C.C.MARTINDALE,S.J.).

The Library of Devotion
Handy editions of the great Devotional books, well edited. Small Pott 8vo. 3s. net and 3s. 6d. net.

Little Books on Art
Well Illustrated. Demy 16mo. Each 5s. net.

Modern Masterpieces
Fcap. 8vo. 3s. 6d. each volume. Pocketable Editions of Works by HILAIRE BELLOC, ARNOLD BENNETT, E. F. BENSON, G. K. CHESTERTON, JOSEPH CONRAD, GEORGE GISSING, KENNETH GRAHAME, W. H. HUDSON, E. V. KNOX, JACK LONDON, E. V. LUCAS, ROBERT LYND, JOHN MASEFIELD, A. A. MILNE, ARTHUR MORRISON, EDEN PHILLPOTTS, AND R. L. STEVENSON.

Sport Series
Mostly Illustrated. Fcap. 8vo. 2s. net to 5s. net each. Handy books on all branches of sport by experts.

8 MESSRS. METHUEN'S PUBLICATIONS

Methuen's Half-Crown Library
Crown 8vo and Fcap. 8vo.

Methuen's Two Shilling Library
Fcap. 8vo.

Two series of cheap editions of popular books.

Write for complete lists

The Wayfarer Series of Books for Travellers
Crown 8vo. 7s. 6d. net each. Well illustrated and with maps. The volumes are :—Alsace, Czecho-Slovakia,

The Dolomites, Egypt, Hungary, Ireland, The Loire, Provence, Spain, Sweden, Switzerland, Unfamiliar Japan, Unknown Tuscany.

The Westminster Commentaries
Demy 8vo. 8s. 6d. net to 16s. net.
Edited by W. LOCK, D.D., and D. C. SIMPSON, D.D.
The object of these commentaries is primarily to interpret the author's meaning to the present generation, taking the English text in the Revised Version as their basis.

THE LITTLE GUIDES

Small Pott 8vo. Illustrated and with Maps

THE 62 VOLUMES IN THE SERIES ARE :—

BEDFORDSHIRE AND HUNTINGDONSHIRE 4s. net.
BERKSHIRE 4s. net.
BRITTANY 4s. net.
BUCKINGHAMSHIRE 4s. net.
CAMBRIDGE AND COLLEGES 4s. net.
CAMBRIDGESHIRE 4s. net.
CATHEDRAL CITIES OF ENGLAND AND WALES 6s. net
CHANNEL ISLANDS 5s. net
CHESHIRE 5s. net
CORNWALL 4s. net.
CUMBERLAND AND WESTMORLAND 6s. net
DERBYSHIRE 4s. net.
DEVON 4s. net.
DORSET 5s. 6d. net
DURHAM 6s. net
ENGLISH LAKES 6s. net
ESSEX 5s. net
GLOUCESTERSHIRE 4s. net
GRAY'S INN AND LINCOLN'S INN 6s. net
HAMPSHIRE 4s. net.
HEREFORDSHIRE 4s. 6d. net
HERTFORDSHIRE 4s. net.
ISLE OF MAN 6s. net
ISLE OF WIGHT 4s. net.
KENT 5s. net
KERRY 4s. net
LANCASHIRE 6s. net
LEICESTERSHIRE AND RUTLAND 5s. net
LINCOLNSHIRE 6s. net
LONDON 5s. net

MALVERN COUNTRY 4s. net.
MIDDLESEX 4s. net.
MONMOUTHSHIRE 6s. net
NORFOLK 5s. net
NORMANDY 5s. net
NORTHAMPTONSHIRE 4s. net.
NORTHUMBERLAND 7s. 6d. net
NORTH WALES 6s. net
NOTTINGHAMSHIRE 4s. net.
OXFORD AND COLLEGES 4s. net.
OXFORDSHIRE 4s. net.
ROME 5s. net
ST. PAUL'S CATHEDRAL 4s. net
SHAKESPEARE'S COUNTRY 4s. net
SHROPSHIRE 5s. net.
SICILY 4s. net.
SNOWDONIA 6s. net
SOMERSET 4s. net.
SOUTH WALES 4s. net.
STAFFORDSHIRE 5s. net
SUFFOLK 4s. net.
SURREY 5s. net
SUSSEX 4s. net.
TEMPLE 4s. net.
WARWICKSHIRE 5s. net
WESTMINSTER ABBEY 5s. net
WILTSHIRE 6s. net
WORCESTERSHIRE 6s. net
YORKSHIRE EAST RIDING 5s. net
YORKSHIRE NORTH RIDING 4s. net.
YORKSHIRE WEST RIDING 7s. 6d. net
YORK 6s. net

METHUEN & CO. LTD., 36 ESSEX STREET, LONDON, W.C.2.

327